Empowering Gifted Minds

Educational Advocacy That Works

Best wishes
empowering the gifted children
Close to your heart.
Barbie Gilman

Empowering Gifted Minds

Educational Advocacy That Works

By

Barbara Jackson Gilman, M.S.

With Observations on the Inner Experience of Giftedness

By

Quinn O'Leary

DeLeon Publishing
Denver, Colorado

Cover design by Concepts Unlimited, Inc. 2003

Published by:
DeLeon Publishing, Inc.
P.O. Box 461027
Denver, CO 80246
www.deleonpub.com

ISBN 1-932186-02-6   (pbk)

04 05 06 07 08   0 9 8 7 6 5 4 3 2

For Nick,
the experimental child,
who handled undeserved educational difficulties
with uncommon grace

Table of Contents

Chapter 7
Successful Programs for Gifted Students.................. 211

Chapter 8
Models of Advocacy for Parents....................241

Chapter 9
Teachers of the Gifted..............................261

Approaches to Teaching the Gifted

Chapter 10
Charter Schools... 311

Chapter 11

Foreword

by Linda Kreger Silverman, Ph.D.

It is a joy for me to write the Foreword to this important new book on advocacy for the gifted. *Empowering Gifted Minds* is an essential resource for all who care about gifted children—school board members, principals, coordinators, teachers, teacher-educators, counselors and psychologists—as well as parents. It contains a wealth of concrete information about the nature of giftedness, assessment, appropriate curriculum and instruction, dealing with underachievement, twice exceptional children, programming at all grade levels, advocacy models, exemplary teachers, charter schools, developing individual educational plans (IEPs), and long-range educational planning for the gifted. Replete with portrayals of real children, the book is laced with the poetic insights of Quinn O'Leary, a profoundly gifted young writer who shares his own bittersweet experiences in public schools.

Years of designing IEPs for gifted children and twice exceptional learners (gifted children with learning disabilities) laid the groundwork for this manual. Based on research, clinical experience and irrefutable logic, *Empowering Gifted Minds* is poignant, easy to read, and simply makes perfect sense. It would be hard for anyone to discount the wisdom found in every chapter. This concise volume is packed with wonderful ideas that can be implemented immediately in a child's program. *Empowering Gifted Minds* is destined to become a classic handbook on advocating for the gifted.

Many acknowledge that moderately, highly, exceptionally and profoundly gifted children need interventions of

increasing intensity, but very few programs offer differenti-
ated services related to the student's level of advancement.
Empowering Gifted Minds outlines specific alternatives that
need to be considered at each of these levels of giftedness.

In no other book have I seen achievement scores of gifted
children tracked from the early primary grades to middle
school. This documentation of the rapid growth of basic
skills over time highlights the importance of accelerated
work to keep pace with the exponential advancement of the
child. Another unique feature of this book is Barbara
(Bobbie) Gilman's detailed treatment of the testing process,
and the translation of assessment data into provisions
tailored to the needs of the child. *Empowering Gifted Minds*
serves as a complete guide for examiners of the gifted, as
well as parents seeking assessment.

The most commanding sections of *Empowering Gifted
Minds* are the in-depth discussions of various causes and
treatments for underachievement; the infusion of the most
up-to-date information about the latest intelligence scales;
a comprehensive discussion of gifted children with learning
disabilities; a step-by-step guide for advocating for a child
from kindergarten through high school; sample individual
educational plans; tips from exemplary teachers; essential
resources; successful programs for the gifted; homeschooling; online courses; and advice on how to create a
charter school. Other topics addressed include definitions of
giftedness; attitudes about giftedness; identifying characteristics; levels of ability; the meaning of intelligence tests;
achievement tests; diagnostic assessment; preparing a child
for assessment; asynchrony; personality traits of the gifted;
overexcitabilities; introversion; social development; going
underground; poor study and organizational skills; gender
issues; AD/HD; teaching to the child's level, pace, and
learning style; diagnostic-prescriptive curricula; instructional
methods; acceleration; grouping strategies; magnet schools;
empowering students; flexibility; and giftedness in adults.

Empowering Gifted Minds is beautifully written. Bobbie's writing style is powerful and engaging, drawing the reader into the experiences of the children whose lives she has touched. As I consumed the book, I was keenly aware that no one else could have written this book, because no one else has had Bobbie's experiences as an examiner, parent, charter school developer, curriculum writer, and passionate advocate for the gifted.

Bobbie Gilman has been a treasured asset of the Gifted Development Center for over a decade. She is our Director of Staff Development, responsible for guiding our doctoral interns in the intricacies of assessment, and carefully reviewing the reports of staff members. Whenever I have a question about assessment, I seek out Bobbie's expertise. Bobbie is also a specialist on parent advocacy and curriculum development for the gifted. Her knowledge of the education, psychology and assessment of gifted children is vast. In addition, as the parent of two profoundly gifted boys, she has experienced firsthand the triumphs and setbacks of advocating for her own children. Her personal journey served as the impetus for writing this volume; she is committed to helping other parents successfully navigate the educational system. All of the wisdom Bobbie has gained personally and professionally has been woven into the tapestry of this book.

Bobbie affirms parents in her post-test counseling sessions, phone consultations, parent seminars and workshops, and her professional writing. She thinks outside the box, advising parents to take the responsibility for their child's education into their own hands, designing new combinations of options, as their child's needs change. This is a book that clearly empowers parents of the gifted, which, in turn, empowers children. Everyone who reads *Empowering Gifted Minds* will be moved by it.

Introduction

This book could only have been written by a parent. No amount of training in issues of the gifted or generalized desire to help others could create the insistence that fuels this book. That can only come from the outrage a parent feels when a child has been hurt. In this case, the hurt was not physical, but it was profound. Our older son, a very highly gifted boy with tremendous promise, dropped out of high school on the Monday following senior prom. By the time it happened, we actually supported his choice because no one that ambivalent about school for that long needed to be there. But, he had joined the ranks of high school dropouts, about a quarter of which (the Gifted and Talented coordinator at our high school insists) are gifted. Whatever happened from then on would certainly not be straight-forward or particularly easy. At the very least, we would all be in for difficult times ahead, with the greatest burden borne by the most intense individual in our family.

Even more frightening to me, because I work with gifted children at the Gifted Development Center in Denver, was the fact that the sequence of events leading up to our son's decision was so similar to that of many gifted children. Offered essentially traditional educational programs with little or no accommodation for giftedness, many are at risk. Moreover, parents may not realize the extent of damage being done to these children until it is too late to stop the progression—at least for a long time. At some point, a frustration sets in with school that is highly resistant to change.

Because I had a testing background before I had my family, I was fairly aware of our first son's abilities. I had not tested him, and would not have wanted to test him myself, but had seen his strong reasoning abilities. What I had completely misjudged, however, was the likelihood that his needs would be reasonably met in public school. I had no reason to question his placement there. After all, we lived in the West, where people had trusted public schools for generations and the middle class had not moved its commitment to private schools, as had occurred in some other parts of the country. And, my husband and I had done well enough in public schools.

My husband grew up in California during the space race and cold war, at a time when the nation highly valued gifted young science prospects. His mother recalled the principal of his neighborhood junior high school calling her to his office. "You need to start planning now to send Bob to a good school—I don't just mean a good school, but a GOOD school." It was on his advice that my mother-in-law began a real estate career that would allow her to be at home with Bob when she needed to be and save for what turned out to be Cal Tech. Likewise, my mother recalls being called to a meeting at my elementary school when I was in fifth grade. The parents were told that their children were gifted, and the repercussion of that meeting, as I look back on it, was probably that we were all tracked in higher level classes (at least in some academic areas) through junior high and high school. Tracking was a system of dividing students into levels based on assessed ability, with students generally placed at the chosen level in all academic subjects. I was never aware of that at the time, but I recall always being in classes with the same friends: Sally, who later became teacher of the year in Colorado; David, who won all the math and science awards; Janet, who graduated first in her medical school class; and similar others. I remember most of us being challenged most of the time. I didn't realize how different our son's experience in school would be. Moreover, I didn't anticipate the reactions of school personnel to his giftedness. Not only was he underchallenged, but the schools were resistant to identifying him as a gifted student. And they certainly would not have initiated the discussion, as school personnel had done for Bob and me.

The school reform movement of the 1980s and early 1990s brought an end to tracking and an emphasis on the hetero-geneous grouping of students for instruction. Valid concerns had been raised about the difficulty of students moving to a different track (such systems were often quite rigid), about poor teachers being given lower track classes, about lower classes emphasizing discipline over course content, and about the fact that students might need coursework at varying levels in different academic areas. Tracking was an overly simple system with serious flaws. However, tracking for gifted students had been very successful when the course content was varied from that of lower-level classes.

It was unfortunate that some form of hybrid system was not devised that allowed higher level classes with more flexible access to them, but, instead, an equally extreme emphasis on heterogeneous grouping began. For gifted students, the result was placement in considerably less challenging classes. Rather than being seen as needing faster paced, higher level instruction, the gifted were increasingly viewed as role models for the heterogeneous class and teachers' helpers. Cooperative Learning, an instructional method in which children learn in small groups, often earning group grades, became the favored approach to teaching in the '90s and the perfect complement to heterogeneous grouping (cooperative learning groups were usually deliberately heterogeneous)—unless a student was not average. Teachers in our district were pushed to increase the percentage of time that this method was being used year by year, so that its use could be maximized. In theory, all children benefited from this approach. Gifted children helped to pull up the other students and were the classroom leaders. Exposure to high achievers helped the other students who were struggling. All benefited from learning to work together in an increasingly team-oriented world.

Yet, many gifted students were frustrated by being held to grade-level work through this approach, which certainly had a *leveling* influence, and by being pressured to serve as leaders/teachers for other students or else earn low grades. Karen Rogers' 1991 statistical meta-analysis of ability grouping research (sponsored by the National Research Center on the Gifted and Talented) concluded that, as yet, there was no research showing such an approach to be beneficial to the gifted, while there was considerable research documenting the huge gains gifted students make when grouped for instruction and provided instructional content appropriate to their learning needs.

Adding to the emphasis on heterogeneous grouping was Middle School philosophy, another change that occurred since my husband and I attended junior high. An attempt to supplant junior high schools with programs more appropriate to bridge the gap between elementary and high schools, middle schools became some of the strongest proponents of heterogeneous grouping for instruction. Not only was it viewed as a more ethical way to teach students, but it was also the natural outcome of grouping children into *pods* or smaller groupings within a grade for all their courses to provide the additional support adolescents were felt to need. Most middle schools established several groupings of students within each grade, each tied to a team of teachers. The students would, more or less, stay together, creating a more intimate, supportive experience. However, for all to stay together, students had to take classes at the same level. Most middle schools eliminated or severely restricted honors or more advanced classes (some offered honors math).

It was into this unknown (to us) world of education that our son went. Identified as a talented and gifted (TAG) student in second grade, little was done differently for him in the classroom. We had originally *nominated* him for TAG because he wanted to advance in math in first grade. However, we had to study first and second-grade math books with him on our own and then no modifications were made in his second grade math instruction. We thought a tutor was initially possible; that finally materialized in the form of a high school girl coming to his elementary school once a week in third grade during her lunch hour. When we asked why they were simply playing math games, we were told, "We wouldn't want to interfere with classroom instruction." Of course, interfering with classroom instruction was exactly what our son needed, but he didn't get it. Finally, in fifth grade his teacher moved him to a sixth-grade math book and he worked independently. Sadly, the teacher was forced to take a medical retirement midyear and an inexperienced substitute for the remainder of the year made our son do the regular fifth-grade work, as well. He was afraid there would be holes in our son's knowledge, he explained, and he also told him that he would only grade the fifth-grade work. The effect of this decision, coupled with the fact that the teacher was extremely punitive (he punished the entire class when-ever one student misbehaved and regularly made children cry each day) was dramatic in our son's life. He began having difficulty getting to sleep, he cried frequently, and didn't want to go to school. In short—he was clinically depressed. To his credit, he stood up one day for another student who was unfairly treated and told the teacher what he thought of him. The entire class applauded. Our son then voluntarily went to the principal and explained what he had done and why. The teacher did not return to school for three days and, although he finished the last few weeks of the year, was not hired as a permanent teacher at the school. The depression ended, but hopes that middle school would finally offer the classes he needed went unfulfilled.

It was at this time that I attended a panel discussion on the social and emotional needs of gifted children. On the panel was a psychologist, Linda Kreger Silverman, the Director of the Gifted Development Center in Denver. Listening to her speak, I learned why so many since have viewed her as the expert with the most relevant understanding of gifted children and their needs, and the most complete knowledge of the field. With a double major Ph.D. in both educational psychology and special education, Linda began her career tutoring children with learning disabilities and teaching gifted children. She approached the gifted as she did those with special education needs. She assessed their needs and designed programs to meet them. For her, gifted education had always been about accommodating children with discrepant educational needs and never about providing advantages for the elite. Because Linda also viewed these children as a psychologist and knew them through counseling, she was equally knowledgeable about both the education and psychology of the gifted. Intuition told me that this was a woman who truly did understand children such as mine and I made plans to pursue assessment and consultation at the Gifted Development Center (GDC).

The testing at the GDC yielded information we desperately needed and support for the advocacy we would have to provide for our children. It documented the reasons why our son's educational program was a poor fit for him and gave us, as parents, support for the concerns we had had through the years of his education.

However, even gaining a better feel for what needed to happen for our son and advocating more strongly, we encountered many barriers. The most immutable were found in our beautiful new middle school that offered virtually no challenge. By eighth grade, our disgusted son's mostly A grades dropped, beginning a pattern of resistance to school and haphazardly done work that improved only occasionally with special teachers until he dropped out of school.

Meanwhile, we had also learned at the Center, as so many parents before us had, that where there is one gifted child in the family, there are likely more. Our younger son's testing at age six actually took place at a much more propitious

time, which allowed us to advocate for him much earlier.
The GDC not only became a support system for our family,
but I returned to work as a tester there and began to work
with other families in our same situation. My husband and
I became more aggressive, careful consumers of education,
joined advocacy committees, and even helped create a
charter middle school (not for the faint of heart!).

Now in my second decade at the Gifted Development Center,
I continue to be amazed at the dearth of truly appropriate
educational programs for gifted children, especially in the
public schools. For this reason, there is a necessity for
parents to be extremely knowledgeable advocates, if they are
going to prevent real damage to their children. We offer
lengthy consultations following testing that attempt to
answer parents' questions, but we are only able to scratch
the surface in the time we have. The majority of our parents
come from out of state, leaving within a day or two after
testing, and I frequently feel that we have barely given them
a fighting chance at advocacy. We've discussed, at length,
those issues that are uppermost to them now, but rarely
have time to explore future issues or the broader questions
about educating and parenting the gifted. Unfortunately,
I share with many parents the sense that our firstborn was
forced to be the *experimental* child, who taught his parents
what we needed to know to advocate for his sibling, too late
to benefit himself. This book is meant to be a crash course
in everything you need to know to advocate for your gifted
child—immediately. It is meant to share with you the
experience of the GDC staff in Denver, Colorado about the
relevant issues regarding giftedness.

Our family has been fortunate to see our older son begin to
rebound from the experiences that cost him so dearly.
However, some parents have lost their children permanently.
It is my sincere hope that you will find these pages helpful,
that you will find support for your own good judgment, and

that your children will mature with their love of learning intact.

References

Rogers, K. B. (1991). *The relationship of grouping practices to the education of the gifted and talented learner.* (Research-Based Decision Making Series). Storrs, CT: National Research Center on the Gifted and Talented, University of Connecticut.

1

The Experience of Giftedness

Six-year-old Zachary was brought to the Gifted Development
Center (GDC) because he was extremely unhappy in kindergarten. His mother hoped we could assess his needs and
give her guidance. Placed in a respected private school
because he was unusually advanced, Zachary was supposed
to be challenged and motivated by his first year in school.
Instead, he was miserable and his confidence was shaken.
The school he attended was teaching him little that he had
not known before. In addition, his teacher found his personality characteristics, interests, and favorite activities so
unusual for a kindergartener, that she began to criticize
Zach and blame his mother's child-rearing techniques.
Behaviors that had at first appeared eccentric seemed
increasingly pathological to his teacher.

Although Zachary was an excellent reader when he entered
school, interested in world events, he stopped watching the
news and reading the newspaper after his teacher called
him an "information junkie," who "already had too much
information." He resisted *inventive spelling* because he didn't
want to misspell known words. He refused to continue doing
simple addition problems because "the answers will always
be the same; they never will change, so why do we do them
day after day?" Zach came to believe that nothing he did
was right for his teacher. His teacher believed he was overly

sensitive and a "cry baby" due to separation anxiety. He said
he "was just a dolphin jumping through hoops." He had
been instructed not to say "but what if..." or "that depends"
and he was now limited to "one curious question per day."

Zachary finally came home from school reporting that he
had "emotional problems" and had been referred to the
school psychologist. When contacted, the psychologist said
that Zach did not have emotional problems, but did need
praise instead of criticism from his teacher. Zach experienced
stomachaches, did not want to go to school, and finally
developed chest pain and a rapid heart rate related to
stress. His high degree of sensitivity, mature reasoning
ability, and advanced reading and math skills were highly
unusual, but nothing about him was pathological.

Advanced Developmental History

Zachary's past history was that of a very highly gifted child,
developing at a faster pace than normal children. Since
birth, he was noted to have a long attention span and a high
energy level. In fact, his mother did not recall him ever
napping (a characteristic we see occasionally) and he had
continued to view sleep as "a waste of time." Zach reached
developmental milestones early, especially in the intellectual
and verbal domains. He said his first word at five months
and spoke in sentences at nine months. He sight-read an
easy reader at two years, three months and sounded out
new words at two years, 11 months. He wrote his first word
at three years. Zachary developed within the normal range
physically; he sat without support at six months of age and
walked at 13 months. Initially ambidextrous, he had become
right-handed.

Because Zachary was clearly not progressing as baby books
described typical development, his mother kept careful
records of his activities. He was an intensely curious child
with a wide range of mature interests. He would frequently

wake his mother during the night to ask questions and had studied fields as varied as Native American tribes, dinosaurs, aircraft and flight, the solar system and space, the Gulf War, and anatomy. His mother wrote, "Zachary didn't go through the terrible twos"... he "was too busy learning." Zach's love of reading had resulted in a collection of 1500 books, which were kept in a closet in which he loved to spend time. Also at age two, Zach told his grandmother that he had a "B-R-I-T-E" idea and he spelled the word for her.

By age three, he was asking questions that were difficult to answer without research ("does a shark have a tongue and, if so, does it have an epiglottis?"). In addition, he was so preoccupied with the concept of time that his family bought him six clocks to inform him of the time in major cities around the world. That same year, he was concerned with the lack of NASA funding, world crises, natural disasters, and ecological problems.

At age four, Zachary began to tell everyone he was six so that they wouldn't tell him he was too young to do things. This actually worked quite well and helped him cope. He routinely checked to see how various stocks were doing, studied adult literature and poetry, became a vegetarian to avoid "hurting wildlife," studied 25 separate tribes of Native Americans (wearing a loin cloth and cloth leggings whenever possible), and concluded about the Aztecs that, "just because they do things we do not approve of does not mean that we should not study who they were."

Zachary's sensitivity and compassion were evident at a very young age. At nine months, he was a participant in a university child development study. Asked to pick up a tiny pill and put it in a pillbox, he performed perfectly. However, when asked to turn a girl doll over and spank it three times, he was reluctant. Zach finally spanked the doll, then glared at the examiner and refused to return it. He hugged it repeatedly. This compassion had continued and was reflected in concern for the well-being of friends and relatives, as well as global concerns.

Zachary was previously tested at the age of four years, 11 months on the Wechsler Preschool and Primary Scale of Intelligence-Revised (*WPPSI-R*) and reportedly earned a Full Scale IQ score of 150[+]. It was this assessment that resulted in the recommendation to find a highly challenging school. Zach's score, in the highly gifted range, was probably a minimal estimate of his abilities, given his history. However, his teacher's contention that Zachary "had more of a 105 IQ than a 150" left his mother uncertain about both his educational needs and his actual abilities. And, it left Zachary devastated. A full evaluation was scheduled at the GDC to address these issues.

Testing Confirms Ability

Once Zachary and his mother arrived at the GDC, she revealed privately that he was quite worried about the testing because he felt it would determine whether the kindergarten teacher's low assessment of him was correct. We asked her to have Zach bring some of his favorite toys and he brought along dinosaur books and plastic dinosaurs to share. Taking time to discuss the dinosaurs was both an icebreaker and an opportunity to observe Zach. He spoke precisely and in depth about various dinosaurs, passages in the books he had brought, dinosaurs in movies, and museum experiences. Calmer almost immediately, Zach was soon smiling and talkative. He was concerned with details and was careful to place his books back in his backpack in a preferred order. During the testing, he generally appeared confident. Occasionally, with only the most difficult questions, he would bite his nails and was reluctant to guess. He was sensitive to the conditions of the room and his clothing (he stopped several times to adjust his socks). When the IQ scores were given to his mother from the

WISC-III and Stanford-Binet L-M, and it was clear that Zachary had scored within the highly gifted range again, she chose to share them with her son. Aware of his teacher's comments, he already knew that high scores provided some justification for his differences. When told what the scores were, he held his arms out from his sides, breathed a sigh of relief, and said, "I am finally free."

Unnecessary Damage

Such a story, of absolutely unnecessary damage to a child, is both heartrending and telling. In a nation that has done an excellent job of valuing education for all citizens, we lack understanding about the needs of our most able learners and permit considerable pressure for these children to simply fit in. The goal to educate all to at least a moderate degree falls short for gifted students. Worst of all, the failure to nurture our best minds can result in a failure to reach full potential, with both personal and national ramifications.

Zachary's story is typical of the situations that are most damaging to gifted children in school. Not only are they inadequately challenged day after day, which could certainly undermine their motivation to learn, but their self-esteem also suffers as they sense subtle (or not so subtle) disapproval for their differences. Gifted children, as a group, don't fit the expectations of teachers or curriculum developers because of development that is proceeding at a much more rapid pace than is typical for the average child. It is their degree of difference from the norm that defines them as a special needs population, requiring special accommodations in school. However, because these accommodations are rarely offered (few strong mandates exist in this country), we see these children suffering.

Teach to Their Level, Pace, and Learning Style

Gifted students need educational programs designed to meet
their needs, just as the regular curriculum is designed for
the majority of children it serves. Such programs must
consider their level of content mastery, pace of learning,
learning style, and effective instructional approaches. An
impediment to the simple consideration of gifted students
and their educational needs is the perception that they are
advantaged. Must the second-grade teacher teach above-
level material to the child who has mastered second-grade
work or simply feel that her job is done where that child is
concerned? If a child is already advanced, do we really have
an obligation to help him or her progress further? Couldn't
this child simply help others to learn so that all students
could end their year at more or less the same point of
mastery? The experience of many gifted children attests to
the fact that their needs must be met adequately enough to
avoid destroying their motivation to learn or limiting the
realization of their potential.

All gifted children, typically 98th percentile and above, have
difficulty with educational programs planned for the
majority of students. Their learning rates outpace such
programs, they need higher-level material earlier, and they
can and need to reason abstractly before most children are
ready for it. Likewise, children who score at the 2nd percentile
and below are considered discrepant enough from typical
children that they have mandated special education modifications in school to accommodate their slower learning rates
and other specific needs. Children between these extremes
may also need modifications at times (teachers must be
sensitive to the needs of all children), but we know gifted
and developmentally delayed children will need accommodations and we must plan for them.

The issue of making accommodations for the gifted has
never been about satisfied, high-achievers whose parents

demand special privileges—a sort of "tax credits for the rich" issue. On the contrary, it has always been about more basic, universal values that all parents share about the education of their children: maintaining a child's interest in school, developing healthy self-esteem, nurturing social development, teaching a strong work ethic, and preparing a child for a satisfying life. Such values are never elitist by themselves and gifted education only becomes elitist when it is denied to children without means. This can occur when the public school system denies appropriate education to gifted children and only those with the financial means to afford private schools are able to obtain the educational programs they need.

We have a responsibility to educate all children to reach their full potential and inappropriate educational strategies can derail a child's learning altogether. The gifted high school dropout is as much a failure of our system as the less able dropout who has struggled and received insufficient help. The issues are the same for all children; children have specific needs and we are obligated to find ways to serve them.

An analogy to the plight of the gifted may be helpful. What if, for example, we were to mandate the grouping of all average children with mildly retarded children of IQ 70 and somewhat below? Knowing that developmentally delayed children require significantly more drill and practice to master concepts, we would need to create a curriculum with sufficient practice to meet the needs of our slowest learner. Because we could no longer cover as many topics during the year, we would need to reorganize the scope and sequence of our multi-year curriculum and add years of education prior to high school graduation. We believe the plan would be a significant improvement because we would be supporting egalitarian ideals and because, eventually, even more students would reach a level of high school graduate competency.

There is little doubt that there would be an outcry as more average students became frustrated in the classroom. Most would complain of boredom and many would condemn the extra years required in school to earn the credits necessary for graduation. They would insist that the extra drill and practice is counterproductive to children who don't need it and harmful to a positive attitude about learning. Of course, they would be right; but, when exactly the same situation occurs for the gifted in average classrooms, there is resistance to the very same expressed concerns. Sometimes, gifted children are even admonished to be satisfied in order to get along with others in the world. What seems clearly inappropriate for one group is character building for the other... unless the gifted child is close to us and we see the genuine suffering that can occur. Gifted children are too *discrepant* for the educational programs that generally serve them. Moreover, their personality characteristics and interests are out-of-sync with those of age peers.

Personality Characteristics

Gifted children can, for example, become knowledgeable enough in a subject area that they appear quite eccentric when compared with more average children their age. Some teachers find that disturbing. Often, the written observations we receive from teachers contain a concern that Heather or Ryan "just have time to be a kid." Mature interests and abilities may be assumed to be the result of pushing by parents, rather than natural tendencies of the child. Surely, a child wouldn't choose such interests independently!

Our experience has shown exactly the opposite; gifted children do choose to pursue unusual interests (or perhaps their curiosities reach a mature level quickly and that appears unusual). Parents don't tend to push, but usually struggle themselves to keep up with these curious, high-energy children. It can be exhausting to answer their incessant questions and support the interests they express. It can be financially difficult to provide the enrichment opportunities such children crave. These are not the parents who show their children flash cards in the high chair and push to give them a competitive edge in life. They are, more likely, barely hanging on and in need of both sleep and support for trying to meet needs that few adults around them appreciate.

Gifted children also exhibit other differences that come with the territory. Their high degree of sensitivity, intensity and concern for injustice can send up psychological red flags for teachers. Their tendency to want to make their own decisions about life at an early age can be frustrating to adults working with them. Because teachers often have little background in gifted education, these differences may not be understood as a normal part of the domain of giftedness. In fact, they are part of a larger group of characteristics we recognize as typical of advanced development. They characterize giftedness far better than simply high achievement in one or more subject areas in school.

Where teachers are supportive of the differences gifted children display, other students may not be. The gifted child in elementary school may be isolated by his peers not only for his unusual interests, but due to his adult speech. Young children may be quick to exercise prejudice against a gifted child who is different, just as they might a child with racial or ethnic differences, or a disabled child. Teachers may feel less comfortable addressing prejudice against the gifted, as in the case of Matthew.

Matthew came to us as a fourth-grader, feeling very isolated in his public school classroom. A boy with an unusual interest in history—particularly military history—he enjoyed discussing military leaders, their campaigns and their strategies. He spoke so articulately about these interests that I could visualize the adult Matthew teaching university

courses in history and spending considerable time
researching and debating his passion.

His classmates, however, were not impressed and he was
the target of the class bully, who did everything possible to
make his life miserable. The bully consistently rallied others
against Matthew, making the situation for him almost
unbearable. He spoke of recurring nightmares about the
bully and dreams in which the bully "flew off the earth."
That, he admitted, was what he most wished could happen.
Unfortunately, his teacher did not intervene because she
believed children needed to resolve such matters themselves.
Matthew's sensitivity and introversion made this highly
unlikely and he was miserable.

Social Development

What was also of concern in Matthew's case was his social
development. There is a common misconception that gifted
children must be placed with age peers for social development to progress. But, it is exactly Matthew's type of
situation that halts social development. Children who must
constantly defend themselves do not make strides socially.
Rather, they need to find others with similar interests, from
which friendships develop. It is within the context of friendship that social development occurs. This is undoubtedly
why, with all of the pressure to place children with age peers
in school, we have seen the best social development in gifted
children who attend schools or full-time programs for the
gifted. Because they are accepted by others and are confident
that they *fit in*, they learn how to be good friends. Surprisingly,
they seem to be more tolerant and open to others with
diverse backgrounds, interests and abilities than gifted
children placed in heterogeneous groups. Most of the latter
experience persecution to some degree and lose some of
their tolerance. Because Matthew earned gifted-level IQ
scores and so desperately needed a program that would

support not only his interests and learning needs but also his personality characteristics, we strongly recommended placement in a school or full-day program for the gifted.

Out-of-Sync With Middle School

As gifted children mature and leave elementary school, we see new problems arise. Older gifted students, particularly in middle school, may be tormented for caring too much about their studies. Possibly arising out of the emphasis on heterogeneous grouping and "excellence for all," many writers have commented on the "anti-intellectualism" prevalent in middle schools. We have seen gifted students struggle for acceptance, enduring slights ranging from name calling ("school boy," "school girl") to bumper stickers proclaiming "MY KID BEAT UP YOUR HONOR STUDENT." Gifted middle-level students may perceive themselves as so different from what is considered popular that they wonder if something is wrong with them. They may see no point to the activities their classmates value so highly and may find virtually nothing relevant in the classroom. Kathryn was one such young lady.

Kathryn came to the GDC at age 12 because she was finding the pace of academic work in seventh grade "stultifying" and because she was feeling very different and isolated from her peers. Although Kathryn still maintained a 4.0 average, she had hated school since sixth grade and complained that it was painfully boring. Many gifted students reach this point after the accumulation of years in elementary school, moving at too slow a pace. They hold out hope that middle school, with its greater choice of courses, will afford them the opportunity to finally have more challenging coursework. Regrettably, most find sixth grade a disappointment, with emphasis on fairly basic skills and grade inflation common. They then view their middle school prospects with considerably less optimism, as did Kathryn.

Whereas school personnel had been cooperative, meetings with her mother every few weeks had not been practical or effective. Kathryn's mother felt her daughter was a bright, delightful, sensitive, and aware girl. Moreover, she wrote that Kathryn "has a fine character and more understanding and concern for the world than many adults." Yet, Kathryn had had difficulty finding others with similar interests and concerns, forcing her to "choose between being herself and fitting in." Middle school coursework had been particularly disappointing. Kathryn liked math best; it was the only class that was ability-grouped and, therefore, came closest to offering the high-level material and fast instructional pace that she needed.

Kathryn arrived for the testing feeling both anxious and relieved that she would finally be evaluated. She explained that plans had been made to test her at the age of nine, but they were changed and the evaluation was never done. It seemed very important to her at this time to finally have information about her abilities and she was visibly nervous about performing well. Nevertheless, she was friendly and poised, displaying a warm smile and a subtle sense of humor. When asked how she liked middle school, Kathryn replied that she spent most of her time coloring. She added that the work was very concrete because "we don't have abstract reasoning ability until we're 13 to 15."

Kathryn's test scores explained her sense of isolation. She missed only two items on the *Stanford-Binet L-M,* the IQ test with the highest ceiling available at the time. Her IQ score of 170⁺ (the plus meaning that she failed to reach a point where she could no longer answer questions correctly in one or more domains and might, therefore, score higher if tested on an instrument with a higher ceiling) was in the exceptionally gifted range, with an equivalent mental age of 22 years, four months. In the conference, she tearfully described how poorly she fit in at her school. She said, "I will never be pretty or popular... All I have is my grades." A lovely, sensitive person, Kathryn was suffering from considerable loss of self-esteem for no justifiable reason. It was simply the result of being too discrepant from her age peers in a program designed to fit the majority of students.

Mental Age

The mental age computed on the test Kathryn took has actually been an excellent estimate of a child's level of functioning. It is based on the notion that the child is mentally one age and chronologically another and is useful when describing both advanced and delayed development. This is the conceptual basis of the Intelligence Quotient or IQ. Originally, the mental age divided by the chronological age times 100 equaled the IQ score. Although this calculation is somewhat modified on modern tests, perceived mental age is helpful in estimating a child's ability. For example, a child who is comfortable with age peers in a typical school is likely to have a mental age close to his or her chronological age. If the mental age and chronological age are the same, their ratio is equal to 1. Multiplied by 100, this yields an IQ score of 100, which is considered *average* and at the 50th percentile for children of that chronological age. On the other hand, a six-year-old child who is generally uncomfortable with age peers and prefers to play with 12 year olds may well have an IQ score approaching 200.

Kathryn's mental age of 22 years, four months placed her totally outside the realm of more typical middle school students and rendered her unable to fit in. Thinking at so different a level, Kathryn could only hope to accelerate to a higher grade level, where her mental age would not be so discrepant, or to a school with more advanced students. It would be ludicrous to assume that she could happily exist as a middle-schooler—that the same things would be important to her as were important to her age peers. Moreover, it would be cruel to insist that she continue in this environment based on conventional wisdom. Parents frequently receive advice that acceleration will harm their children socially or are told that their child "can't have everything her way" and must learn to fit in. Such a moralistic approach has no place when a child suffers to this degree.

Because Kathryn was a straight-A student who was highly advanced academically, we suggested she skip eighth grade and enter a high school program with a large number of Advanced Placement courses or an International Baccalaureate program. Research on acceleration has been largely positive, providing the child concurs with the placement. In Kathryn's case, she was miserable in her current placement and was likely to be considerably happier in high school. There, she would be a better fit, although still more advanced than most and a considerably faster learner. These differences would persist, even after acceleration or movement to a different school, and Kathryn's academic program would need to be frequently reevaluated. Even placed in a school for the gifted, Kathryn would advance through the curriculum so quickly that an Individualized Educational Plan would be needed to adjust her academic program. Such a school would best meet the needs of children with IQs just into the gifted range: 130 and up. The curriculum would not be designed for someone like Kathryn, but it would come closer to meeting her needs and offer more emotional support. There would be the chance of finding a friend there, a true peer who might share Kathryn's interests, understand her views, and appreciate her humor.

Underachieving Older Boys

In the last few years, the GDC has seen an increasing number of middle and high school-age boys. All have been brought by worried parents due to underachievement in school, failing some courses, refusing to go to school, about to be kicked out of school, or in danger of not graduating. Many high school students are in attendance trouble, their ambivalence about school causing them to skip classes or arrive late. Sadly, current high school policies (designed for good students not suffering from this type of angst) are quick to remove course credit for such problems, effectively pushing these students out of school.

Most of these boys share a pattern of highly gifted reasoning ability, increasing boredom with the regular curriculum, and a drop from mostly A grades to poor ones in middle school. The change from junior high schools with honors classes to middle schools with few or no honors classes seems to be a factor in the increasing number of older boys we are seeing. Such students could well be bored in honors classes. Without them, they have few, if any, options.

These boys need a faster-paced, higher-level educational program that allows them to move ahead when they have mastered concepts. Such a program needs to be available before they assert their independence too strongly and before too much cumulative damage has been done in programs that are underchallenging for them.

Poor Study and Organizational Skills

The more challenging program not only engages these boys more effectively, but teaches good work habits and strong organizational skills. Gifted children don't tend to learn effective study and organizational skills until their work is difficult enough to require them. Why learn to take notes when you can remember everything the teacher says in class that will be needed for the test? Why schedule work for a large assignment you can pull together impressively at the last minute? Failure to learn such skills may prevent some boys, bored with middle school, from succeeding in International Baccalaureate or other challenging high school programs that, one would think, would rekindle their interest. Such programs usually carry with them an impressive homework load, as well as more challenging, enjoyable work. These students are not really prepared and are so upset when they initially struggle, that their confidence is shaken. Teachers may be less than understanding when students are obviously talented and underachieving, and these highly sensitive boys take their criticism to heart. They may not be able to continue in the challenging program, creating a negative cycle that may take years to resolve. Boys do tend to react more overtly in defiance of a system that is hurting them. Although parents instinctively counsel them to continue trying to do their best in order to keep as many options open as possible, we must acknowledge their just cause. They rebel against educational programs that ignore their needs and undermine their natural love of learning. Unfortunately, the ramifications of their rebellion may include years of struggle to regain options appropriate and essential for their happiness as adults.

Girls: Suffering Silently or *Going Underground*

Whereas many boys underachieve to protest an educational program that they perceive to be harmful to them, many girls tend to suffer silently, at great cost to themselves. They may maintain the highest grades, as Kathryn did, or they may go underground with their giftedness, appearing to be only as intelligent as any group in which they are placed. Girls are particularly adept at sensing the social expectations others have for them and too frequently choose the path that pleases others. Such was the case for 13-year-old Cynthia.

Previously tested and found to have gifted-level abilities, Cynthia's parents brought her to us for additional evaluation and advice regarding her needs for a high school program. She was an eighth-grader, taking honors algebra and a gifted language arts class. Her middle school provided more than the usual offerings. Although she was proud to be an *A student*, she wasn't working particularly hard and preferred to invest more of herself in her social life. Somewhat concerned, her parents wanted her to consider an International Baccalaureate or other highly challenging high school program, but Cynthia resisted. She liked being the top student in her less challenging classes and enjoyed some degree of leadership in her social group. She frankly did not want to work any harder, but still planned to become a pediatrician. Pursuing a school program at the academic level popular with her friends was not going to support her career goals adequately. As Cynthia participated in the post-test conference, we were able to share our concerns with her. Dr. Linda Silverman remarked that, in our experience, most 13-year-old girls would have expressed similar socially based goals. "But," she said to Cynthia, "you have to understand that the world wants you to become a secretary." These girls often lose their determination to challenge themselves and find it extremely difficult to diverge from the pathways others have chosen. The failure of academic programs to push such students more is a failure to nurture giftedness.

The tendency for women to hide or deny their gifts and pursue more socially acceptable activities has persisted for generations. We often see mothers of clients at the GDC beginning to accept their own giftedness only after their children's evaluations. When some initially claim their children inherited their intelligence from their fathers, we suggest that the mothers must have had a hand in this, too. The underestimation of self that these mothers have accepted has often led to less-than-challenging early careers. We are always pleased to see such mothers move ahead with additional education or a new career pathway as they accept their own capabilities, following the evaluations of their children. Many have proven to be enormously talented individuals, often highly committed to the plight of the gifted. Girls, and even adult women, require substantial encouragement to realize their full potential. Every effort must be made to support their interests, develop their talents, and find true peers who will appreciate their abilities. Gifted females can support each other and friendship can minimize social pressures.

Teachers Vary in Their Knowledge of the Gifted

Teachers are the most important variable in the success of gifted students in the classroom. Because most states lack strong mandates for gifted education, they require only minimal education for teachers in meeting the needs of the gifted. Training in *gifted* may amount to only a small portion of an Exceptional Child course emphasizing special education needs. As a result, teachers vary tremendously in their ability to create appropriate learning experiences for gifted students. Although most teachers sincerely have their students' best interests at heart, they lack the expertise and experience to consistently challenge their gifted students and ensure their continuous progress. Without this experience, teachers are likely to underestimate the degree of accommodation needed and are vulnerable to misconceptions about the gifted. Such misconceptions tend to proliferate and may be compounded by agreement with other teachers in the same school building.

For example, the belief that gifted children will be fine, regardless of their situation, begs for nothing to be done for them. Reflecting confusion between gifted students and high achievers, it suggests that the gifted, when given lemons, will make lemonade. In actuality, gifted students often fare poorly in the wrong learning environment and do not necessarily earn high grades. They are more likely to be high achievers in challenging classroom environments, but may be lackluster students when more basic, grade-level material is stressed. Teachers should not withhold more challenging work solely because a child fails to impress them with basic achievement.

Parents have also been warned, "If you put your child in a school for the gifted, he or she will just shut down socially." Reflecting the common concern that children must be placed with *normal children,* particularly chronological age peers, for proper social development, this view keeps schools from considering acceleration more frequently. In fact, research on acceleration has generally been positive, provided the child concurs with the placement. We have seen gifted children relate better to mental age peers and to develop socially when they feel confident they *fit in.* Children for whom we've recommended acceleration (with their permission) have fared very well. In fact, it is surprising what a nonissue grade skipping has been for many of our clients after only a short time in the new classroom.

The prevalent notion that "gifted children just need a little enrichment" seems to have guided the development of some fairly ineffective gifted programs. Enrichment in the class- room that truly increases the depth and breadth of the material studied would be an improvement for the gifted student, but the term *enrichment* can be used in almost any context. Programs that maintain traditional whole-class instruction in classrooms for all children but add a few extracurricular *enrichment* outings for the gifted group both fail to make a significant contribution to meeting their needs and incur the wrath of the parents of non-gifted children. Why gifted children, and not others, would receive special advantages not directly related to their educational needs is, indeed, a reason for concern and such concerns can lead to the discontinuance of a gifted program before a more appropriate program can be developed. Likewise, opportuni- ties for gifted students to commiserate with each other about their inflexible programs during a monthly brown-bag lunch will never be adequate to meet their needs. The damage to gifted children results from an inappropriate educational program that must be endured six hours a day, five days a week, week after week, year after year. Most programs limited to activities outside the classroom arise because there is resistance by classroom teachers to modify regular schoolwork. Although such programs represent a commitment to do something for gifted students, they do little to save children from the frustration they feel. Significant accommodations must be made in the daily classwork the gifted child completes, the pace at which he or she is allowed to progress, and the instructional approaches taken.

There is a pressing need for teachers to gain experience in gifted education and for gifted students to be placed in the classrooms of teachers with expertise. I have known incredible teachers of the gifted and have been amazed by their life-changing influence on students. However, we need many more of these teachers than we currently have and the quality of the teacher is critical for any child with special needs. The natural good fit of the curriculum is not there for such children to fall back on if chemistry with the teacher is poor. Unlike special education children who have federally mandated programming, the gifted are completely dependent upon the teacher's willingness to voluntarily provide appropriate learning experiences, and his or her knowledge of what that is. That is quite a tall order with some of these children.

Of course, one must also ask whether it is fair to expect teachers to do a good job with each and every student, when in large heterogeneous classrooms, students vary in ability from developmentally delayed to profoundly gifted. It is a wonder, given the range of student needs, that even a master teacher can provide something appropriate for all on a consistent basis. Yet, there is currently a very strong preference within public school districts to meet the needs of the gifted within the regular classroom and self-contained gifted programs continue to be very rare.

Gifted Introverts are Vulnerable

Gifted children are vulnerable to teachers who insist on grade-level curriculum. Teachers may be honestly unaware of students' higher levels of mastery before they teach them. Because gifted students are largely introverts, they are not likely to reveal to teachers that the work is too easy. Identifying the gifted in schools (to inform teachers that such a child will be in their class) and frequently assessing children in the classroom (through the use of pre- and post-testing, casual assessment, and standardized tests) ensures teaching at the right level. Ignoring children's abilities and requiring them to complete work on concepts they've already mastered has the effect of confusing and devaluing them. If their advanced skills were worthwhile, surely they would be noticed and applauded by the teacher. Why wouldn't gifted children react negatively when forced to complete all regular assignments when they have already mastered the material in question?

Two kindergarten-age girls seen at the GDC, who both earned IQ scores in the 130s (moderately gifted range), typify this problem. Both girls had learned to read before entering school, both felt horribly out of place in the kindergarten classroom, and neither was offered any accommodations. Savannah, age six years, two months, had advanced through the developmental milestones related to reading so quickly that she needed very accelerated reading in kindergarten. She recognized letters at 17 months of age and sight read her first word at age three. At three years, 10 months, she could sound out words and read easy readers at age four. When we saw her, her mother noted on our Developmental Questionnaire that, in the summer, Savannah liked to read from 8:00 P.M. to midnight and sleep until 11:00 A.M. On our sentence completion test, Savannah completed the sentence stem "When I wake up at night..." with, "I read some books and go back to sleep."

She particularly enjoyed reading the *American Girl, Bobbsey Twins,* and *Berenstain Bears* series. Savannah was frustrated learning her ABCs and numbers at school, having no opportunities whatsoever to work at her actual level in reading. She liked only *Choice Time,* during which she taught other children to use the computer. She needed acceleration in reading immediately and her needs would have been better served in a school for the gifted, where she could avoid becoming a teacher's helper and progress academically. Savannah was also very sensitive and sometimes prone to regressing to baby talk when stressed. If not placed in a more suitable environment, she could not be expected to handle her situation well for long.

Sierra, also a kindergartener, felt so out of place that she told her parents the other children were "babies" and began to make up excuses that would keep her from leaving for school. She had difficulty finding appropriate clothes in her closet—nothing was right for each day—and her parents were, frankly, frightened by her behavior. She simply could not be the student her teacher expected and she was reluctant to continue trying.

Children like these are usually better placed in first grade, with, perhaps, even higher-level reading instruction. Skipping kindergarten is typically the least problematic grade acceleration. Unfortunately, the school district serving both girls had ended its program to allow some children to enter public school in first grade. All had to begin as kindergarteners, with acceleration to first grade possible only after a short period in kindergarten and with the agreement of school personnel that acceleration was appropriate. Though not optimal for gifted children, such a change (from placement in kindergarten to placement in first grade within the first few months) would be better than remaining in kindergarten.

A National Discomfort With Giftedness

American society has always exhibited conflict between egalitarian ideals and respect for high intellectual ability. We both honor our most brilliant thinkers and assert that all men are created equal. We have difficulty deciding whether *equality* in education means supporting *all* students to reach an equal level of performance, or *each and every* student to reach his or her full potential. Whereas many adults remember when high ability and achievement were celebrated in school, there is considerable reluctance now to acknowledge it. Some schools stubbornly assert that "all of our students are gifted," effectively eliminating efforts to meet the needs of advanced learners. In addition, the contrast is marked between acceptance of intellectual differences and acknowledgement of differences in a variety of talent areas. We not only ask our children to accept that they may be less talented in sports, but to "toughen up" when they sit on the bench or fail to make the team. However, our discomfort with the concept of giftedness limits our ability to handle differential educational needs effectively.

Egalitarian ideals such as those being stressed in middle schools have superceded rational consideration of special needs. For example, the "Middle School Essentials" of a local school district stresses "inclusion of all students regardless of abilities, needs, backgrounds and interests, in common learning environments" (heterogeneous grouping) as a means to ensure that "all children will achieve excellence." Ideology underpins this educational philosophy, not empirical data about how well children with different needs and abilities learn together. If the desire to meet the needs of all children is sincere, then the effectiveness of our educational policies must stand up to scrutiny. The prevalence of *whole class instruction* in these schools virtually guarantees problems for children at the extremes of ability, but special education mandates do provide further support for those students with limited abilities. The gifted face a considerably more uncertain future in such schools.

The Need for Vigilant Advocacy

Parents of the gifted, usually gifted themselves, exhibit the same sensitivity, compassion, and introversion that their children display. They usually find it very difficult to advocate strongly for their children with resistant teachers and can be as uncomfortable with the term *gifted* as critical opponents of special services. Usually sensitive to the plight of all special needs students, parents of the gifted are reluctant to push their own students' agendas too far in fear of communicating insensitivity to the needs of others. The fact that advocacy for the gifted is unpopular in our increasingly egalitarian society makes it even more difficult. For these reasons, parents of the gifted may be too trusting of the education their children are receiving for too long, placing their students at considerably greater risk than they would ever deliberately allow. Parents need to educate themselves as fully as possible about their children's needs and accept the role of advocate early in their students' educational careers.

Parents faced with advocacy for their gifted children or educators who accept this role will need to be more than casual observers of the fit between each gifted child and his or her educational program. A child's academic achievement must be constantly monitored to determine if the work he or she is doing is appropriate. When a concept is mastered, is the child allowed to move on to new material? Gifted children reach mastery before other children, creating the problem of what to do with them while the others finish. Is the gifted student learning something new every day or is the bulk of instruction and assignments related to known material? Is learning restricted to grade-level work? Can a first-grader learn multiplication or a fifth-grader begin algebra?

Most advocates discover that they need considerably more information than they have to do this job well. They must understand giftedness and have some idea of the educational needs gifted students have. Some estimation of the child's general level of ability, as well as strengths, weaknesses, and learning style, becomes critical. Advocates need familiarity with the forms *gifted education* can take so that they can determine what an acceptable request is. They must have an idea of the options available for a child at his or her school and the people who can provide them. To whom does one go for help—the teacher, the G/T coordinator, the principal? If parent requests for help at school are denied, what options does the parent have? Is help available at the district or state level? Where can supportive teachers obtain guidance? Are there laws pertaining to gifted education? Are other schools more appropriate and how does one find them? Are there tutors, mentors, or other resources outside of school for instruction in various subject areas? To what degree can one circumvent school limitations to meet needs?

To educate themselves more fully, many advocates become avid readers and gifted conference attendees. They frequent computer bulletin boards, learning what they can (sometimes to an impressive degree) to negotiate a labyrinth of educational complications. What they have is love for these children and determination; what they don't have is considerable time. The learning discrepancy between young gifted children and their age peers only increases, making accommodations increasingly necessary. And, the accumulation of frustrating experiences grows, threatening the inborn curiosity and love of learning that so characterizes gifted children from their first years of life. This book will hopefully serve as a guide for advocates to better understand what giftedness is and nurture it in their children or students—in time.

Quinn O'Leary...Observations on the Inner Experience of Giftedness

"Today," grated the pedantic nasal caw that served the white-haired, wizened, tired-bodied teacher for a voice, "We will be writing about..." Her drone paused as she peeled the previous day's date from the department-store calendar full of ostensibly inventive ways to "inspire young writers." Mrs. "K" siphoned these ideas verbatim from the pastel-colored paper with the blaze-orange $4.99 sticker still clinging to the plastic backing. This admittedly ingenious plan saved her both the effort of actual invention and the risk of facing self-spawned creativity from her students.

The fishlike movement of her lips as she silently read the calendar's suggestion lent her the aspect of an idiot. After a moment's consideration, she smiled and addressed the class. "Complete the following poem, 'I hope to have a horse one day, a beautiful pony to run and play...' " The last words were spoken slowly so that the by-and-large-at-least-mildly-attentive class could copy them.

Throughout this, I had not raised my eyes or my pen from the page of my lovingly ragged notebook. Mrs. K had apparently noted this lack of attention and, as soon as she finished proclaiming the four-line assignment's due date as the following day, she approached and read over my shoulder. The obscure instinct of insecure writers dictated that I shift my free hand to cover the unfinished piece, a childish shard of a story concerning a tragic love between a toaster and a mouse.

"That doesn't look like the assignment, Quinn," rasped the venomous voice of authority. "Perhaps you would be more successful in my class if you spent as much time on the material I assign as you do daydreaming."

The remark raised an equally venomous titter from the class. I felt the subtle flush of shame heat and stain my cheeks, and hurriedly turned the page, breaking off my tale to turn out a partly plagiarized poem.

"I suppose you expect me to read the assignment that you weren't paying attention to again," grumbled Mrs. K, turning away to retrieve the calendar cum lesson plan.

Without looking up, in the quiet voice that later teachers would learn meant I was being defiant, I recited, "I hope to have a horse one day...a beautiful pony to run and play," in a mockingly unsubtle singsong. Mrs. K clapped slowly, dramatically sarcastic.

"I'm sure all your classmates are impressed, Quinn. Now stop showing off and get to work. Your poem is due today instead of tomorrow." Her acidic tone and pinched, strained demeanor brought a surreptitious smile to my lips. I had touched a nerve, bested someone my senior more than four times over. Five minutes later, I handed her this poem:

Shod hooves stamping, steady beat
Cool wind banishing summer's heat
Travel lands both fey and fair
My horsey takes me anywhere.

Satisfied in my ability, I returned to my seat and finished my toaster tragedy. Two minutes before the end-of-class bell, Mrs. K called me to her desk. When I approached she said nothing, but handed me my poem, slashed in the angry red angles of an "F." Her textbook perfect handwriting arched below it. "Perhaps I should have reread the assignment after all. You won't go far with the attitude you're showing."

I regained my seat, staring dumbfounded at the first failing grade of my life, though certainly not the last. The sharp sting of tears compelled me to hide my face in my folded arms as I quietly wept.

For Further Reading

Kearney, K. (1993). Discrimination against excellence. *Understanding Our Gifted, 6*(2), 16.

Kerr, B. A. (1997). *Smart girls: A new psychology of girls, women and giftedness.* Scottsdale, AZ: Gifted Psychology Press.

Kerr, B. A., & Cohn, S. J. (2001). *Smart boys: Talent, manhood, and the search for meaning.* Scottsdale, AZ: Gifted Psychology Press.

Morelock, M. (1992). Giftedness: The view from within. *Understanding Our Gifted, 4*(3), 1, 11-15. http://www.ditd.org/floater.php?location=17 (23 Feb. 2003).

Silverman, L. K. (1986). What happens to the gifted girl? In C. J. Maker (Ed.), *Critical issues in gifted education, Vol. 1: Defensible programs for the gifted* (pp. 43-89). Austin, TX: Pro-Ed.

Sykes, C. J. (1995). *Dumbing down our kids: Why America's children feel good about themselves, but can't read, write or add.* New York: St. Martin's Press.

Tomlinson, C. A. (1992). Gifted education and the middle school movement: Two voices on teaching the academically talented. *Journal for the Education of the Gifted, 15*(3), 206-238.

Tomlinson, C. A. (1994). Gifted learners: The boomerang kids of middle school? *Roeper Review, 16*(3), 177-182.

Webb, J. T., Meckstroth, E. A. & Tolan, S. S. (1982). *Guiding the gifted child.* Columbus, OH: Ohio Psychology Publishing Company.

2

What Do We Mean by *Gifted*?

Giftedness is asynchronous development in which advanced cognitive abilities and heightened intensity combine to create inner experiences and awareness that are qualitatively different from the norm. This asynchrony increases with higher intellectual capacity. The uniqueness of the gifted renders them particularly vulnerable and requires modifications in parenting, teaching and counseling in order for them to develop optimally.

The Columbus Group, 1991

Parents advocating for a precocious child must necessarily understand how their local schools define giftedness. Today, we see a surprising range of definitions, many of which reflect our national discomfort with the notion of giftedness. Are we indeed all equal or are some more equal than others? Do we respect high intellectual ability in children and try to ensure that it is nurtured appropriately? Or, to maintain egalitarian ideals, do we back away from concern about the nation's most able learners, identify as *gifted* a far larger percentage of students—or even *all* students? How a child's school views this issue can affect not only the child's admission to a program, but also the level of services provided.

For example, one public elementary school in a local district requires IQ scores of at least 140 (130 is typically considered *gifted*) because the school has a particularly able student body and feels its program can provide for the needs of many gifted students without special accommodations. Yet, we have also encountered programs for which only *above average* ability, creativity, and task commitment are sufficient for entrance. The top 1% or the top 30% may be admitted, or the school may assert that, "All our children are gifted," effectively eliminating most effective accommodations for the highly able. Even schools within a district may differ if each has chosen its own method of identification, so parents need to research this issue carefully. Schools should be able to supply literature describing gifted and talented services and outlining admission requirements. Such documents usually provide insight into the school's perception of giftedness and commitment to supporting it. The following pages provide an overview of the current thinking on giftedness, as well as its recent history.

Definitions

The G Word

The term *gifted* is an unfortunate one in a society highly sensitive to the meanings of words and their political ramifications. Originally used simply to describe a level of intellectual functioning (adjectives can be difficult to find for this purpose), it has unfortunate connotations for some. Perhaps labeling only some children *gifted* comes too close to suggesting that all children are not the special gifts to their families that they are...or offends by the fact that some children have gifts that are neither earned nor deserved. Furthermore, though we speak of nurturing giftedness, we don't usually speak of developing it from scratch. We acknowledge it as largely inborn—running in families just as learning disabilities and other deficits do—a fact that rankles many. For whatever reason, it invites criticism.

Susan Winebrenner, in an article in *Understanding Our Gifted* (1994, p. 8), suggested an alternative. Because what we are really trying to describe is children who are *Discrepant In Learning From Age PeerS*, she proposed that DILFAPS might be a better choice. The term would refer to all students for whom the regular curriculum and instruction are not appropriate. "All DILFAPS need different pacing or complexity, and have learning styles that require atypical teaching methods," she wrote. But, whereas DILFAPS would remove some of the emotional loading that *gifted* has, the term is not exactly mellifluous and might be slow to catch on. So many attempts have been made to rename and reframe the problem that they tend to confuse the critical issues. One of the latest replaces the term *gifted* with *talented*, a problem because *talented* already has accepted meanings to some who don't want its usage changed. Comedian George Carlin observes that when Americans can't *solve* a problem, they *rename* it, usually with a longer, more complex name (1990). He offers as an example the terms we have applied to the traumatic effects soldiers experience from combat: *shell shock* in World War I, *battle fatigue* in World War II, *operational exhaustion* in the Korean war, and *post-traumatic stress disorder* in Viet Nam. He notes that each longer name increasingly conceals the pain involved and "has the humanity squeezed out of the phrase." If Carlin is correct, we may simply prefer to keep *gifted* and avoid something far more cumbersome, impersonal, and (likely) devoid of any suggestion that being gifted is a good thing. Either way, the advocacy issues surrounding gifted children demand the time such an argument about terminology would take away.

The 130 IQ

The term *gifted* is a long-standing descriptor of high-level cognitive functioning. When I was an undergraduate psychology major, taking my first Individual Differences course, it meant one thing: individuals with IQ scores of 130 or higher on standardized tests of intelligence, generally the Wechsler or Stanford-Binet. The *average* level included scores from 90 to 109 (on a Wechsler test), high *average* encompassed scores from 110 to 119, and *superior* ranged from 120 to 129. The *gifted* level reflected scores two standard deviations above the mean of 100 and at the 98th percentile, when compared with other individuals of the same age. The 2% of the population labeled *gifted* corresponded with the 2% of the population considered retarded, with both groups exhibiting needs so discrepant from those of average individuals that special provisions were assumed to be necessary. The Wechsler scales used a standard deviation of 15; hence, 130 was the beginning of the gifted or *very superior* range. The Stanford-Binet tests utilized a standard deviation of 16, so 132 was considered the gifted level. Many clinicians have defined a *highly gifted* level, as well, beginning at three standard deviations above the mean (145 on a Wechsler test or 148 on the Stanford-Binet tests). Wechsler tests have ceilings of 160, effectively limiting the identification of higher levels of ability than *highly gifted*. Stanford-Binet scales, through the Form L-M, extended the range to 200 or more, allowing for the identification of even higher levels of giftedness than *highly gifted* (possible when the child is young enough to avoid reaching the test's ceiling). However, the Stanford-Binet: Fourth Edition was introduced in 1986 with a ceiling of 164 because it was felt that too few children scored in the extreme ranges to warrant the necessary extra test items. As of this writing, Riverside Publishing is introducing the Stanford-Binet: Fifth Edition, with provisions to raise the ceiling once again. Psychologists working with profoundly gifted children, as well as programs attempting to meet their needs, desperately need the information that the higher ceiling affords (see chapter 3 for a discussion of this issue).

Children whose IQ scores identify them as being within the gifted range represent only about the top 2% of the population. However, at the Gifted Development Center, we identify more children as gifted than just 2%, due mostly to the fact that we work with many *twice exceptional* children who exhibit not only highly advanced reasoning abilities, but also learning disabilities and other deficits that lower their IQ scores. These children are the *learning disabled/gifted*. They absolutely require educational accommodations for giftedness, but coupled with support for their deficits. We also occasionally see a child whose high abilities are apparent in our clinical observations, but whose giftedness can't be documented with our tests for one reason or another. In these rare cases, we try to gain entrance for these children into gifted programs on a trial basis. The combination of all of these types of *giftedness* yields a larger percentage than just 2%, perhaps 3 to 5%, but these children remain a very small minority in our society.

What Do IQ tests test?

Most scholars who study intelligence agree that it consists predominantly of abstract reasoning ability (Snyderman & Rothman, 1988), which manifests itself in various domains such as verbal reasoning, spatial reasoning or mathematical reasoning. Abstract reasoning is the hallmark of giftedness. Intelligence tests assess reasoning ability by presenting the test taker with such tasks as finding similarities between concepts, discerning a mathematical pattern in a series, asking why certain things are done, or copying designs with blocks. Most have vocabulary measures, as well, because the acquisition of words in a language and the ability to define them is a strong indicator of general intelligence, even for children from deprived backgrounds. IQ tests also assess other abilities in addition to reasoning that are felt to be clinically significant. Most have measures of visual and auditory memory (either short or long term), visual-motor coordination, visual perception, attention to visual detail, and, increasingly, processing speed. The actual items on an intelligence test reflect the test maker's conception of intelligence. For example, the WISC-III (Wechsler Intelligence Scale for Children—Third Edition) manual describes the late David Wechsler's original view that intelligence is not a particular ability, but an aggregate and global entity, the "capacity of the individual to act purposefully, to think rationally, and to deal effectively with his or her environment" (1991, p. 1). Wechsler explained,

> ...the subtests are chosen, therefore, to tap many different mental abilities, which all together reflect a child's general intellectual ability. Some subtests require the child to reason abstractly, some call on the child's memory, some call for certain perceptual skills, and so forth. All of these abilities are valued to varying degrees by our culture, and all relate to behavior that is generally accepted as intelligent behavior in one way or another.

Test items are usually designed to assess a combination of *fluid* and *crystallized* abilities (Cattell, 1963). Fluid reasoning is general reasoning ability—"thinking on one's feet" in novel situations—especially perceiving relations in figural and spatial material. Crystallized abilities are the result of acculturation and education, accessed by tapping a child's general store of knowledge, verbal and quantitative reasoning, sequential memory, vocabulary, and reading comprehension.

Intelligence tests are excellent measures of how discrepant a child is from others in terms of typical developmental expectations because they compare the child's abilities to those of other children the same age. The greater the variance from the mean of 100, the more discrepant or asynchronous the child is. Determining giftedness based on high IQ test scores is a reasonable approach to the identification of gifted children, provided there is flexibility in the choice of tests to document the particular strengths of the child (see Chapter 3—Testing Considerations). IQ testing is preferable to basing identification solely on performance in school, teacher recommendation, or individual interview.

High Achievement

Although most children earning IQ scores of 130 and above on individual intelligence tests would be labeled *gifted* by their schools and accepted for a gifted program, some schools insist upon performance-related definitions that require accomplishment in one or more academic areas. A child has to earn top grades in one or more subjects and show high-level mastery of the school's curriculum. Such requirements reveal a fundamental confusion between giftedness and high achievement. The gifted can process more conceptually complex material, need to be taught at a higher level, and learn at a considerably faster pace because they master concepts more easily. High achievers, by definition, perform well in a given subject area. Certainly some, but not all, high achievers are gifted. Many gifted students are high achievers; some are not. Gifted students who have been underchallenged for a considerable length of time or for whom the school's curriculum is, otherwise, a poor fit, may not produce impressive work. One reason testing is avoided by schools is due to concern that certain children, especially minority children and those without means, will be underidentified. Yet, an identification process for giftedness that focuses on high achievement in school may miss *these* children as well as other underachieving gifted students who are considerably at risk. The result is th schools fail to provide accommodations to those who need them most.

Whereas performance-related definitions of giftedness may feel more ethical to schools (one must earn giftedness), and tend to identify more children, they have other disconcerting ramifications. A child may be considered gifted in some subjects, but not others, and be identified as gifted at some times, but not others, based on performance. Certainly, schools want to offer services to gifted children most in need at a given time, but giftedness is a more generalized advanced cognitive ability, or intelligence, that is relatively stable over time. It does not come and go and should not be measured simply by performance in the classroom at a given time. Intelligence tests do a better job of finding gifted children, especially those at-risk students who are not performing well in school. IQ test scores tend to be fairly stable, so that the child who was once documented as gifted remains so, unless there has been serious illness or injury to the brain. Scores may rise as interventions are under-taken for disabilities. But, in general, a gifted child who has been identified should stay identified and be continuously monitored to meet special needs as they occur.

Teacher Recommendations and Student Interviews

Some schools place considerable weight on teacher recom-mendations to find gifted children. However, we often see cases in which teachers have difficulty seeing the giftedness in introverted students, who may simply meet expectations and prefer not to stand out in the classroom. Likewise, teachers may not recognize giftedness in children who have become behavior problems when a program is a poor fit. Most teachers believe that their teaching is sufficiently engaging for all children in their classrooms—so a child's abilities should be evident in his or her classwork. Unfortunately, this is not always the case.

Interviews with the child can also result in inappropriate conclusions when the interviewer is less familiar with giftedness. One first-grade boy who was turned down for his school's G/T program (a program that considered only teacher recommendations, a parent questionnaire, and interview with the child) wryly commented that he should have said his favorite TV program at that time was *Mr. Wizard*, instead of *You Can't Do That On Television*. Those who still remember the latter program would be aware that this first-grader liked a comedy program for middle school-aged children, certainly a *gifted* choice. The next year, the same boy actually said his favorite program was *Mr. Wizard*, made unexpectedly fast progress in reading (primary teachers usually expect that a gifted child will be an advanced reader), and was accepted to the G/T program.

Educational Definitions of Giftedness

If a high score on an intelligence test is not the standard used to judge giftedness in children, what other definitions of giftedness or high intelligence should parents be familiar with in order to obtain services for their children? The operational definitions of giftedness schools are using are becoming more inclusive, including more children who demonstrate giftedness in more diverse ways. This can be good or bad, depending upon the individual child's needs, as the more inclusive definition can lead to overidentification of gifted children and make it less likely the school can meet their needs. For example, a definition used by my children's school district, around 1991, defined giftedness as follows:

> *Gifted students are those who possess excep-*
> *tional intellectual and/or academic capabilities.*
> *Their demonstrated or potential ability is so*
> *outstanding that it becomes essential to provide*
> *them with qualitatively different educational*
> *programming which is individually prescribed.*

Note that the above definition includes both children acknowledged for high intelligence (probably those able to supply high IQ test scores would be accepted) and those who are high achievers in school. But, compare that to the following definition promoted by the state of Colorado in 1998:

> *Gifted and talented children...means those... whose abilities, talents, and potential for accomplishment are so exceptional or develop- mentally advanced that they require special provisions to meet their educational needs...Gifted and talented students are capable of high performance, exceptional production, or exceptional learning behavior by virtue of any or a combination of these areas:*
>
> *(1) general or specific intellectual ability,*
>
> *(2) specific academic aptitude,*
>
> *(3) creative or productive thinking,*
>
> *(4) leadership and human relations abilities,*
>
> *(5) visual arts, performing arts, spatial, or musical abilities, and*
>
> *(6) psychomotor abilities.*

Multiple Intelligences

Clearly the second definition is responding to high ability in more diverse areas and requires the school to extend its services for the gifted. Educators respond to popular theories of intelligence and this latter definition reflects the influence of Howard Gardner's Multiple Intelligences (MI), as described in his 1983 book, *Frames of Mind*. Gardner initially proposed a group of more or less discrete *intelligences* including the following: Verbal/Linguistic, Logical/ Mathematical, Spatial, Bodily/Kinesthetic, Musical,

Interpersonal, Intrapersonal, with an eighth added later: Naturalist. Gardner continued his MI tradition in his 1999 *Intelligence Reframed*, with a discussion of whether Spiritual, Existential, and Moral intelligences should be added to the list. Existential was deemed closest to meeting Gardner's requirements for an intelligence.

Although *intelligence* seems another poor choice of words when discussing such things as Bodily/Kinesthetic abilities, the theory does acknowledge the different ways in which ability manifests itself in different individuals. Some schools have chosen to support these *intelligences* in their students, as evidenced by student performance in the classroom. Schools are to be commended for efforts to support all advanced abilities in their students; however, it is important that they not overextend to promise support they cannot practically offer. Schools have typically been in the business of providing instruction in traditional curricular areas (e.g., in mathematics, science, and written composition), but not of supporting the serious ballet student or child whose piano accomplishments have already eclipsed the knowledge of the school's music teacher (although outside involvement might certainly become a part of the child's educational program). Schools feel pulled to increase their gifted identification to please an ever-widening population of families. When class sizes are large, teachers are hard-pressed to accommodate the needs of all students.

Disappointingly, we have seen some schools extend Gardner's views to suggest that every individual must be gifted in at least one intelligence, a conclusion not intended by the author. In some schools, this misinterpretation has led to individualized learning plans for all students to support the *giftedness* of all. Supporting the learning strengths of any student is important, but the assumption that all are gifted tends to dilute accommodations for students who need significant changes made to their educational programs. And, as one teacher noted, the faculty in her school had to concede very quickly that some students did not excel in any of Gardner's areas, an uncomfortable realization the school might have avoided with a plan more carefully designed to meet previously unmet needs.

One positive result of Gardner's theory, however, has been an increased interest in teaching to the appropriate learning style of each student, as his intelligences suggest certain teaching strategies. We have been convinced for many years at the GDC that children clearly vary in their learning styles and that instructional approaches geared to their learning are more successful than approaches that are at odds with their strengths. Children often display a preference for learning through a particular sense modality: auditory, visual, or kinesthetic. They may prefer either verbal or spatial tasks (or be adept at both), and learn more successfully through either a sequential or gestalt approach. Because these elements of learning style lend themselves well to Gardner's intelligences, his theory has been extended to teachers' manuals to support instructional approaches for a range of learners. Teaching has traditionally been highly verbal and sequential (emphasizing a lecture style and provision of some new information each day to build upon what was presented the day before). Any help for teachers to expand their instructional approaches to include visual aids and models, hands-on experiences, music and rhythm, etc., benefits many students with more atypical learning styles.

Parents of children who have a significant need for modification in their academic programs will need to find their way through the labyrinth of gifted identification in each school. Accomplishing this is a first step to being granted the privilege of accommodations, to the degree they are possible. Every effort should be made to fully understand the school's view of giftedness and how it can be demonstrated by the child, so that identification progresses smoothly. In some cases, it may become apparent that the school's perception of giftedness is inadequate to meet the child's needs.

For example, a highly gifted child in a program where 30% of children are identified and accommodations are minimal may want to consider a different school. Only if the child can be identified and receive meaningful accommodations is the gifted program worth pursuing (some do little more than identify).

Whereas the educational definitions of giftedness speak to the need for modifications in school, they do little to help parents understand the inner experience of giftedness in their children. There is one definition, however, that goes further.

Dealing With Asynchrony

Giftedness as Asynchronous Development

In 1991, a group, including Dr. Linda Silverman, met in Columbus, Ohio to consider the question of what giftedness actually is. Still referred to as the Columbus Group, this group of clinicians, theorists and parents was concerned about definitions of giftedness based solely on external performance. Our experiences at the GDC suggested giftedness was not only advanced abstract reasoning ability, but also a quality of experience that involved higher levels of sensitivity, intensity and moral development. The possibility that it could be defined merely by high achievement in a subject area placed many gifted students at considerable risk. If they were not also high achievers, they would fall through the cracks of our educational system and fail to reach their full potential. Striving to agree on a more comprehensive definition that would reflect the totality and inner experience of giftedness, the Columbus Group wrote:

> *Giftedness is asynchronous development in which advanced cognitive abilities and heightened intensity combine to create inner*

experiences and awareness that are qualita-
tively different from the norm. This asynchrony
increases with higher intellectual capacity. The
uniqueness of the gifted renders them particu-
larly vulnerable and requires modifications in
parenting, teaching and counseling in order for
them to develop optimally. (unpublished transcript)

This definition, which we strongly support, respects the
unique experience of being gifted and its academic, social
and emotional ramifications. Asynchrony in the gifted means
that the child experiences special difficulties because his
abilities are not developing typically and in concert with
each other. Reasoning ability may outpace physical development and fail to support emotional needs. The highly
asynchronous child develops in a minefield of potential
problems and should not spark the envy of those who are
concerned about his being *advantaged* or *elite*.

The Asynchrony of Advanced Mental Age

The most notable asynchrony is the child's advanced *mental
age* when compared with chronological age.

Mental age predicts the amount of knowledge
he or she has mastered, the rate at which the
child learns, sophistication of play, age of true
peers, maturity of the child's sense of humor,
ethical judgment, and awareness of the world.
In contrast, chronological age predicts the
child's height, physical coordination, hand-
writing speed, emotional needs, and social
skills (Silverman, 1995).

For example, one child may have higher standards for the
creation of a drawing than her physical fine-motor coordination can yet support; another may dictate terrific stories to
his mother, but quit in frustration when asked to write them

by hand. The asynchrony of the child's higher aspirations and more limited physical coordination can cause considerable dismay. Teachers gear instructional approaches to what is likely to work best with children of a particular *age*, and in many cases these approaches are at odds with the needs of the gifted. For example, many young gifted students are reluctant to use the *inventive spelling* their kindergarten and first-grade teachers encourage (to enable students to begin writing) because they immediately grasp the importance of correct spelling. This can paralyze their developing composition skills until they learn to spell enough words correctly that they're willing to take the risk. In one case, a boy was horrified to learn that his teacher had been saying his spelling was fine when it was, in fact, incorrect. "She lied to me," he wailed, and insisted that his teacher had actually taught him to misspell. Considering that some of these children learn with only one presentation of material, this could have been true in his case. As is true for the developmentally delayed child with an eight-year-old body and a five-year-old mind, development is full of pitfalls. The child must struggle daily with age expectations that cannot be met. The gifted child with the eight-year-old mind trapped in the body of a five-year old functions intellectually as an eight-year-old with eight-year-old aspirations, perfectionism and reasoning abilities, but is treated like a five-year-old.

The Further Complication of Emotional Age

The fact that emotional needs are tied to chronological age renders gifted children more vulnerable. Whenever advanced cognition makes them aware of information for which there is insufficient emotional maturity for understanding, their suffering can be heartrending. For example, young children strongly need the stability their parents' love and support provides. But when the preschool-age gifted child becomes aware that parents may die, this is very difficult information to accept. "Nothing's going to happen to Mommy or Daddy" is an unacceptable statement on logical grounds (we can never be certain disaster will not strike), even when the child has an age-appropriate need to believe it. Likewise, during recent wars in the Middle East and Afghanistan, we saw many children devastated by the incongruity of adults killing other adults for a cause when children are taught to "fight with words" because physical aggression is not right. Such highly conflicting realizations are encountered on a regular basis by these children.

We see the chronological age aspects of gifted children remaining fairly steady (although some of these children reach physical developmental milestones such as walking early), while the mental age qualities are usually very advanced (with notable lapses, parents insist), and emotional maturity varies with the situation. These children can appear extremely mature in some situations and highly immature in others. Parents are forced to deal with a child of many *ages* at the same time—no simple matter.

Achievement vs. Developmental Advancement

In her 1995 keynote address at the Eleventh World Conference on Gifted and Talented Children in Hong Kong, Linda Silverman spoke on "The Universal Experience of Being Out-of Sync." She emphasized that just as some want to move away from giftedness being determined by intelligence tests, a performance or achievement-oriented definition invites other criticisms. She noted that as early as 1926, Leta Hollingworth pointed out that achievement is very much a function of opportunity and those who have greater financial resources have more opportunity to succeed. Moreover, she reported that George, Margolin, and Sapon-Shevin have even claimed that the notion of *giftedness* is culturally biased (even racist), related to socio-economic opportunity, and a social construction to maintain hierarchical power relations. Linda concluded that this is difficult to refute when children are identified by high achievement. Furthermore, giftedness as achievement is culturally determined, so that the same performance may be judged differentially by members of different groups.

Conversely, if giftedness is viewed as developmental advancement, Linda observed that there are children in every culture who

> *...develop at a faster pace from early childhood on, are inquisitive to a greater degree than their agemates, generalize concepts earlier than their peers, demonstrate advanced verbal or spatial capacities at an early age, have superb memories, grasp abstract concepts, love to learn, have a sophisticated sense of humor, prefer complexity, are extraordinarily insightful, have a passion for justice, are profoundly aware, and experience life with great intensity.*

These qualities may or may not lead to world renown or success. In some societies they are applauded, whereas in others they are punished.

Personality and Other Traits of the Gifted

Extensive experience, not only testing gifted children but also counseling them, caused Linda Silverman to note typical personality characteristics common to the group. Not only did these children reason well, but they also exhibited many of the same personality traits. These traits applied regardless of the way intelligence was manifested—in advanced mathematical/spatial reasoning or in remarkable verbal reasoning abilities. Over the years, she has revised her original list and retained items most predictive of high IQ scores. The following list is used at the GDC as a screener for giftedness and is available on our website.

When parents endorse at least 18 of the 25 characteristics as typical of their child's personality, our in-house research indicates there is an 84% chance that the child will earn an IQ score of 120 or above.

When parents agree with virtually every item and insist that most are not just *true*, but *especially true* for their child, a profoundly gifted child can usually be predicted. This happens often, but not always, with this particular group.

Characteristics of Giftedness in Children

Linda Kreger Silverman, Ph.D.

Reasons well (good thinker)

Learns rapidly

Has extensive vocabulary

Has an excellent memory

Has a long attention span*

Sensitive (feelings hurt easily)

Shows compassion

Perfectionistic

Intense

Morally sensitive

Has strong curiosity

Perseverant when interested*

Has a high degree of energy

Prefers older companions/adults

Has a wide range of interests

Has a great sense of humor

Early or avid reader**

Concerned with justice, fairness

Judgment mature for age *at times*

Is a keen observer

Has a vivid imagination

Is highly creative

Tends to question authority

Shows ability with numbers

Good at jigsaw puzzles

*(Long attention span or perseverant if interested. Does the child stay with tasks for long periods of time?)

**(If the child is too young to read, is intensely interested in books.)

Working with these children over the years, we have become accustomed to their personalities. They love to reason, consider ideas, and debate. They are rapid learners in the sense that they do not require as much instruction as other children. Although the average child may need eight or nine repetitions to learn material, these children need far less explanation, with drill and practice considerably reduced. Some are also fast processors (while others are more reflective), but concepts are more easily grasped by all gifted children. They tend not to need the review that is provided in school every fall to ensure students have not forgotten last year's work. Their memories are usually excellent and parents often note that they remember verbal material discussed only once, months or years before, or seem to have a perfect visual memory, perhaps of a place they've been. Vocabulary is generally strong, regardless of socioeconomic background. Their speech usually resembles that of older children, adding to the social distance they experience with age peers from the earliest grades in school.

These children have long attention spans for material of interest, almost without exception. Even gifted children with attentional deficits have the capacity to *hyperfocus* for long periods of time in areas of interest. Sensitivity (getting feelings hurt easily) abounds and tends to magnify the disparity between these children and others. Their differences are often not appreciated by other children, and they are made even more vulnerable to signs of rejection because of their heightened sensitivity. They may also be quite compassionate and empathetic about the plights of others. This is accompanied by moral sensitivity that allows them to consider deeply the events around them. Perfectionism is almost always seen in these children, as well. It is evidence that they perceive a higher possible level of achievement than is expected and that they aspire to something better. It is the rare gifted child who is less than *intense*. As I talk to parents, they clearly view their children as challenging, exhausting, high-strung, or high maintenance; these are not children characterized by being easygoing or happy to just go along with the decisions of a group. Many show intense curiosity about the world, often leading to a wide range of interests.

Highly motivated to learn and accomplish, they can persevere to unusual degrees for children. Their energy level is usually described as high and most require less sleep than others (many also stopped napping earlier as small children). They commonly prefer to interact with older children and adults (and sometimes younger children) rather than with same-age peers. This is due to developmental advancement that makes them more similar to older children in both cognitive abilities and interests. Most sincerely enjoy humor and appreciate it during test sessions. In fact, when Linda Silverman taught at the University of Denver, she and colleague Ken Seeley proposed (with tongue in cheek) the Silverman-Seeley Pun Test of Giftedness, in which a teacher makes a rather sophisticated, humorous comment to the class and watches to see who falls out of a chair. Gifted children are clever and generally appreciate puns or funny situations. They particularly enjoy the Verbal Absurdities items on the Stanford-Binet L-M that require them to find what is foolish or silly about a verbal statement. They also enjoy the reading subtest of the Kaufman Test of Educational Achievement because it asks them to read passages and respond appropriately in pantomime. If they pantomime correctly, then they obviously understand the written passage, but they enjoy the humor of the situation.

Most gifted children are also early or avid readers. Many have taught themselves to read; those who learn later may learn very quickly. Reading provides, to such a large degree, the information they crave that it is important to virtually all of them (gifted children with AD/HD may be less avid readers of books, preferring periodicals or browsing in non-fiction books). Concern for justice and fairness is enormously important to this population. Fueled by their reasoning ability and high moral development, these are children who will go to great lengths to ensure that life is fair. We have seen children who had nightmares during the Gulf War and who began "Save the Elephants" campaigns. Their higher-level moral development is oftentimes even more impressive than their problem-solving abilities. Their judgment can be very mature and they will question authority if it seems appropriate. Creativity and a vivid imagination may accompany the above traits, as well, and we often see unusual ability with numbers or puzzles. Some children even insist on assembling puzzles with the pieces upside down to increase the difficulty!

Other Gifted Characteristics

Beyond the characteristics that are included on the Giftedness in Children scale, there are others we have noted, as well. Young gifted children typically progress through the developmental milestones more quickly than usual, at least in some areas. They may talk quite early, walk or ride a bicycle early. However, there are some who will wait until they can walk, talk, or ride the bike almost perfectly before they show us, going through an extended period of mental rehearsal. The gifted also tend to exhibit physical, as well as emotional, sensitivities and frequently have allergies, asthma, food sensitivities, or a history of colic in infancy. Tactile sensitivities to clothing are very common, most often with rough fabrics (some can wear only soft cotton knits), tags in the necks of garments, and seams in socks. Hypersensitivities to bright lights and loud noises are also seen frequently within the gifted population.

Introversion

Most gifted children are introverts, whereas the general population is predominantly extraverted. This is a concern because society provides considerable support for extraversion, but little for introversion. Mothers do not admonish their children to stay in and read, but, rather, to go out and play with other children. When a child shows introverted characteristics, there is usually pressure to *help* him change his maladaptive style. Yet, gifted introverts replenish their energy through time alone or with close family members, so respect for and accommodation of their more introverted personality traits is very important. They need more time to observe and reflect before entering into discussions or answering a teacher's questions. Because introversion makes it more difficult for a child to be the *squeaky wheel* whose behavior forces some accommodation from teachers, we may need to intervene and advocate more strongly for introverted gifted children, even when they are older.

Early Self-Efficacy

Elizabeth (Betty) Maxwell, Associate Director of the Gifted Development Center, has proposed that gifted children show early self-efficacy (1998). Not content to simply model their actions after adults until well through childhood, these children often insist while quite young that they should make many decisions pertinent to their lives by themselves. For example, one three-year-old profoundly gifted boy I tested had insisted upon making even the simplest decision since he could talk. His mother explained that he had been quite a challenge to handle because most children do not question virtually every decision made for them by parents as he routinely did. When tested in the spring, he had just informed his preschool teacher, "Now, I will write," after refusing written work all year. Such children do not seem to come from parents who are overly indulgent, but show these tendencies regardless of the response they get from adults. They generally view themselves as more in charge than others their age, although they may be refusing to do some things until they can perform them well enough to meet their own high standards. More typical children would not think to make such decisions and could not be taught to try.

Familial Histories of Giftedness

Gifted children have familial histories of giftedness. A question on the Gifted Development Center Developmental Questionnaire asks if parents or grandparents had indications of giftedness. Whereas most relatives have no test data to reference (a few note that they were given an IQ test but were never told the results), their answers frequently include academic honors and high SAT scores. Sometimes, parents mention skipped grades or relatives beginning college at a young age, or they describe unusual accomplishments. They may also include references to underachievement—struggles in public school and elsewhere due to the discrepancy between their high ability levels and program offerings. The following response was notable for the number of highly accomplished relatives mentioned:

> Mom—in gifted pull-out program in Middle School. PSAT-National Merit Scholar. GRE—790 math, 800 analytical, 710 English. Music very important—played flute/piccolo throughout grad. school and professionally. Ph.D. in Molecular Ecology. Dad—not interested in school, but got good grades, finished a Ph.D. in Plant Physiological Ecology and is now a college professor. Paternal Grandfather—Ph.D.

*Recognized as the leading _____ in U.S.
and probably worldwide. Harvard professor 30
yrs. Currently at Princeton. Paternal
Grandmother—artist-deceased. Maternal
Grandfather—Master's in Business, obvious
intelligent underachiever! Maternal
Grandmother—author of children's rhyming
books-but unpublished. Also—Great
Grandfather founder of [major corporation].
Great-great grandfather invented [high tech
gasket]. Great-great-great uncle was the
[European] painter _____, Grand Uncle
important inventor.*

Although few children have histories like the one above, it is especially helpful in evaluating a child to have information about relatives. For example, a child who earns lower scores on an IQ test, but has a highly gifted sibling and parents who are successful professionals in their respective fields is likely to be far brighter than we can document at that time. In such cases, the likelihood of learning disabilities or other deficits lowering scores is very strong. Given support for strengths as well as disabilities, such a child can become a late bloomer whose giftedness becomes apparent as he or she matures.

Gifted adults show similar personality characteristics to those of gifted children. We use an adult scale, which expands the characteristics listed on the child scale. It includes the following:

Giftedness in Adults

Linda Kreger Silverman, Ph.D.

Are you a good problem solver?
Do you understand new ideas quickly?
Do you have an extensive vocabulary?

Do you have good long-term memory?

Can you concentrate for long periods of time?

Are you highly sensitive?

Are you unusually compassionate?

Are you perfectionistic?

Do you have passionate, intense feelings?

Do you have strong moral convictions?

Are you very curious?

Do you persevere with your interests?

Do you have a great deal of energy?

Do you often feel out-of-sync with others?

Do you feel overwhelmed by many interests or abilities?

Do you have an extraordinary sense of humor?

Are you an avid reader?

Do you often take a stand against injustice?

As a child were you considered mature for your age?

Are you a keen observer?

Do you have a vivid imagination?

Do you feel driven by your creativity?

Do you often question authority?

Do you have facility with numbers?

Do you spend time doing puzzles?

Do you love ardent discussions?

Are you perceptive or insightful?

Do you have organized collections?

Do you need periods of contemplation?

Do you often connect seemingly unrelated ideas?

Do you thrive on challenge?

Do you often search for meaning in your life?

Are you fascinated with paradoxes?

Do you have extraordinary abilities and deficits?

Are you often aware of things that others are not?

Do you set high standards or goals for yourself?

Do you have unusual ideas or perceptions?

Are you a complex person?

Such characteristics run in our gifted families, allowing parents some innate ability to cope with the issues of their gifted children. The highly sensitive child usually has a highly sensitive parent who is nurturing to the degree necessary. The highly curious child usually has a parent who is equally anxious to find out the answers and will make that trip to the library, museum, or Internet site. Only in rare cases do we see parents who are baffled by children with unexpected or unappreciated personality character- istics. When this does occur, it is essential that the parents understand all that goes with the territory of giftedness. No gifted child can "stop being so sensitive" or "stop asking questions" or "stop thinking life should be fair." Under- standing the psychological territory of giftedness is essential to supporting, planning for, and appreciating the gifted child.

Levels of Giftedness

Schools usually acknowledge only a single level of giftedness, identifying students as gifted or not gifted, but the range of ability above 130 is far-reaching and the differences between children profound. Some of the most advanced children have earned IQ scores above 250 on the Stanford-Binet L-M, more than seven standard deviations above children scoring 130 (two standard deviations above the mean). Though all gifted children require accommoda- tions in their educational programs, the accommodations may be quite different, based on the needs of the child.

The Moderately Gifted

The *moderately gifted* range, from 130 to 144 (or 132-147 on a Stanford-Binet L-M) comprises about 1.5 percent of the total population and, by far, the largest group within the gifted population. Most children we test earn IQ scores within this range and most of the literature about giftedness pertains to these children. They not only have gifted abstract reasoning abilities, but also the accompanying personality characteristics discussed above. This is the group public schools try to accommodate most, although programs are limited. Most schools specifically for the gifted, whether public or private, plan curricula and instructional approaches based on the needs and learning pace of this group (more highly gifted children usually require an Individual Educational Plan in such programs to meet individual needs).

All gifted children can be assumed to need considerably less drill and practice and to progress more quickly through new material. In fact, a common rule of thumb is that these children can learn in about half the time. They do not require the review of material in the fall that most children need and they have usually mastered some of the material that will be taught ahead of time. The rest they will learn much more quickly. They tend to be better at reading comprehension (understanding a passage) than decoding (identifying and pronouncing a word correctly). Their special gift of abstract reasoning allows them to discern a word's meaning from the context in which the word is found. Likewise, most gifted children are stronger at math reasoning than calculation. They hate the drill and practice required to learn math facts and many fall somewhat behind learning their multiplication tables. Strategies to make this learning more fun and much quicker are needed. Moderately gifted students will generally need modifications in their educational programs in more than one academic area.

Almost never are the needs of children in this range fully met in heterogeneous classrooms with whole-class instruction. Likewise, it is a rare moderately gifted child whose special needs are served by simply assigning an extra project or providing services outside the classroom, in addition to the *regular* work. They all need consistent modification of their daily instruction to provide higher level material and accommodate their faster learning pace. This is best accomplished by developing an Individual Educational Plan each year that sets performance goals in each academic subject area based on current achievement levels. Moderately gifted children should be assessed frequently to monitor their progress and modify the yearly IEP if necessary. These children must be allowed to move ahead when they have mastered new material. Ensuring their *continuous progress* supports their motivation to learn. If they become too advanced for the general work of the class, they may need to advance a full grade or attend a higher-grade-level classroom for one or more subjects. Failure to acknowledge their need to progress further and/or any attempt to restrict their progress can place these students seriously at risk. Enrichment programs offered by colleges, museums, etc., are particularly helpful for the gifted and may provide a means to accelerate in a subject area. Likewise, correspondence or online courses, as well as tutors, can increase the options of moderately gifted students in public schools.

All gifted children have a need for true peers and it is essential that a child find friends with whom he or she shares interests to promote social development. This generally requires access to other gifted children or those who are older. Of all gifted children, those at the moderately gifted level are most likely to value high achievement in school and be excellent students. But, they absolutely need the highest level classes schools can provide (honors classes may not be challenging enough), along with additional relevant enrichment and possible acceleration to reach their full potential. Self-contained schools or programs for the gifted, whether public or private, can generally best meet the academic, social and emotional needs of these students.

What concerns do parents have about these children? Consider Katelyn, who was brought for an evaluation because her mother felt she was not adequately challenged in school and recognized in Katelyn some of her own "gifted-girl-in-hiding" traits. A seven-year-old girl in second grade, Katelyn was just beginning to underachieve. Her mother wrote that she could learn with "...blazing speed when she's interested; otherwise, she just cruises." Katelyn's mom feared that she already knew "the system" and would finish her work first to gain time to read or other rewards, while remaining unchallenged. Because parents largely share their children's giftedness, they may also share having their own giftedness go unsupported. Many hope to prevent problems in their children that they experienced themselves. Katelyn's mother knew the pressures on girls to deny their giftedness and hoped her daughter would avoid that particular trap. Yet, the signs were already there, at age seven, that there would be difficulties ahead. We documented Katelyn's giftedness for admission to school programs and strongly recommended a full-time school for the gifted to address her academic, social, and emotional needs. We noted that if such a placement proved impossible, Katelyn would need advancement in reading and possible grade acceleration to the next grade level. We also suggested that her love of drama, music, and singing be strongly supported and her talents developed. Supporting the strengths of the gifted is always of uppermost importance in supporting the self. Katelyn would also benefit from contact with other gifted girls, with whom she could be herself and share her gifts. Where there is appropriate educational programming and similarly gifted peers, children such as Katelyn have a much better chance of reaching their full potential.

The Highly Gifted

The *highly gifted* differ from the moderately gifted in their
pace of learning and in the intensity of their personality
characteristics. They are even more asynchronous. Usually
highly articulate, these children may learn simply upon one
presentation of material (if they are paying attention), with
no drill and practice. Comprising IQ scores from 145 to 159
on Wechsler tests, or 148 to 159 on the Stanford-Binet tests,
many need more extensive acceleration (perhaps two or
more years). This group will often show high school-graduate
grade equivalents in reading and pre-algebra math before
they complete elementary school. They also tend to make
dramatic leaps in basic skills (e.g., reading) which necessitate
very frequent evaluation to avoid teaching them material
they have already mastered. A highly gifted kindergartener
I may have tested last year for school admission, who merely
knew her letters then, may be at the third-grade level in
reading when tested at the same time this year. Likewise,
math skills may be learned very quickly and it is important
for the child to move on to something new.

Continuously reviewing already mastered material is very
difficult for the highly gifted child—and deadly for the child's
love of learning and appreciation of school. These children
may become valedictorians or may find few reasons to earn
A's. They will often perform best in high-level classes with
favorite teachers and less well in *easier* classes, or classes
taught by teachers they don't respect. Alienation may be a
considerable problem as few others share their abilities or
interests. Moreover, they may perceive school to be antithetical
to their needs. They need true peers and opportunities to
find them. In addition to taking all of the highest level
courses available, they should take advantage of Talent
Search or other courses offered by colleges for younger
students, distance-learning opportunities, computer-based
coursework, opportunities to attend high school and college
concurrently, tutors, etc.

Nine-year-old Kirk demonstrates the issues highly ⟨ children face. A boy who was "born intense," accordin⸳ his mother, he has enormous energy and a determination to focus himself and figure things out. Consistently somewhat reserved around other people and cautious regarding new situations (a strong introvert), he continues to be reticent about expressing his emotions. Kirk's feelings about school have changed dramatically; what he once loved, he now resents when there is too much homework and too much wasted time during the school day. Third grade was a traumatic year for Kirk, with a teacher who was unable to individualize work for him and Kirk responding with crying, sleeplessness, and refusal to go to school. He didn't understand why other students were happy with school and he was not. Finally, his mother arranged to have the Woodcock-Johnson-Revised (WJ-R) achievement tests administered to Kirk. He placed at the high school and college level in most subjects. His mother then homeschooled him for the last two months of third grade, covering most of the fourth-grade curriculum, as well. At this point, Kirk was willing to enter the district's magnet school for academically advanced students as a fifth-grader. These changes have helped tremendously, but Kirk continues to express many complaints about school.

The Exceptionally and Profoundly Gifted

Beyond the highly gifted category, there is less agreement about what to call children who earn even higher IQ scores. The *exceptionally gifted* form a group we define as having IQ scores of 160 to 174, whereas the *profoundly gifted* comprise the IQ range from 175 on. Because these populations are statistically very small (an IQ score of 160 represents approximately the 99.99[th] percentile), few professionals have worked with individuals at these levels. However, specializing in work with the gifted, we have felt it quite important to acknowledge them because their needs are so unique, documentation of their abilities is so essential, and recommendations for them differ so much from those for other gifted children.

In January of 1985, Linda Silverman created a support group for parents of children with IQ scores of 160 and above. The group named itself POGO (Parents of Gifted Offspring) and continues today with local Colorado chapters and members who communicate by email from much more distant locations. POGO provides families support and information (through correspondence and family conferences) to deal with the daunting needs of children at this level. (The Hollingworth Center, based in Maine, and started by Kathi Kearney a year earlier, is a similar group for individuals with IQ scores three or more standard deviations above the mean. It offers support, publications, and has held excellent conferences.)

Such groups assist parents in learning how to provide extremely fast-paced, high-level instruction to allow a child to make relatively continuous progress in school. Progress this rapid is virtually impossible to ensure all the time, but these parents must try. Reevaluation of their children's situations must be ongoing, with revised educational plans often needed because a child makes unexpected progress and needs to move on. Resource information is critical and, in some cases, parents have had to create the resources. They have helped to start charter schools, have provided homeschooling for their own children, or have started small educational groups in their homes. They have found colleges willing to accept their much younger children for one or more courses, or college programs for high school-age students. Frequently, they have had to move their children from program to program trying to create a reasonable educational sequence where none exists in a single school building or district.

These children may make incredible learning strides and graduate from college as pre-adolescents, or they may choose to accelerate only as much as is absolutely necessary. We have seen a surprising range of solutions be ultimately successful. Exceptionally and profoundly gifted children are considerably more vulnerable, however, than gifted children at lower IQ levels, to damage from an ill-fitting program. Extremely sensitive and aware of every nuance of their predicament, they are unlikely to be a good fit with classmates until graduate school. But, placing them with older, more advanced students helps considerably and is necessary even in schools for the gifted.

Exceptionally and profoundly gifted students are often not our best students, in terms of grades or academic performance. Even more philosophical than the highly gifted about the importance (or lack thereof) of grades, these students may excel or become dropouts. One who excelled won a recent national science competition and, at 15, began attending a top college utilizing her $50,000 scholarship prize. She moved directly from sixth grade to high school, and completed math coursework from Algebra I to Calculus in one year via computer-based instruction from a university. Yet, many other exceptionally and profoundly gifted students tread a winding and uncertain educational path.

A few years ago, a group of POGO children and teenagers was assembled at the GDC to assist a television production company researching high levels of giftedness. The company was not planning to make public any information from this meeting, but hoped to gain some background perspective to help create a program on the subject. Virtually every student who attended had a story to tell about being terribly alienated in the classroom, of a teacher becoming defensive, and of being personally attacked (publicly criticized or humiliated). One girl described an incident in elementary school when she was being taught subtraction. When asked by the teacher if a larger number could be subtracted from a smaller number, the girl replied, "Yes," knowing the answer would be a negative number. Her teacher insisted this was not true and became so upset when she couldn't exact agreement from the little girl, that the girl's mother had to remove her from the class and homeschool her. In fact, quite a few had been removed from school by their parents and educated at home. A teenage boy in a black leather jacket described how an International Baccalaureate Program at his high school had decided he was *not appropriate* for their program (some of these programs have homework demands that exceptionally gifted students neither need nor see as important). The students agreed it was not worth the personal cost to try to *fit in* in some of these situations; one had to give up too much of oneself for acceptance. A high school counselor working with a National Merit Scholarship contender failing his high school classes advised him to leave school immediately and take his G.E.D. She felt he despised high school so much that remaining could only injure him further.

Children With the Highest IQ Scores

We have defined levels through the *profoundly gifted*; however, there are children whose abilities are significantly greater and whose needs usually cannot be met by creative acceleration in schools. Children with IQ scores above 200 are generally homeschooled because their differences from age peers are too extreme and they are unable to meet typical expectations.

As IQ scores rise from the moderately gifted level (130) to higher levels, we see increasing dissatisfaction with schools (even schools for the gifted), angst, and unwillingness to "play the game" expected of typical students. More highly gifted children tend to value grades less and struggle more to meet average expectations (another good reason to avoid performance-based identification—these students may never appear *gifted*). At the moderately gifted level, we see many high achieving students, whereas at the highly gifted level, we find some valedictorians and many underachievers.

From the exceptionally gifted level on, students are increasingly at risk, with dropping out of school and even suicide potential dangers. The most highly gifted children, above 200 IQ usually cannot continue in school for long. Many are at least partially homeschooled and take college courses quite early.

Such children push the envelope of asynchronous development and experience its profound implications every moment of their lives. Few would consider their challenges enviable or their needs elitist. They experience the sensitive aspects of their existence to the most joyful and most painful degrees. Their needs simply are what they are—just as the needs of the most profoundly retarded child present themselves and must be accommodated. By acknowledging and labeling their giftedness, we merely recognize them as individuals who need our help.

Quinn O'Leary...What is Giftedness?

It was 5:37 in the morning by my watch when I stepped off my skateboard and mounted the slatted steps to my porch. The fog, thick and reminiscent of televised thrillers set in London, was melting swiftly as the world's colors shifted and climbed from greyness. The clouds lowering over the distant mountains were showing the first touches of blushing dawn, just as the grass-swarded pond bordering the street in front of my home was showing the nascent green of the amorous touches of uncertain mountain spring.

Instead of entering my house, I laid my skateboard across my knees and sat on my porch, heels gently thumping over the edge. The awefully hushed quality of a foggy night was breaking up as birds woken by the traintrack clatter of my wheels against the sidewalk's sections trilled and warbled morning noise. The sighing breathing of the nearby highway was rousing itself from its nighttime lassitude as early-morning drivers bustled. I played careful fingertips over the wax-smooth skin of the apple that had ridden the night in my coat pocket, savoring the poignance of hunger and stilling the quiet concussion of my boot heels against the deck, willing for a moment the peaceful silence to remain.

The slight depression of the pond held the fog longer against the morn's incursion but its edges were consistently nibbled up like water swallowing a tidal island. In the still-predawn dark, a black shape dropped almost vertically into the fog. Startled, I peered hard for it until the familiar tri-note warble of a red-winged blackbird clarified.

As the fog grew increasingly less dense, the reflections in the glass-still, gem-smooth lake became more apparent, the fan of a skeletal tree becoming a drab pinwheel of intricate pattern. Close beside, the oddly oriental ornament of a stilt-legged heron doubled itself with the sedate stillness of its species.

The chill of the air, ignored in my nightlong exertions, made itself startlingly apparent, the chafing weight of my clothes notwithstanding. The part-rain scent of the fog's departure wafted from the tiny wildness, misting my mind with nostalgia befitting someone far older.

Breathing deep of the new day, I felt myself somehow restored by its newness, made purer by its potential, made peaceful by its birth. When I bit into the apple, it tasted of spring.

References

Carlin, G. (Writer & Performer), Urbisci, R. (Director), Hamza, J. & Carlin, B. (Executive Producers). (1990). *Doin' it again* [videotape]. (Available from Columbia Tristar Home Video, 3400 Riverside Drive, Burbank, CA 91505)

Cattell, R. B. (1963). Theory of fluid and crystallized intelligence: A critical experiment. *Journal of Educational Psychology, 54,* 1-22.

Columbus Group (1991, July). Unpublished transcript of the meeting of the Columbus Group, Columbus, OH.

Gardner, H. (1983). *The theory of multiple intelligences.* New York: Basic Books.

Gardner, H. (1999). *Intelligence reframed: Multiple intelligences for the 21ˢᵗ century.* New York: Basic Books.

Maxwell, E. (1998). "I can do it myself!" Reflections on early self-efficacy. *Roeper Review, 20,* 183-187.

Silverman, L. K. *Characteristics of Giftedness Scale.* © Copyright held by Linda Kreger Silverman, August, 1990. Gifted Development Center, 1452 Marion Street, Denver, CO 80218. (303) 837-8378. http://www.gifteddevelopment.com (13 Oct. 2002).

Silverman, L. K. *Giftedness in Adults.* (January, 1998). © Copyright held by Linda Kreger Silverman, Gifted Development Center, 1452 Marion Street, Denver, CO 80218. (303) 837-8378. http://www.gifteddevelopment.com (13 Oct. 2002).

Silverman, L. K. (1995). The universal experience of being out-of-sync. In L. K. Silverman (Ed.), *Advanced development: A collection of works on giftedness in adults* (pp. 1-12). Denver: Institute for the Study of Advanced Development.

Snyderman, M. & Rothman, S. (1988). *The IQ controversy, the media and public policy.* New Brunswick, NJ: Transaction Books.

Winebrenner, S. (1994, July-August). How gifted kids can survive in inclusion classrooms. *Understanding Our Gifted, 6*(6), 1, 8.

Wechsler, D. (1991, p. 1). *Wechsler Intelligence Scale for Children-Third Edition Manual.* San Antonio, TX: The Psychological Corporation, Harcourt Brace.

For Further Reading

Gross, M. (1993). *Exceptionally gifted children.* New York: Routledge.

Morelock, M. (1992). Giftedness: The view from within. *Understanding Our Gifted, 4*(3), 1, 11-15.
http://www.ditd.org/floater.php?location=17 (23 Feb. 2003).

Silverman, L. K. (1997). The construct of asynchronous development. *Peabody Journal of Education, 72*(3&4), 36-58.

Silverman, L. K. (1988). On introversion. *Understanding Our Gifted, 1*(2), 11.

Silverman, L. K. (1993a). The gifted individual. In L. K. Silverman (Ed.), *Counseling the gifted and talented* (pp. 3-28). Denver, CO: Love.

Silverman, L. K. (1993b). A developmental model for counseling the gifted. In L. K. Silverman (Ed.), *Counseling the gifted and talented* (pp. 51-78). Denver, CO: Love.

Silverman, L. K. (2002). *Upside-down brilliance: The visual-spatial learner.* Denver, CO: DeLeon Publishing.

Silverman, L. & Kearney, K. (1989). Parents of the extraordinarily gifted. *Advanced Development, 1*, 41-56.
http://www.ditd.org/floater.php?location=126 (23 Feb. 2003).

Tolan, S. S. (1996). *Is it a Cheetah?*
http://www.stephanietolan.com/is_it_a_cheetah.htm
(23 Feb. 2003).

3

Testing Considerations

Few experiences are more fascinating to me than testing a gifted child. From the first moments of meeting the child, a picture of that child's pattern of abilities and, perhaps, relative weaknesses is becoming apparent. Once we begin the IQ test, I am observing verbal abstract reasoning, spatial reasoning, general knowledge, vision, audition, memory, motor skills, processing speed, attention and a host of subtle cues that help to further explain the scores the child earns. The sessions are usually very engaging for these children; the inherent challenge of the tests often eclipses what they experience at school. They are usually happy, frequently quite humorous, and virtually always well-motivated to do their best. But for me, amidst the enjoyment of getting to know them, the pieces of a puzzle are being put into place and the final puzzle seems always to be unique from all of the others that I have watched coalesce.

The IQ test was developed as a tool to observe the behavior of individuals under controlled conditions and it is, indeed, a very useful tool, especially when used in conjunction with other observations. Those of us experienced in testing the gifted can usually make close estimates of the scores children will earn based on our initial conversations with them. Those qualities that we have learned to recognize as gifted, or highly or profoundly gifted, become recognizable.

Likewise, the developmental history of a child is critical information in judging apparent or potential ability levels. However, the tests offer us tools to further explore a child's intellectual functioning and document it. They shortcut the process of observing the child's responses to myriad situations over the course of days or months into two to three hours. Because they provide normative comparisons with age peers, we are able to tell exactly how advanced, typical, or delayed a child's abilities are.

I am always surprised to read a scathing condemnation of IQ testing. For example, the view that IQ scores offer an elitist way to rank order individuals in our society according to some misguided scale of personal worth seems shocking to me. I view IQ tests as a means to clarify the educational needs of children who are discrepant from the average and to provide information needed to create an appropriate educational program for them. (Sometimes adults take these tests, as well, to answer long-held questions about their own strengths, weaknesses or learning style.) Although the performance of average children is important in norming these tests, the tests are rarely used for average children experiencing no problems in school. They are used most with developmentally delayed children, those with learning disabilities or other deficits, and the gifted because typical educational programs are not working well for these children. Even when the scores are impressively high, parents know to keep the information private except when working with educators; the scores don't impress other children or parents and will never make a child more popular. But, they help parents make child-rearing decisions and they provide excellent input about educational needs. They also provide documentation that what the parent thinks about the child's abilities has been confirmed by a professional. Parents are so often put in the difficult position of justifying why they believe their children are gifted that testing becomes essential to provide a factual basis for discussion.

The information to follow draws heavily from my experience testing predominantly gifted children at the Gifted Development Center in Denver. It is offered to familiarize parents and teachers with the relevant issues surrounding the assessment of gifted children. Because a wide range of testing and related services are offered by testers, those available in a given location may or may not closely resemble the services described on the following pages. However, this information can provide a starting point for any family considering testing, and suggest questions to be asked of potential testers.

Choosing a Tester

The decision of where to have the testing done is an important one (resources are provided at the end of this chapter, and the book, to help). While private testing of the gifted is costly, free testing at school has some limitations. Generally, school psychologists are hired with special education funding and are not available to test gifted children. When their services are offered, they often lack experience with the gifted. This can affect the interpretation of test score profiles. For example, relative disabilities that would concern us at the Gifted Development Center because they represent a significant weakness when compared with often remarkable strengths, might not appear to a school psychologist to be an issue when viewed on an absolute scale. I have seen reports that failed to view a discrepancy of 30 points between Verbal and Performance IQ scores on a Wechsler IQ test as indicative of anything, when the lowest score is still within the average range (the test manual confirms that such a discrepancy is highly significant). If the child is scoring within the gifted range in Verbal IQ and the average range in Performance, this is suggestive of vision problems and the need for further evaluation of both acuity and visual processing difficulties. The Verbal items on the test are presented auditorially and the Performance items are presented visually. We have become aware in our practice that vision intervention (often with vision exercises) may well produce higher Performance scores upon retesting a year later. It is a travesty, therefore, to simply interpret the higher Verbal IQ score as a *strength*, ignoring the diagnostic implications of the lower score, when parents could easily address vision.

Moreover, practiced testers with little experience testing the gifted may rush these children, being used to testing taking a shorter amount of time. It generally takes longer to test gifted children because their thinking is more complex and they answer more items correctly before the discontinue criteria are reached. Many gifted children continue to hone their answers until a point when they are finally satisfied. However, if the tester rushes to the next item, the child is quickly *trained* to offer the quick, concise answer that may not score as high. Allowing the reflective, gifted child the proper time to contemplate is as important as learning how to offer a speedy administration to the gifted child who is an especially fast processor and may lose focus if administration is too slow. Testers familiar with this population learn these necessary skills to support optimum performance from gifted children. It is generally advisable to have a gifted child tested by a psychologist or center with experience with many gifted children over the range of giftedness, not just the occasional child.

Although extensive testing by school psychologists using individual IQ and achievement tests is not usually available for assessment of the gifted, most schools offer some form of brief individual or group testing to qualify children for gifted programs. The tests are usually unprotected tests that can be administered by teachers or paraprofessionals, as opposed to protected tests (e.g., Wechsler, Stanford-Binet, etc.), which must be administered under the supervision of a licensed psychologist trained to administer the particular test. The items on protected tests are kept strictly confidential, so the test remains a valid measure of abilities. The brief tests we often see schools administer include the Cognitive Abilities Test (CogAT), the Ravens Progressive Matrices Test (a nonverbal reasoning test), the Otis-Lennon, the SAGES, and the Slosson Full Range Intelligence Test (Slosson FRIT). We rarely obtain scores on major individual IQ tests that are lower than scores from these brief instruments, but we often obtain higher scores.

Brief measures appear particularly inadequate for documenting the giftedness of twice exceptional (both gifted and learning disabled) children and they frequently fail to document high levels of giftedness. For example, we have seen profoundly gifted children (175$^+$) score in the 130s on the CogAT. Research as early as 1959, by Pegnato and Birch, showed that highly capable children often expand the meaning of the multiple-choice questions on brief tests beyond what the test writer had in mind, and they may answer incorrectly. The major protected IQ tests, which are more extensive and detailed, use open-ended questions and prevent this problem. My personal favorite of the brief tests is probably the Slosson FRIT because it is a reasonable test of both verbal abstract and spatial reasoning and seems to have a higher ceiling that allows for more scores above the 130-140 range. But, individual IQ testing on the major tests is always preferable where the accuracy of the results is important. Sadly, some schools will only allow children to be assessed on the brief test(s) they use, believing that they must test all students on the same test to be fair. Tests and their limitations differ, so this is a poor policy if the school sincerely wants to identify all gifted students. It is fairest to all children to allow outside testing by a licensed psychologist and the opportunity for the child to be tested on a test that best documents his or her ability. Most schools will accept outside testing, but it is important to find out the school's policies to be certain.

Private testing has advantages in addition to providing access to the major individual IQ tests. If private testing is chosen, the parents have the opportunity to assess the results before deciding what to do with them. Reports are given only to the parents unless the tester is instructed by the parents to send the report elsewhere (with a specific signed release form). This can be advantageous for a variety of reasons. For example, parents may want to have a child assessed before choosing a school that is a good fit. Based on the child's results, a tester experienced with the gifted can suggest a variety of programs or schools for further consideration by a family. A private tester works for the benefit of the child, not as a gatekeeper determining whether or not the child may enter a specific program.

Furthermore, if the child is tested by a particular school or program, it can be difficult to obtain a full report of the scores, and interpretation of the results may be minimal. The test has been given to satisfy the needs of the program, not the needs of the family for information. The test(s) given usually can't be readministered for a period of time. Major protected individual IQ tests cannot be given again for one year. We have seen cases where the school would not relinquish scores because they are considered a part of the confidential admissions process (parents should research the legality of this type of policy in their home state). One mother called me to request testing of her young daughter, under age six, on the WPPSI-R. Because the little girl was tested several months previously for admission into a private school on the WPPSI-R, we could not readminister it yet. The school was only willing to provide scores in a few more months, after its final admission decisions had been made for the coming year, and viewed releasing scores early as a threat to its highly selective, confidential process. Having a child tested privately ensures that scores are available as needed. Results from school testing are also often brief and offer little or no interpretation or recommendations.

In addition, many parents have been uncertain who did the testing within private schools.

Testers experienced with the gifted are particularly concerned about documenting strengths, not just weaknesses, as it is the developmental advancement of these children that most often requires educational accommodations. This is different for the school psychologist who must primarily document weaknesses to gain educational accommodations for children with learning problems. Both are responsible for gaining admission for children to programs that will help them. And, both want to make strong cases for these children to be included in programs that they need. However, the documentation of strengths as a prime emphasis is not the way most psychologists are trained. Parents need to know that gifted programs can be swayed in their willingness to accept a gifted child if it appears that the child has too many weaknesses or the report focuses most on the weaknesses. Experienced testers of the gifted are used to emphasizing the level of strengths and the need for appropriate accommodations for giftedness. Where there are also weaknesses, a case is made for appropriate support for the child in those areas, as well. Twice exceptional children require a two-pronged approach; we argue strongly that a child should be taught to his or her strengths first, with gifted accommodations offered appropriately, followed by support for weaknesses.

The final choice of a tester must depend upon all of these issues. How does a parent find the appropriate person? Parents are wise to attend local gifted conferences and presentations and to seek recommendations from professionals and parents of other gifted children via local organizations (gifted support groups, state and local associations for the gifted) or the Internet. The resource sites in this book offer lists of testers that can be updated as circumstances change. This helps to ensure professional competency and boosts our ability to find a professional who can advocate appropriately for the gifted.

A psychologist or center testing gifted children should be able to suggest specific services to support each child's individual needs. Talking with the tester, or a representative of the center, about such needs at length can not only be a good way to obtain advice about what tests are needed, but also provides a means of gauging the *comfort level* with the professional(s) involved. Do the suggestions seem reasonable? Are the issues of the child grasped and appreciated quickly? Does the professional fully recognize the different educational needs of the gifted child? Does he or she understand the child's frustrations? As a tester and parent, I would want to know not only that the tester or center was professionally competent and experienced with gifted children, but also that we agreed on basic issues of gifted advocacy (gifted children won't necessarily be "just fine" in a typical public school program, but will need significant accommodations). Furthermore, I would want to have a gut-level feeling of trust for that person by the end of the conversation.

I would also want to know that the person testing my child genuinely liked working with gifted children and was a person with whom my child would enjoy spending time. A psychologist who has built a practice around work with the gifted or spends significant time testing gifted children would be more likely to have good rapport with them. Likewise, a center or group practice specializing in assessment of the gifted is more likely to draw professionals who will delight in the special qualities these children possess: their interests, humor, and characteristic reasoning. They will understand when the little girl who misses an item begins to cry because she's used to getting everything right at school. They will be willing to spend considerable time supporting these children and answering any questions they are allowed to answer during test administration. I am always pleased when our office manager, Lee Ann Powell, says, "You guys have been having entirely too much fun in there," because she has heard laughter emanating from a testing room. The tester's enjoyment of these children, and comfort with high levels of sensitivity, reflectivity, perfectionism, and curiosity makes for a more comfortable session for the child. It also contributes to reports oriented to appreciating and helping the whole child in whatever ways seem appropriate, as opposed to being provided for a single purpose (such as program admission), utilizing only the options available at a child's school.

The Cost of Testing

The cost of private testing is based on the time spent by a professional actually administering tests to the child individually, scoring the instruments, interpreting the scores and observations of the child, having a conference with the parents (possibly including the child) and writing the report for that child. Our experience at the GDC may be illustrative. We generally spend at least four to five hours in actual testing and 15 to 20 hours total for an IQ test, self-perception test, and achievement test (a combination of tests frequently requested), with their consequent report writing times and post-test consultation. Additional tests and services require additional time and, usually, additional days, as testers are reluctant to push children too hard for too long. Prices may be assessed for each test administered and service provided, or may be based on hourly rates. These are generally about the same, with contract prices reflecting an hourly rate appropriate for professionals in the field. However, in rare circumstances, a tester assessing a child who takes considerably longer to test may need to ask for additional compensation. We have had several children who because of significant learning disabilities or other disorders have proven very time-consuming to test. One took three days to complete an achievement test that usually requires no more than 1½ hours. Testers are generally very reluctant to ask for additional compensation and it happens rarely, but additional trips to the office and possible rescheduling of other appointments makes it necessary. If a parent is planning to have such a child tested, it would be wise to discuss the probable difficulties the tester might anticipate and ask how the costs will be calculated to avoid surprises. Likewise, a child with documented disabilities and a history of testing will require more report writing time. Testers are professionally obligated to review past testing to understand the child and to report relevant assessment results. Some children have had multiple batteries of tests through their lifetimes, which require summation in the report.

After the measures are administered, they are then scored and interpreted by the tester as part of the contracted price. Most parents choose to include a post-test conference to understand the test results more fully and discuss how they relate to the child's academic, social, and emotional needs. Billed according to length of time and the professionals involved, costs can vary. The GDC, for example, utilizes two-hour conferences that include the tester, another senior staff member, and the parents. Other people (including teachers, grandparents, the child, etc.) may attend the conference at the request of the parents. Testers share test results and observations, and the parents offer their input. The second professional ensures maximum expertise in interpreting results and providing helpful recommendations. One thing to inquire about is the type of documentation of test results and recommendations that will be available at the conference, pending receipt of the formal report. If results are needed immediately at school, how can information be transferred quickly? At the GDC, we provide an Evaluation Summary at the end of the conference (the recommendations are completed as we reach conclusions during the conference) that lists all of the test scores, as well as recommendations stated briefly. This signed summary can serve as the documentation of results until the formal report is received, or parents can request that scores be faxed or have the tester call the school (with a signed release).

Particularly time-consuming and requiring additional weeks for writing and review, the formal reports are highly individualized and lengthy. Most GDC testers estimate that they spend about an hour per page writing these (this accounts for a significant portion of the testing cost); however, we feel they are extremely important as the major documentation of need for gifted services. The entire process is very different from the machine-scored ability or achievement tests administered at school that yield, at best, a short, computer-generated report. Each test is described, along with resulting scores and their interpretation. Test behavior is noted and all results are combined and summarized, with a lengthy list of recommendations geared to the specific needs of each child. A child's report will probably be used on a number of occasions throughout school to help determine educational needs, so it must be of sufficient quality for this purpose. Just as an example, our youngest son's report from the Gifted Development Center (completed at age six, modified at age seven to reflect an IQ test with a higher ceiling, and augmented several more times to add later individual achievement testing) was used many times. Submitted to his elementary school, it was used to identify him as a gifted student in first grade, was consulted when planning his second-grade program, and was pivotal in the consideration to skip him from second to fourth grade. It was also considered when he entered a private school in sixth grade, was used for admission (in lieu of SAT scores) to a Talent Search math class following sixth grade, and, along with samples of writing and descriptions of classes taken in seventh and eighth grade, facilitated his skipping most freshman and sophomore courses in high school. It might be prudent to ask for a sample of the type of report parents can expect from a tester to determine if it will meet such standards.

There may also be other services provided, depending on specific needs. For example, extra time may need to be scheduled to get to know a child who is particularly anxious about the upcoming evaluation (some parents request this), or a clinical interview with the parents before testing may be advisable to understand a complicated situation better. Parents should also allow some flexibility for the tester to follow up on any observations of diagnostic significance (e.g., the tester might want to add a reading subtest or two, to clarify a reading problem). Alternatively, he or she may suggest that adding an additional test or subtest will further document a child's strength in some area. In such cases, the tester should discuss supplementary tests (and their costs) with parents as the need arises. At the GDC, minor additions to the planned battery of tests are billed at an hourly rate and usually add little to the total cost; however, they can contribute significantly to the case we make for accommodations at school. Other services might include creating an Individual Educational Plan (IEP) for implementation at school. This is helpful when a school is willing to make accommodations but is uncertain about what is needed.

Costs are usually limited to one major individual intelligence test as IQ scores remain relatively stable. Children need not be tested again and again on an intelligence test to obtain *current* assessments of ability unless there has been a brain injury or serious illness, or there are disabilities that are likely to improve with interventions. One child with whom I worked had been originally diagnosed with pervasive developmental delay, autism, and sensory-motor integration problems, based on initial testing as a young child. By age 12, he had completed years of therapy with several types of interventions and finally tested within the exceptionally gifted range, after receiving considerably lower scores years earlier. Such a child might be tested several times to assess progress. However, few children show such a pattern and most who have only minor weaknesses earn scores that are fairly consistent if testing is repeated. Sometimes the child's test scores are felt to be an underestimate due to immaturity. When this occurs, the child might benefit from being retested when somewhat older. We suggest this when the child refuses to do parts of the tests or is reluctant to guess unless absolutely certain of an answer. Parents may also be advised to have a child tested on an intelligence test with a higher ceiling if the child's abilities appear to be beyond the limits of the test taken. However, this is a matter of documenting the full range of abilities, not of expecting it to change. (See Ceiling Problems: Scoring Beyond the Limits of IQ Tests on page 87.)

In most cases, the only testing parents may want to consider doing several times is individual achievement testing, in order to evaluate the child's academic progress and determine whether grade placement is reasonable. Individual achievement tests provide a way to document achievement levels higher than those typically assessed on grade-level tests at school. Achievement tests can be given alone—there is usually no need to repeat the other tests—and are usually available from good testers close to home.

As I have thought about the cost of testing our children, I have felt it was probably the best money we spent to support their giftedness. Whereas tutoring, enrichment classes, summer foreign language camp, and private school for a brief time were all helpful, the testing was the most essential, as it documented our children's abilities and provided us with a game plan for advocacy. When families lack the means to afford individual testing, it is worth inquiring about low-cost options. We are beginning to see some private funding become available for this purpose and many testing centers offer a limited amount of low-cost testing done by supervised interns in training.

Which Tests Should Be Given?

Most testers of the gifted suggest several tests to provide different kinds of necessary information. To answer questions about general ability level, relative strengths and weaknesses (including learning disabilities), and whether a child meets requirements for entrance into a particular school or program for the gifted, an individual intelligence test will be needed. In addition, an achievement test is important to answer questions about current achievement levels for various reasons: to evaluate the effectiveness of the child's educational program, help with planning a home-schooling curriculum, determine grade placement, or provide support for acceleration. We currently also add a brief self-perception test for all of our children to rule out areas of concern for the child. Some have had their confidence and self-esteem affected by negative circumstances. Personality tests (we routinely evaluate children for intro-version/extraversion) can provide more information about the child's personality style and how he or she may fit into the family or classroom environment, whereas emotional inventories and projective tests can further elucidate children's concerns. A number of diagnostic tests may also be used to evaluate apparent problems (e.g., visual-motor integration, AD/HD, auditory processing, etc.).

Such tests all provide important data to consider when evaluating a gifted child's needs, but are not all needed for every child. Ideally, testers of the gifted should carefully assess the testing needs and suggest tests that will be most helpful for an individual child. Then, parents can make an informed decision about what they want, can afford, and will be most relevant in their efforts to obtain educational accommodations. Here is what parents most need to know about the various types of tests used to assess gifted children.

IQ Tests

IQ tests reflect the test developers' philosophy of intelligence, but have many elements in common. Abstract reasoning ability is considered by most psychologists to be the most essential element of intelligence (Snyderman & Rothman, 1988); however, other abilities are assessed, as well. There are measures of memory: both visual and auditory, meaningful and non-meaningful, short-term and long-term, and *working* (where the test taker is asked to manipulate remembered material in some way). There are assessments of visual/motor/perceptual abilities and processing speed. There are measures of attentional focus. Most IQ tests ask questions that assess both *fluid* and *crystallized* abilities, in terms of Cattell's two-factor theory of intelligence (1963). Fluid abilities can be tested by questions that require the child to solve novel problems, especially those involving spatial relationships. Crystallized abilities are those that are constantly augmented through experience. For example, vocabulary and general store of knowledge reflect the child's curiosity, exposure to information, and long-term memory. Because the major IQ tests are *protected*, the questions must be kept confidential. A child cannot prepare for an IQ test, but parents can always support learning and encourage reasoning at home.

As previously noted, the major IQ tests all have some diagnostic capacity, beyond providing an estimate of intellectual level. Because they have been given for many years to large numbers of children, recognizable scoring patterns have emerged that suggest various deficits and disabilities. Sometimes, for example, auditory memory seems poor in a child with a history of ear infections, even though an audiologist has previously found no permanent hearing damage. The child may miss mental math questions because he has difficulty keeping the question, or his mental calculation, in memory. Or, the child can't repeat strings of digits; her memory for non-meaningful material is quickly lost. This could be Central Auditory Processing Disorder, a rather common problem for which new therapies are being developed. Or, these symptoms could be caused by attentional deficits, which should be further evaluated. Likewise, visual processing problems (e.g., visual perception, visual tracking, focus, accommodation, etc.) may be apparent in testing, suggesting the need for a vision evaluation. The child may appear to have good spatial reasoning ability, but experiences visual confusion copying designs with blocks or assembling puzzles. Problems with tasks of visual-motor speed can indicate inadequate functioning of the visual system, fine-motor coordination problems, or attentional deficits (because the child loses interest in the boring task and cannot maintain focus).

When suspicious scoring patterns occur, supported by the observations of an experienced tester, it is reported to the parents and recommended that further evaluation take place with specialists. Testers often receive reports back from these specialists after the child has had further evaluation, so the testers obtain feedback about what was an apparent concern in testing. Over time, experienced testers improve in their ability to find subtle issues and parents are wise to follow through on further evaluation where indicated. In most cases, weaknesses in the gifted are *relative* to their unusual strengths and are not serious by absolute standards. However, because many respond to interventions, it's important to find them. In some cases, the weakness is seriously hampering the functioning of the child and has been masked by the gifted child's ability to compensate. If further evaluation with a specialist is undertaken, it is important to share the testing information with the specialist. Gifted children have been known to *compensate* in other evaluations, as well.

At the GDC, we typically begin with an IQ test that is acceptable to most schools, followed by additional IQ measures if the child scores beyond the ceiling of the test or shows a need for a different type of test (e.g., a nonverbal measure). Tests acceptable to schools are usually the newest versions of nationally recognized instruments. IQ tests are generally revised and renormed every 15 to 20 years, and new versions of several major tests have recently been released. Testers are ethically bound to use current tests or justify the use of an older test; however, monetary limitations may determine how fast school districts and individual clinicians replace their tests. Schools may vary in their requirements for private testing, so it is always wise to ask not only *which test* is acceptable, but *which version* of a test is required when a child is going to be tested outside of the school.

Wechsler tests are favored by schools and are strong measures of reasoning and diagnostic information for children earning IQ scores as high as the 140s (occasionally the low 150s). Released in 2002, the Wechsler Preschool and Primary Scale of Intelligence-Third Edition (WPPSI-III) replaced the WPPSI-R (Revised). The WPPSI-III features a shorter version for ages two and three (only four subtests are required) and child-friendly, streamlined version requiring seven subtests for ages four and five. Both offer supplementary subtests. The WPPSI-III subtests used to calculate the IQ score emphasize abstract reasoning well. Verbal, Performance, and Full Scale IQ scores are important for gifted identification; Processing Speed is not.

The Wechsler Intelligence Scale for Children-Fourth Edition (WISC-IV), for ages 6-16, replaced the WISC-III in 2003. This version adds more advanced questions at the upper ends of a number of subtests, which is helpful when testing the gifted. It is largely untimed in the areas that emphasize reasoning: Verbal Comprehension and Perceptual Reasoning, which provide the best measure of giftedness.

The Wechsler Adult Intelligence Scale-Third Edition (WAIS-III), for ages 16 and up, revised in 1997, provides older

teenagers and adults with Verbal, Performance, and Full
Scale IQ scores (a Working Memory score is optional).

These newest Wechsler revisions reflect structural changes
important to gifted identification. Previous Wechsler IQ tests
were divided into Verbal subtests (presented auditorially)
and Performance subtests (presented visually), and yielded
Verbal IQ, Performance IQ and Full Scale IQ scores. The
subtests assessed abstract reasoning (verbal, mathematical,
spatial), as well as some acquired knowledge and processing
skills (short-term memory, processing speed). Perhaps
because processing skills are limiting factors for lower-
functioning children, their weight has increased in Full
Scale IQ scores on the newest tests, rendering these scores
less predictive of giftedness. The WISC-IV has dispensed
with Verbal and Performance IQ scores, in favor of a Full
Scale IQ and four Composite scores: Verbal Comprehension,
Perceptual Reasoning, Working Memory, and Processing
Speed. This was done despite the fact that the gifted group
in the normative sample, reported in the technical manual
(p. 77), scored lower in these latter two areas, potentially
confounding results. Verbal Comprehension and Perceptual
Reasoning better identify giftedness. When Composite scores
show extreme variance, a Full Scale score should not be
used. Information about such ongoing testing issues is
available on the GDC website (www.gifteddevelopment.com).

Also released in 2003 was the Stanford-Binet Intelligence
Scales, Fifth Edition (SB5) for ages 2-86+, replacing the
Stanford-Binet Intelligence Scale: Fourth Edition (SB-IV).
The SB5 is the second wholly reformulated Stanford-Binet
test since the Form L-M (1972), which was the culmination
of decades of tests that were successful assessing the gifted.
Binets through the L-M were organized into age levels, each
containing a selection of different types of questions a
normal child of that age could answer. The tester worked
through the age levels to determine a Mental Age; then a
ratio-based IQ score, placed in a normed comparison,

yielded the single IQ score. The tests offered excellent reasoning items (especially verbal) and had much higher ceilings and lower floors, extending the range of testing beyond the limits of Wechsler tests. The SB-IV was a departure to a Wechsler-like test with subtests assessing different kinds of abilities, and a more limited scoring range. The SB5 reflects a return to a test with wider range, structure akin to the L-M, and toys, a favorite feature of earlier Binets for young children. Based on a five-part model of intelligence, the SB5 taps Fluid Reasoning, Knowledge, Quantitative Reasoning, Visual-Spatial, and Working Memory, with verbal and nonverbal items to assess each. The SB5 has extremely advanced visual-spatial and mathematical reasoning items, but many of the *verbal* items are *verbally-presented* math problems or spatial reasoning items, rather than items that measure the verbal abstract reasoning abilities emphasized in gifted classrooms (e.g., comparing and contrasting, making inferences, making social judgments). While more verbal reasoning items would have been preferable, test developers did understand the reflective nature of many gifted children and virtually eliminated timing in the administration of the test. Author Gale Roid also notes that questions from one section out of the five (e.g., Working Memory) might be omitted and an overall score prorated from the other four sections, if those questions prove to be less relevant in identification of the gifted (G. Roid, personal communication February 12, 2003). To utilize this test for the gifted, testers need to consider any score over 120 a *gifted* score, as the test scores quite low using the regular scoring tables, and testers should be familiar with alternate scoring approaches discussed in the test's Interpretive Manual and on Riverside Publishing's website. Endorsed by the publisher, these are appropriate for use with the gifted, provided they are reported as a change in typical procedure. Rasch-ratio IQ scores, comparing age equivalents with a child's chronological age, can document extraordinary reasoning levels with scores as high as 200+ ("Profoundly Advanced").

The Stanford-Binet Intelligence Scale-Form L-M is useful as a supplemental test to assess the full range of intelligence for children who demonstrate abilities beyond the limits of other current tests. It is best for children under the age of 10 (see the discussion of "Ceiling Problems" to follow). This heavily verbal, largely untimed instrument has stood the test of time identifying the gifted mind, sometimes at extraordinary levels. It is, perhaps, the test that emphasizes abstract reasoning most, with meaningful questions gifted children find engaging.

The Developmental Ability Scales (DAS) is another IQ test we like, especially for older gifted children (it has less emphasis on timing), but some schools are unfamiliar with it. The Woodcock-Johnson III Tests of Cognitive Abilities (WJ-III) is most useful to us in exploring deficits and fine-tuning recommendations for a child needing accommodations. It is less helpful in identifying gifted potential, as it strongly emphasizes processing skills, rather than abstract reasoning, and usually produces lower IQ scores in children who test in the gifted range on other tests. The Ravens Progressive Matrices Test and Naglieri Nonverbal Abilities Test are popular nonverbal intelligence measures to use with children who show visual-spatial strengths, are from culturally-diverse backgrounds, are deaf or hard of hearing, or are limited English-speaking.

Test authors strive to create tests that meet the broadest range of needs possible, which may or may not serve the gifted well. Using some tests, or portions of tests, and avoiding others makes sense. Most testers agree that gifted individuals are best identified by tests that maximize abstract reasoning (verbal, mathematical, spatial) and minimize diagnostic assessment (memory, processing speed, fine-motor coordination). This best identifies the children who need the characteristic gifted classroom that

emphasizes fast-paced, advanced instruction and the development of higher-level thinking skills. Whenever tests are
revised, we need to find which tests, or portions of them,
best serve different gifted children and advise parents
accordingly.

Ceiling Problems: Scoring Beyond the Limits of IQ Tests

Gifted children may experience ceiling effects on intelligence
tests. Every test has a ceiling in terms of the highest scores
possible and the most difficult items included. Once a child
can correctly answer the hardest questions on a test, he or
she has reached the ceiling. If the child is young enough
that the ceiling level performance is remarkable, the score
will be quite high. However, if the same child is tested
several more times on the same test, over the next few
years, and can answer no additional questions because
there are no harder ones, the child's score will go down
because his or her performance will become less and less
remarkable. Is the child's intelligence declining? Of course
not. There are simply ceiling problems restricting the scores.
What is needed is a test with a higher ceiling and more
difficult items. However, if no such test is available, it is
important to test the child early enough on an available test
to obtain the best score and avoid a score reflecting any
decline. In this case, the first test score would usually be the
best estimate of the child's true abilities if the test session
went well. Any gifted child who has been tested on a test
with a sufficient ceiling (the child cannot yet answer the
most difficult items) and earned high scores should use
those scores throughout childhood for program admissions.
It is not appropriate to ask a considerably older child who
was tested previously for *current* scores to document
giftedness, as it will be more difficult to obtain an accurate
measurement.

Several major IQ tests have important ceiling limitations
for the gifted. First, they have maximum possible IQ scores
around 160, with the highest earned scores generally
occurring in the 140s (with an occasional 150+). These
highest scoring children may earn their scores with just
enough raw score points on each subtest to qualify for them
or they may earn considerably more raw score points than
needed to qualify for the highest IQ scores. Their overall
scores cannot go higher. Children with a range of abilities
score at the top level of every test: those that barely reach
the top level and those that meet and exceed it to varying
degrees. The Wechsler Intelligence Scale for Children-Fourth
Edition (WISC-IV), Wechsler Preschool and Adult scales
(WPPSI-III and WAIS-III), and Differential Ability Scales
(DAS) all have ceilings around 160. Scores of 145 through
the 150s document at least highly gifted abilities, but may
mask considerably higher abilities beyond the ceilings of the
tests. To those who do not work with the gifted, this issue
may seem trivial. What difference does it make if a child is
actually more capable than the test can measure? Do we
need to know if a 145 IQ is an underestimate? At this level,
does it really matter? It matters considerably because we
would advise parents differently about child-rearing issues
and educational choices based on the level of scores above
this ceiling.

Currently, the preferred test with a higher ceiling is the
older Stanford-Binet Intelligence Scale—Form L-M. Having
last normed this test in 1972, Riverside Publishing still
supports its use for testing the extreme limits of intelligence
and for research. The Form L-M can produce scores as high
as 200+ in children not old enough to have surpassed its
ceiling. Generally, we use the L-M with children whose
abilities are beyond the limits of the other tests (we obtain
several ceiling-level subtest scores). Children who are nine
or younger are the best candidates, because they are less
likely to encounter a ceiling. Sometimes, we are able to
document higher ability with slightly older children, and

sometimes even children younger than nine can do the most difficult items.

There is some current confusion about the higher scores sometimes obtained on Form L-M. Some believe that children always score higher on the L-M, and that the higher scores are due simply to older norms. Neither is true. Children do not always score higher on the L-M; those that score near the top of the other tests will earn a range of scores from around the same score (or occasionally a bit lower) to scores that are much higher, with the majority of children scoring nearer their previous scores. Those that score lower on the other tests, for example in the 120's, will usually score similarly on the L-M, but sometimes higher. Because we are reluctant to suggest a second IQ test unless higher ability is strongly suspected, we recommend retesting for only those children with certain scoring patterns on other tests in order to maximize our chances of finding those likely to score higher. For example, children who earn 99th percentile scores or higher on two or more of the Verbal Comprehension subtests of the WISC-III or IV (Information, Similarities, Vocabulary and Comprehension) should be retested because our research at the GDC indicates they are likely to score higher on the Binet. Ceiling-level scores on subtests with the highest loading for abstract reasoning are indicative of intellectual abilities beyond the limits of the test.

Changes in scores of the magnitude we sometimes see cannot be explained by old norms. The Flynn Effect has been defined as the general tendency of the population to score higher on intelligence tests over time (1984, 1999). This gradual increase in intelligence amounts to about 1/3 of an IQ point per year and is cause for renorming tests. Although it is uncertain whether or not the Flynn Effect applies at the extreme limits of ability, it would only account for a point difference equal to 1/3 the number of years since the 1972 norms were published (or less, due to several antiquated items modern children miss). With some rare individuals, we have seen discrepancies between Wechsler and Stanford-Binet L-M scores of greater than 100 points, which can only be explained by extraordinary advancement for a child's age (evident on a test with a high ceiling) and the Binet's normed ratio IQ scores, which allow for greater expansion of scores at the extremes, instead of forcing the scores into a more limited bell curve. These rare scores are sensible to clinicians familiar with the highest levels of giftedness and do, indeed, describe these unique children. John Wasserman, then Director of Psychological Assessments at Riverside Publishing, and project director of the fifth edition of the Stanford-Binet Intelligence Scale, wrote:

> *Although we standardly recommend that the most contemporary norms be utilized for any test, it has not been effectively demonstrated that phenomena such as the Flynn effect (the notion that norms become obsolete over time due to improvements in population intelligence) apply to changes in abilities at the extreme ranges (i.e., for individuals at very high or very low levels of ability). Indeed, there are sound statistical reasons for assuming that there may be only very minimal changes at the extremes of ability and that most of the changes in question occur for children and adults near the population mean. Moreover, Form L-M is one of the few reasonable options given the dearth of intelligence tests with sufficient ceiling to assess extremely gifted children...*
> (J. D. Wasserman, personal communication, December 23, 1997)

For children needing this type of higher-level assessment in the future, it will be important to seek out the best available instrument or combination of tests at that time, along with literature explaining why the high scores are justified (for schools and programs). The SB5 offers both Rasch-ratio IQ scores and an Extended IQ scale, which allows the highest scorers on the total test scores up to 200+. These scoring methods, determined after initial release of the test, are offered by the SB5's developers and are explained in the test's Interpretive Manual. It remains to be seen whether or not they have created a test as successful as the Stanford-Binet-Form L-M in identifying high levels of giftedness. Experience with this new test is needed to tell us more, but the SB5 appears to emphasize nonverbal and spatial/mathematical reasoning more than the L-M does, with less emphasis on verbal reasoning (although both have very advanced vocabulary lists). One test may not be a substitute for the other—both may be of value—with the SB5 offering a way to identify different (more visual-spatial) children. Defining intelligence in a new manner that is still meaningful at the highest levels of ability is a daunting task. Still, we appreciate the commitment of test developers to assessing children in the higher ranges of giftedness, as these children are at considerable risk. Unable to find them with traditional tests with limited ceilings, we threaten our most able minds.

IQ Tests and Minorities

Concerns have become prevalent about IQ tests favoring specific groups and failing to document strengths in minorities. These concerns are largely based on the fact that older tests did not utilize normative data on a large range of population groups and may have been less relevant measures of ability for minorities. Modern tests, however, have generally been subjected to intense scrutiny and testing with many population groups. They are normed using a more diverse population and test items are chosen that are equally relevant to all groups. Most schools have made efforts to use tests to assess giftedness that are more culturally fair. However, their good intentions have produced both positive and negative results.

Since schools typically have more limited testing capacity than private psychologists, they cannot provide a battery of tests to each child. Most schools rely on one or two multiple-choice screeners of intelligence, designed to be administered quickly. Sometimes a single test is chosen because it appears more equitable to insist that all children score high on the same test. Severely limiting test options lessens the quality of identification procedures for the gifted, including gifted children from minority groups.

Every test tends to emphasize certain types of abilities. In individual testing at the GDC, we begin with a frequently administered IQ test and then use additional assessment measures to clarify any weaknesses apparent on the original test and to further document strengths the child exhibits. If the child's particular strengths would be better documented by another test, we suggest administering it. The benefits of this type of approach are obvious; the choice of tests is dependent upon the needs of the child. Group testing in schools can't provide this level of diagnosis and the limited test use may or may not document a child's high abilities. *Whether the test is fair to a child needing accommodations for the gifted depends upon whether it can document the child's unusually high abilities.* Children who have strong visual-spatial abilities will not do as well on a highly verbal test; likewise, highly verbal children will not be identified as gifted on a nonverbal test. Most tests include different types of items, but vary in the balance they achieve. Some tests specifically test only one type of ability, e.g., the Raven's Progressive Matrices Test. An excellent identifier of nonverbal reasoning ability through pattern recognition, the Raven's would not be a good single identifier because it would not document the high abilities of children with strong verbal reasoning abilities. Different populations tend to exhibit certain strengths (although individuals within a group may exhibit very different strengths), so it is important to offer different measures.

The concern of schools to provide culture-fair tests sometimes backfires. For example, one district in California decided it was unfair to test less verbal children with a verbal test, so the decision was made to use only the Raven's Progressive Matrices. The nonverbal test would, presumably, provide a level playing field for all taking the test. However, knowing that African-Americans tend to be highly verbal suggests that this test would fail to identify many gifted African-American children, as well as Caucasians and others who show strong verbal skills, but weaker nonverbal. The assessment would be, from the outset, deliberately unfair to certain groups. A better approach is to provide tests of both verbal and nonverbal/visual-spatial reasoning, and to allow outside testing, in the hope that throwing out a number of different nets will result in a catch of gifted children identified by their strengths in more than one way. No child should be at the mercy of a single test.

Achievement Tests

Tests that assess the academic progress of a gifted child are important to determine specific educational needs, and are essential when acceleration is being considered. The achievement test documents the level of a child's skills in various academic areas, such as reading decoding and comprehension, writing skills, math calculation and reasoning, and spelling. Some tests also offer assessments of acquired knowledge in such areas as science, social studies, and humanities, but we find these measures to be somewhat less useful because school curricula vary considerably. We use individual, continuous tests that sample skills over a large range of grade levels in order to place the child's achievement at a particular level.

Standardized grade-level achievement tests, such as those administered at school, have an important limitation for the gifted. They include relatively few questions above grade level, so we are unable to determine the actual achievement of a child who scores at the highest level of the test (99th percentile). The same child might also score at the highest level if given the test for the next higher grade. We would have to continue administering out-of-level tests for higher and higher grade levels to finally determine the extent of the child's mastery. Continuous tests are less detailed at a particular grade level, but sample knowledge at many grade levels and do a better job of determining the level of achievement for each academic area for the child who is advanced beyond age expectations or asynchronous (e.g., extremely advanced in math, but at grade level in reading). We are able to determine grade equivalents for the various academic subject areas, we can see the kind of work the child has mastered, and we know what he or she is now ready to learn. This allows us to suggest a more specific level of instruction that is about right for the child, and we can easily see the small holes in knowledge that need to be filled.

There are several popular individual tests that can be given. The Woodcock-Johnson III (WJ-III) Tests of Achievement offer standard tests in reading, writing, math, and spelling, with supplementary subtests to explore problems in any of these areas. Our experience with the WJ-III suggests that the fluency measures that assess how quickly a child can read, calculate math problems, and write short sentences may be less relevant measures for the gifted, assuming the child has no significant processing speed difficulties needing accommodation. The most helpful subtests, in the WJ-III standard battery, to document a gifted child's achievement are the following: Letter-Word Identification, Passage Comprehension, Calculation, Applied Problems, Spelling, and Writing Samples. The Wechsler Individual Achievement Test Second Edition 2001 (WIAT-II) offers correlation with Wechsler IQ test scores. We often use the WIAT Written

Expression subtest, which offers a writing prompt and scoring criteria for the composition the child writes. This can be a better choice for the gifted writer than the WJ-III Writing Samples. This subtest involves the writing of 12 structured sentences, but the child who scores especially high will be given six more, and perhaps an additional six more, based on the score! The amount of writing may not be tolerated well when this occurs. Another individual achievement test, the Kaufman Test of Educational Achievement Normative Update (K-TEA/NU) offers both brief and long forms. One form can be used as a retest for the other, or we have used portions of the long form to document detailed achievement information in a particular subject.

The individual characteristics of these tests and ceiling levels are important considerations for specific children. For example, the K-TEA/NU is helpful for younger elementary school-age gifted children and has a particularly enjoyable reading comprehension section in which children pantomime their answers to passages they read. The test has a ceiling of 160 (high school-graduate level), which is adequate for many gifted children, but not all. The WIAT-II also has a ceiling of 160. The Woodcock-Johnson III has a ceiling score of 200 or higher in some subtests, depending on age. Questions sample knowledge as high as the college graduate level, so the test can be quite useful for evaluating profoundly gifted children. The WJ-III also assesses math achievement beyond pre-algebra, whereas the other tests do not, except for the K-TEA long form. Such considerations help guide the choice of achievement tests used to document a gifted child's developing skills. Knowing the child's current achievement levels helps us determine whether his or her academic program is reasonable. A child whose achievement is far beyond that of classmates is unlikely to enjoy that classroom and needs accommodations or an alternative grade or school placement.

Monitoring a child's achievement on an individual achievement test, perhaps every 1½ to 2½ years, is extremely
helpful. The resulting scores help parents determine how
well the child's educational program is working and suggest
an appropriate instructional level. This is important
information to include in an Individual Educational Plan
(IEP) for the next year. Ideally, the child's achievement
scores (calculated as standard scores with a mean of 100)
should approach his or her IQ scores, unless learning
deficits prevent it. Where a child's achievement scores fall
considerably below IQ scores, for no discernible reason, the
educational program may be inadequate. Conversely, when
achievement scores are close to or about the same as IQ
scores, gifted children usually feel challenged and happy.

Personality Tests

At the GDC, we routinely assess introversion/extraversion,
one aspect of personality. The gifted are largely introverted
and living in an extraverted world, so can experience
problems. In psychological terms, introverts replenish their
energy by being alone or with another close individual (often
Mom, in the case of gifted children). In contrast, extraverts
regenerate by being with others—they gain energy from their
multiple interactions. Whereas gifted extraverts often have
unusually well-developed social skills, gifted introverts may
need support for their less common personality style and
accommodation, both at home and at school. We cannot
make extraverts of them, because they are simply wired
differently. Furthermore, respecting their introversion goes a
long way toward acknowledging them as unique individuals
whom we value. We have learned many things about gifted
introverts. For example, an introvert should be disciplined
privately, allowed the extra time needed to adjust to
changes, be given projects to explore in depth, and allowed
time to consider a question before being expected to answer

in public. They don't do as well in large groups, but benefit from one-on-one interaction or small group placements. In addition, we can generally assume that our introverted, gifted students will be reluctant to talk to their teachers about work that is too easy for them, necessitating parent advocacy for such matters, even with older gifted students.

The Myers-Briggs Type Inventory or Murphy-Meisgeier Type Indicator for Children may also be helpful for evaluating other personality characteristics. Understanding a child's personality style can help us suggest approaches for parenting and instruction in the classroom. In addition, on many occasions, we have given the Myers-Briggs to families to help them understand how their underlying personality styles affect their interaction. This has proven to be a very popular and positive use of this test for our clients.

Emotional Inventories and Projective Tests

Emotional indicators are important because the experience of feeling different or out of place is common in the gifted. These children may have particular problems making and keeping friends or coping with the stress of being out-of-sync in the classroom. Perhaps the child has been tormented by a bully or has simply been isolated by other children and feels terribly alone. Or, the child's efforts to move ahead and learn new material have been frustrated by a teacher who insists all students must do identical work. Sometimes, the learning disabled/gifted child is struggling to overcome a disability that is unrecognized and the damage that comes with being considered "lazy." It is important to assess the degree of these pressures and to know the details of the child's concerns in order to suggest strategies to mitigate them. Parents often find this information particularly helpful. They may not have realized their young daughter felt so isolated from classmates or that their gifted teenage son with a learning disability seriously wondered if he were as smart as others. We often learn of needs that can be addressed with teachers, as well as accommodated at home. The older, more verbal child may be asked to answer questions and complete sentences to gain more information about thoughts, concerns and hopes for the future. Or, the younger child may be asked to draw pictures or create stories based on pictures. The patterns of recurring themes in a child's answers help us to understand those issues that are most relevant.

Further Diagnostic Tests

Additional diagnostic measures may be warranted to further investigate a difficulty: explore a reading problem, understand why a child resists writing, rule out AD/HD, etc. The Woodcock-Johnson III supplementary subtests are helpful for exploring problems with phonetic skills, proofreading written work, or understanding basic math concepts. In other cases, the tester may ask to administer another ability measure or portion of an IQ test to substantiate a child's particular strengths. For example, when dealing with children with apparently strong nonverbal/spatial reasoning, we may ask for permission to give one or more of the following: the Naglieri Nonverbal Abilities Test, Ravens Progressive Matrices, or the Universal Nonverbal Intelligence Test (UNIT). Sometimes we even use a portion of an adult test to document extremely advanced abilities in children. The Matrix Reasoning subtest of the Wechsler Adult Intelligence Scale-Third Edition (WAIS-III) is an excellent untimed, nonverbal measure. Demonstrating that a considerably younger child can score high on this test, using norms for 16-year-olds, is convincing evidence to many that the child has a considerable strength. A good tester of the gifted will try to document each child's strengths to the greatest degree possible (to gain accommodations), as well as explore any relative weaknesses that may require support so that the child can be successful. A thorough knowledge of available testing instruments allows the experienced tester of the gifted to accommodate the strengths and weaknesses of any child. The tester should inform parents during testing if another measure might provide invaluable information and add the test, if needed. Parents are paying for a highly individualized evaluation and should gain as much helpful information as possible during the initial assessment, since it is not likely to be repeated.

Preparing Your Child For Testing

Parents are encouraged to prepare their children for testing so that it will be a pleasant experience for all. Our rather introverted young clients need a little time to adjust to the idea. Rather than telling them they will be "playing games," it is better to say they will be involved in activities that help us to find out more about how they think. This information will be used to help them in school. Especially with younger children, parents can provide support by remaining at the office during testing (bring a good book), so as to be there when a child comes out for a short break. We always insist on a suitably lengthy lunch hour that allows the child to get away from the office and the testing for a while. Additional breaks are taken as needed for comfort. Parents are often seen cuddling with their children for a few minutes at such times, or providing healthy snacks to keep blood sugar levels stable. If children are to be tested at school, make sure they will be tested at an agreed-upon time when they are prepared for it. Under no circumstances should a child be unexpectedly pulled out of the classroom for testing or tested without being previously informed that it will occur. Most would be upset and could not be expected to perform well.

Preparing for the Follow-Up Conference

Most parents who bring their children to be tested opt for a
follow-up conference and planning for the conference can
maximize its value. Thinking carefully about what is most
important can ensure that parents' most critical issues are
addressed. Is it understanding the ramifications of a high
level of giftedness or creating a workable educational
program where none exists? Is it helping a twice exceptional
child to understand his strengths and weaknesses or a
lonely gifted child find a friend? Making a list of questions is
a very reasonable approach to take. Parents may bring
grandparents, teachers, or anyone they wish, and some ask
that the session be tape recorded, so that it may be reviewed
at a later time (a great idea as the amount of information
can be a bit overwhelming and both parents are not always
able to attend). We have even used a conference call to unite
our staff and one parent at the Gifted Development Center
with a parent in another location who could not attend.

Providing two experienced clinicians at the conference—the
child's tester and one additional senior member of the
staff—works well at the GDC. The combined contribution of
all parties, parents and professionals, results in conclusions
being drawn about the child's level of intellectual functioning,
strengths and weaknesses, and learning style. Recommendations are then made to support the child's needs, both at
school and at home.

Whereas most parents choose to attend the conference
without their children, deciding later what to share with
them, children are sometimes included at the parents'
discretion. Children can be very helpful joining a conference
toward the end and helping to determine what recommendations should be made to the school, including whether or
not acceleration is an appropriate idea (the child must
concur with this decision for it to be considered). For gifted
children with learning deficits, parents may want to have

these issues explained to the child by the tester. Or, when the child is a teenager or a profoundly gifted child who is terribly asynchronous and needs to understand why, parents may even ask that all of the information given to them be shared with their child, as well. The child may be included in the full conference or brought in for a portion of it, depending on the circumstances and wishes of the parents. Parents who choose to have their child participate in some or all of the conference need to request it. If children are to be involved, clinicians must fully understand what can be shared with them. Some parents would like test results to be limited to general levels, strengths, and areas where the child will need to work a little harder. Others prefer to be very frank and share specific scores. Parents will need to consider the specific characteristics of the child tested to determine this. Also, when siblings are tested, caution is warranted so that children don't become competitive; we do not recommend giving scores to children in such cases. Parents may also attend the conference alone, then set up a separate appointment just for the tester to explain results to the child, according to guidelines discussed within the parent conference.

For children whose scores document gifted-level abilities, the first recommendation is generally placement in a school or full-time program for the gifted, even when one is unavailable where the family resides. Such programs usually meet the academic, social, and emotional needs of gifted children best. And, we have seen families decide to relocate to improve their children's educational options. It is important, whether or not the child eventually attends such a school, to document this need. Other recommendations follow to create a better fit for the child in school, cultivate interests, and nurture talents. Ways to support social and emotional needs are also a priority in the recommendations. Where apparent deficits exist, further evaluation is recommended with specialists.

Testers of the gifted usually offer additional follow-up services, as well. Phone consultations may be available to inquire about issues that have come up since the evaluation, as children mature and move on to different schools. Advocacy services may also be available, whereby the tester consults with school administrators and teachers, or helps create an Individual Educational Plan (IEP) for the child at school. Testers can usually recommend schools locally or offer guidelines for choosing a school out of state. Counseling is often available, as well as resource materials (informative articles, books, and tapes). Once the testing has been completed, parents should have a better understanding of their child's educational needs and have access to the necessary information to advocate for him or her.

Understanding the Gifted Through Testing

Faced with pressure to document claims of a child's giftedness, parents and other advocates usually turn to testing. Individual assessment provides professional acknowledgement that a child has advanced abilities and, therefore, unusual educational needs. Yet the results of assessment are far from trivial—we gain more than simple numerical scores and levels of intelligence. Testing provides us unusual access to understanding the highly complex cognitive abilities of these children and insight into ways to support their rare gifts. Exploring the intricacies of intelligence, we gain information that augments and clarifies our own observations. Because assessment tempers our conjectures with a healthy dose of realistic analysis, it allows us to arrive at more meaningful conclusions about the needs of these unusual children. More confident to make perfectly arguable requests of teachers and school administrators, we become empowered, effective advocates.

Quinn O'Leary...Testing

The test center surprised me. Upon hearing of my multitudinous, albeit somewhat overdramatized and self-pitying problems, a counselor friend had recommended this particular center, but despite her downplaying, I had subconsciously envisioned a stark building of unpainted concrete and mirrored windows, an amalgamation of the latex-and-fluorescent sterility of hospitals I unwillingly frequented as a child and the gently threatening imperson-ality of a government facility. I expected the population to be much the same, a swarm of cookie-cutter professionals in lab coats, toting clipboards and wearing the same empty expression of subtle disdain.

With this picture fermenting in the back of my mind, I nearly walked past the actual testing center. Its entry hunkered like a shy child between and slightly back from the larger street-butted fronts of two venerably encrusted townhouses. It was apparently a converted house, the busy, cramped verdancy of its infinitesimal front yard speaking of a time before the city and its cheek-by-jowl street plan had encroached quite so far.

I navigated the awkward angles of the foyer with a nascent sense of relief already manifesting itself as general good cheer. I greeted the woman working as secretary and was shortly introduced to my tester, a woman whose stature and open, guileless smile put me in mind of an elf from a child's book, kind but capable of a certain brand of gentle mischief. After a brief round of banter, we retired to a spartan room to conduct the testing.

The test itself was a surprise, in that despite my half-panicked feelings, I enjoyed it. A half-day's worth of verbal and visual absurdities, vocabulary, patterns and puzzles of colored blocks. It put me in mind of my first day of school,

*the same hollow anticipatory fear in the pit of my bowels,
similar relief at my apparent capability. The glaring
difference was that the test challenged me and was therefore fun for more than the first fifteen minutes. By the end of
the final subtest, I felt as though my attention had been
sifted like flour through a series of increasingly fine screens
and that every subsequent weave had required more
attention, had demanded more powerfully that I be aware
of the mesh.*

*"Now these scores are a bit less accurate because of your
age. Had you been tested as a younger person, these would
be more indicative of your actual IQ." With these words, my
birdlike tester led me into a concise explanation of what my
scores meant. The numbers, with the slithy mein that is
their wont, slithered quickly from my conscious, but a few
admittedly flattering words filtered through. The phrase that
most caught my attention, however, was offered as an
explanation:* Asynchronous Development. *I was different in
more than attitude; I was singular in awareness.*

*Those two words, their pairing making them almost
incantatory, struck to the core of my worry, slightly
soothed years of self-doubt and guilt, started to abolish
the idea that my always-apparent if somewhat
unsuccessful intellect was nothing more than pedantry
paired with laziness and angst. Relief flooded my head
like liquor and, on my way out the door, I grinned into the
sun with the expression of a joyful madman, reveling in a
sense of well-being that I hadn't felt for years.*

References

Flynn, J. R. (1984). The mean IQ of Americans: Massive gains 1932 to 1978. *Psychological Bulletin, 95,* 29-51.

Flynn, J. R. (1999). Searching for justice: The discovery of IQ gains over time. *American Psychologist, 54,* 5-20.

Pegnato, C. W. & Birch, J. W. (1959). Locating gifted children in junior high schools: A comparison of methods. *Exceptional Children, 25,* 300-304.

Snyderman, M. & Rothman, S. (1988). *The IQ controversy, the media and public policy.* New Brunswick, NJ: Transaction Books.

Wechsler, D. (2003) *WISC-IV Technical and interpretive manual.* San Antonio, TX: The Psychological Corporation, a Harcourt Assessment Company.

Websites With Recommended Testers of the Gifted

Testing and Assessment. Hoagies' Gifted Education Page. (Offers a list of testers by location, testing issues, and articles.) http://www.hoagiesgifted.org/testing.htm (23 Feb. 2003).

Institute for Educational Advancement, Gifted Resource Center. (Offers a database of testers and counselors that can be searched by a number of variables.) http://www.educationaladvancement.org (1 Mar. 2003).

For Further Reading

Gilman, B. J. & Revel, A. (1999, Spring/Summer). Current use of the Stanford-Binet L-M. *Highly Gifted Children, 12*(4), 10-12. http://www.hoagiesgifted.org/current_use.htm (23 Feb. 2003).

Osborn, J. B. (1998, Winter). Assessing gifted children. *Understanding Our Gifted, 10*(2), 9-12. http://www.ditd.org/floater.php?location=84 (23 Feb. 2003).

Silverman, L. K. (1997). Using test scores to support clinical judgment. *Gifted Education Press, 12*(1), 2-5.

Silverman, L. K., & Kearney, K. (1992). The case for the Stanford-Binet L-M as a supplemental test. *Roeper Review, 15,* 34-37.

Silverman, L. K. & Kearney, K. (1992). Don't throw away the old Binet. *Understanding Our Gifted,* 1992, 4(4), 1, 8-10. http://members.aol.com/discanner/dontthrow.html (29 Dec. 2002).

Rimm, S. B., & Lovance, K. J. (1992). How acceleration may prevent underachievement syndrome. *Gifted Child Quarterly, 36*(2), 100-105.

4

Curriculum and Instruction

A Typical Curriculum

Those who have watched a child pass through the public school system have some idea of the curriculum or learning sequence public schools typically provide. Kindergarten stresses the pre-reading skills and basic math concepts that underpin the acquisition of reading and formal math skills. In first grade, children focus heavily on reading and are beginning to learn addition and subtraction. By third grade, basic reading (having a repertoire of recognized words and the ability to sound out words) should be mastered and arithmetic is expanding to include multiplication and division. Teachers are more concerned now about proper spelling, having initially encouraged *inventive spelling* to empower their students to write. Science and social studies topics are presented, as well, at basic levels in primary grades and more complex levels as children mature.

Foreign language is often introduced minimally in elementary school, then taught in classes in middle school. The equivalent of one or two high school-level years in foreign language is offered in middle school, the first usually split into two years. By seventh or eighth grade, most students are concluding arithmetic study, having integrated into their knowledge of the four basic operations (addition, subtraction, multiplication and division) concepts of money and time, decimals, fractions, positive and negative numbers, percentages, and square and cube roots. At this point, it is generally felt that they are ready to learn to solve simple algebraic expressions, first by a "guess and check" method, then by strategies that are taught to them. Algebra instruction, in eighth or ninth grade, introduces a whole new series of higher-level math concepts—logarithms, functions, slope—as students advance to geometry, trigonometry, and finally calculus. In language arts, students have expanded their knowledge of literature, reading age-appropriate selections as they pass from grade to grade. Their writing has progressed from instruction in writing a sentence to learning to write effective paragraphs, and they've probably encountered the three- or five-paragraph essay format. With minor variations, students have learned the same things at about the same ages for a long time. The curriculum has stood the test of time and met the needs of the majority of students.

But, does it work for all students? Curricula are developed by arriving at a consensus about what educated people should know and determining what content and skills must be taught year by year to achieve the desired result after x number of years in school. It must be determined how such knowledge and skills should be taught, beginning with the youngest school-age child. Decisions have to be made about the ways children learn best and about the quantity of material that can be covered in a given period of time. How much review is necessary before concepts are mastered? Must periodic review take place following mastery so that concepts once acquired are not lost? School districts seek to meet the needs of the most students possible, so they determine the level and pace of instruction based on the needs of their average students. This ensures that the educational program will be a good fit for the majority. Yet, some students will learn far faster or slower than the curriculum can accommodate. They will find themselves bored with material they mastered in the past or struggling to keep up with classmates.

What about the first-grader who is multiplying and dividing, the third-grader reading at the seventh-grade level, or the fifth-grader who is ready to start algebra? Gifted children often find the curriculum relevant, but the pacing inappropriate. They may be ready for material much earlier than most children. The typical curriculum can be modified individually for such a child, but not without ramifications. With such an enormous, detailed structure, flexibility is problematic; changing a child's program in just one year threatens the entire sequence and most teachers are reluctant to do this (it is not always readily accepted by the teacher at the next level). Moreover, it is the responsibility of each teacher to prepare a student well over the range of topics that must be covered in that grade level. Teachers take this responsibility seriously and some feel acceleration increases the risk of *holes* in the child's content mastery. Why accelerate when one can have additional time for review?

Sequential Teaching

Most material is taught sequentially in schools because this is the way most children learn. Instruction begins with the most basic concepts and continues with a bit more each day. Yet, we know that all students are not sequential learners. Many (particularly highly gifted and visual-spatial learners) prefer to learn holistically, beginning with an overview of the *whole* and proceeding to the details of the various parts. These students need to know where they're going first in order to integrate new learning into a conceptual framework. They're wonderful systems thinkers and appreciate complexity. Instead of being taught the steps to complete an arithmetic calculation, they may benefit more from being given the answer and asked how the problem must be done. Rather than showing continuous, step-like learning progress, they are more likely to learn in intuitive leaps, mastering large amounts of related material quickly.

Learning Style Needs

Students may also have a strong preference for material presented auditorially, visually or kinesthetically. Whenever the primarily auditory, sequential approach typically used in America's classrooms is not a match with the learning style of the child, teaching will be more problematic. Within the gifted population, we commonly see combinations of ability and learning style that don't fit typical public school programs.

Gifted children may be auditory-sequential learners, better prepared for traditional classrooms, but there are also visual-spatial learners who require different approaches to learn. Linda Silverman has studied these children extensively and finds that they benefit from holistic learning, visual aides and hands-on activities that provide visual input— anything that requires them to visualize. In her book, *Upside-Down Brilliance: The Visual Spatial Learner* (2002), she notes that they often have difficulty following step-by-step instructions and are divergent thinkers. They hate sequential approaches to math calculation (they learn more holistically than sequentially), and are reluctant to "show their work" for credit because they usually arrive at answers in different ways from their teachers. They may fail to excel because instruction is seldom geared to them.

Gifted children who have both auditory-sequential and visual-spatial strengths may be termed "abstract conceptual learners" as the strong abstract reasoning abilities of the gifted characterize their thinking in both domains. They learn readily through both visual and auditory modalities, with holistic or sequential approaches. They can learn with varying teaching styles, but may flounder with instruction too concrete for their needs (e.g., in middle school programs where hands-on instruction for concrete learners is stressed because middle school philosophy assumes that most students have not developed abstract reasoning capacities yet). All gifted children reason abstractly quite early and this capacity needs to be tapped if they are to engage in their studies.

In addition, we see gifted children with other learning styles, such as gifted kinesthetic learners who usually have both visual and auditory deficits. Our highly and profoundly gifted students usually have both auditory-sequential and visual-spatial strengths, along with a preference for holistic learning. Regardless of learning style, all gifted students are efficient learners in the sense of grasping concepts quickly with little drill and practice. They are likely to advance through material very quickly if taught reasonably well.

How do these children, for whom the regular curriculum and instructional approaches are not geared, move through the system successfully? Experience tells us that ignoring their different needs simply does not work and is a dangerous risk to take. Some will suffer silently, but endure the poor program fit and succeed. Some will become under-achievers who lose, at least temporarily, their motivation to learn. Some will become behavior problems to express their frustration about being a captive in a system that is hurting them. Some will drop out of school. Once a gifted student experiences such failures, the final realization of their dreams seems all too dependent on good luck, assuming that they receive strong support from their families. We must take all of their frustrations seriously, despite what should be "fine for all students," because the risks are simply too great to ignore.

How Different are the Gifted as Students?

Learning Rate

Dr. Charlotte Mendosa of Colorado College recalled an anecdote with a teacher in the college's summer enrichment program for gifted children (personal communication, 1993). The teacher wrote to thank her for the opportunity to teach in the program and, particularly, for the daily planning period scheduled into her day. The teacher admitted that, initially, she had thought the planning period would be a waste of time because she had already completed her lesson plans for the entire three-week course before arriving. However, when by Thursday of the first week of class, her students had exhausted everything the teacher had planned for them for the entire course, she was very grateful to have a planning period!

Professor Brian Start (1992) found a difference in learning rates in heterogeneous classrooms of eight to one; the fastest learner learned eight times faster than the slowest. This is an enormous difference with serious ramifications. How can a child who learns at the slowest rate be learning successfully in that classroom without special accommodations? Likewise, how can the fastest learner in that room be challenged adequately enough to learn good work habits and maintain an interest in learning? Unfortunately, needed accommodations are often not available. Although there are stronger laws to support the needs of students with disabilities, the current tendency to mainstream these students sometimes results in less capacity to meet their needs in classrooms where teachers have a wide range of students and class size is large. Gifted children suffer, as well, because teachers have similar limitations dealing with them and because a prevalent lack of teacher training in gifted education restricts understanding of gifted students' learning needs.

The National Research Center on the Gifted and Talented (NRC G/T) published a report entitled, "Why Not Let High Ability Students Start School in January?" (Reis, Westberg, Kulikowich, Caillard, Hebert, & Plucker, 1993) alluding to the fact that gifted students usually do not need the extensive review of material undertaken every fall and could simply begin with new concepts usually taught at the beginning of the new year. Fully 40% to 50% of the material that would typically be taught has already been mastered by these students. In fact, a general rule of thumb is that gifted students can at least progress at twice the normal pace, assuming no disabilities (requiring accommodation) that slow them down, and some may progress more quickly. Yet, virtually no schools are prepared to allow students to progress this fast. The gifted student's pacing difficulties persist throughout his or her schooling. Even when a child skips a grade, he or she is likely to need faster pacing after only a few months in the new grade. The problem is never fully resolved without a program designed for gifted children at the level of the particular child. With regular public school programs (and even gifted programs when the child in question is very highly gifted) parents must be counseled to frequently review their children's programs for appropriate fit and consideration of what to do next.

Typical Test Score Patterns for Younger Gifted Children

The individual achievement testing of gifted children best describes their unusual academic progress. The following is a sampling of actual scores from young children in a school for the gifted in Boulder, Colorado. The test used was the Kaufman Test of Educational Achievement (K-TEA) Brief Form, which assesses pre-algebra mathematics (both calculation and reasoning), reading (both decoding and comprehension), and spelling. Standard scores have a mean of 100 and standard deviation of 15, with levels akin to IQ scores (110 is high average, 120 is superior, 130 is gifted,

145 is highly gifted). This test has a ceiling of 160 (exceptionally gifted range). Note the grade equivalents, which include the grade and month of the school year (5.2 means the second month of fifth grade). Grade equivalents are based on raw scores earned and equate those raw scores with the scores of average children at a particular grade level.

Child A, age 6-6 (6 years, 6 months)

K-TEA Subtests	Standard Score	Percentile Rank	Grade Equivalent
Mathematics	112	79.0	2.0
Reading	160	>99.9	4.8
Spelling	152	>99.9	4.2

Although this school does not have age-based grade levels, it is clear that this young child, who would be a first-grader in most public schools, is very advanced in reading (fourth-grade level) and would have difficulty in a classroom where the basics of reading are stressed for the majority of the school day. This child is also very advanced in spelling, which is not formally taught in most first-grade classes. Most teachers encourage inventive spelling for first-graders to encourage them to begin writing. Such an approach might be frustrating for this child, who would want to know when words were misspelled to avoid learning them incorrectly.

Child B, age 6-8

K-TEA Subtests	Standard Score	Percentile Rank	Grade Equivalent
Mathematics	112	79.0	2.0
Reading	142	99.7	3.5
Spelling	100	50.0	1.7

Of a similar age to Child A, Child B is also very strong in reading, but is at a typical level for a first-grader in Spelling and a high-average level in Mathematics.

Child C, age 6-10

K-TEA Subtests	Standard Score	Percentile Rank	Grade Equivalent
Mathematics	120	93.0	2.5
Reading	160	>99.9	7.3
Spelling	155	>99.9	4.9

Child C is also a very strong reader (seventh-grade level) who would be difficult to challenge even in a school for the gifted. This child will need appropriately challenging books without objectionable content and literature study that engages his or her abstract reasoning. This child's spelling is also so strong that more advanced composition assignments are possible.

Child D, age 6-10

K-TEA Subtests	Standard Score	Percentile Rank	Grade Equivalent
Mathematics	118	88.0	2.4
Reading	160	>99.9	10.8
Spelling	130	98.0	3.3

Child D has an even more remarkable reading level (nearing the end of tenth grade). Such children often start to read early. As parents read to them, they begin to develop their own reading skills. Many parents don't teach formal math skills early, unless the child has pushed to learn certain concepts, so reading is often the more advanced subject at this age. In fact, we have encountered few parents at the

Gifted Development Center who took the lead to teach any formal skills. Rather, these parents usually only respond to curious children's questions.

Note that the children presented up to this point are all six-year-olds! Most would have been placed in the first grade in public schools, based on age, even though reading levels range as high as the tenth-grade level. All of these children would find the typical beginning reading emphasis of first grade stultifying.

Let's look at more children, who are a little older:

Child E, age 7-2

K-TEA Subtests	Standard Score	Percentile Rank	Grade Equivalent
Mathematics	143	99.8	3.8
Reading	148	99.9	4.4
Spelling	116	86.0	2.8

Child E, who was seven at the time of testing, is advanced in both Mathematics and Reading, with Spelling somewhat lower (this is a common pattern for gifted children). Scoring at this level in Mathematics, Child E is probably doing simple multiplication and division, which would not normally be taught in a second grade classroom.

Child F, age 7-6

K-TEA Subtests	Standard Score	Percentile Rank	Grade Equivalent
Mathematics	114	82.0	3.0
Reading	140	99.6	5.2
Spelling	155	>99.9	6.7

This child reads and spells at the fifth- and sixth-grade levels, and would also have serious difficulty being challenged in a second grade classroom.

Child G, age 7-11

K-TEA Subtests	Standard Score	Percentile Rank	Grade Equivalent
Mathematics	160	>99.9	>12.9
Reading	150	>99.9	>12.9
Spelling	156	>99.9	9.2

Child G, another potential second-grader, is remarkably advanced in all areas assessed, scoring at the level of the average high school graduate in reading and pre-algebra math. This demonstrates the rapid progression in achievement we may see, with children exhibiting a widening range of skill levels as they mature.

The children above, a typical mixture of students in a school or program for the gifted, differ in age by only 17 months, yet their grade equivalents vary by 12 grade levels! They would likely be placed in the first or second grade in most public schools. A fair assumption would be that children in the gifted range (IQ 130 to 144) will usually reach the high school-graduate level in one or more academic areas at least during middle school. Highly gifted students (IQ 145 and up) will have reached this point by the end of elementary school. Not only is rapid learning pace to be expected, possibly resulting in extreme advancement, but this assortment of skill levels demonstrates the need for individualized programs for gifted children. Even within a school for the gifted, where instructional pace can be increased for all students, individual accommodations will also be needed.

Choose Achievement Tests Carefully

To consider the academic progress of gifted children as they mature, we have to be very careful to use achievement tests with an adequate ceiling to assess their developing skills. The Woodcock-Johnson III Tests of Achievement is an excellent instrument for such situations as it has a graduate-school ceiling, yields standard scores that can extend in some cases beyond 200, and samples higher-level math (algebra and beyond). Individual achievement tests tend to work better than the standardized group achieve-ment tests given at school as they are largely untimed; some gifted children are very reflective and earn poorer scores when they have to finish a school achievement test within specified time limits. Furthermore, individual achievement tests offer a sampling of material at many grade levels, which is preferable to grade-level tests (ITBS, CAT, Terra Nova, etc.), which sample primarily grade-level material and only a minimal amount of content considered *beyond* grade level. Whereas grade-level tests offer more detailed results about mastery of concepts at the specific grade level, they can obscure very advanced academic progress by the gifted by imposing an inadequate ceiling. If a child earns a 99th percentile score, we know he is at least at the highest level the test assesses; however, we cannot determine additional advancement.

For this reason, it is very helpful to have a child who is advancing quickly tested individually, perhaps every 1½ to 2½ years, to gauge the full range of progress and help make academic decisions. For these purposes, the Kaufman Test of Educational Achievement (long or brief forms), Wechsler Individual Achievement Test, or Woodcock-Johnson Tests of Achievement are fine for early elementary school (profoundly gifted children may need the scoring range of the Woodcock-Johnson), and the Woodcock-Johnson is appropriate for older students. Regardless of school placement or level of achievement (even if well beyond that of the child's classmates), a child should be making reasonable progress each year in school. This means that if we accept as a minimal expectation of annual progress a full grade level's advancement, then the third-grader reading at a seventh-grade level this year should, at least, be reading at the eight-grade level by next year. Of course, the gifted child provided challenging programming should pace more quickly, but under no circumstances should this child's meeting of third-grade expectations this year or fourth-grade expectations next year be cause for doing nothing additional!

Typical Test Score Patterns for Older Gifted Children

A sampling of the grade equivalents of older gifted children confirms that their accelerated learning continues. Variances between gifted children of similar ages are pronounced, and skill levels in the various domains vary for each individual child. The following scores on the Woodcock-Johnson-Revised (WJ-R) Tests of Achievement exemplify the achievement trends of gifted students tested at the Gifted Development Center. (This test was used until its successor, the Woodcock-Johnson III, was introduced in the fall of 2000.)

The WJ-R consists of standard subtests of reading decoding (Letter-Word Identification) and comprehension (Passage Comprehension); math calculation (Calculation) and reasoning (Applied Problems); and spelling, punctuation, and word usage (Dictation). Letter-Word Identification requires the child to read separate words from a list, recognized as whole "sight" words or sounded out phoneti-cally, while Passage Comprehension asks the child to fill in a blank with a single word to complete a sensible passage. Calculation consists of various formal math problems, while Applied Problems is oral word problems, with the child reading along or seeing pictures. Children can do written calculations to answer Applied Problems items if desired.

Child H, age 8-1

WJ-R Subtest	Standard Score	Percentile Rank	Grade Equivalent
Letter-Word Identification	129	97.0	5.4
Passage Comprehension	141	99.7	8.3
Calculation	129	97.0	3.8
Applied Problems	146	99.9	6.3
Dictation	93	33.0	2.2
Broad Reading	135	99.0	6.4
Broad Math	143	99.8	4.7

This child, who would generally be a third-grader, has reading comprehension (Passage Comprehension) at the eighth-grade level. These scores also demonstrate a common pattern among the gifted: reading comprehension typically is stronger than decoding ability (Letter-Word Identification) and math reasoning (Applied Problems) is usually better than Calculation. The gifted use their abstract reasoning ability to their advantage when they read, using contextual clues to aid them, and when they reason mathematically. In contrast, they usually find reading individual words (sounding them out) and doing rote calculations consider-ably less interesting. Most resist learning math facts. Many, like Child H, simply have less well-developed spelling, punctuation and word usage skills (Dictation) and will benefit from spelling and grammar checkers. In fact, note Child H's percentile rankings for the various scores. All are at the 97th to 99.9th percentile, except for Dictation, which is at the 33rd percentile. Clearly, knowledge of spelling and punctuation rules is not strongly related to giftedness!

Child I, age 8-3

WJ-R Subtest	Standard Score	Percentile Rank	Grade Equivalent
Letter-Word Identification	137	99.0	6.7
Passage Comprehension	144	99.8	10.0
Calculation	126	96.0	4.0
Applied Problems	118	88.0	4.0
Dictation	128	97.0	5.2
Broad Reading	139	99.5	7.7
Broad Math	124	95.0	4.0

This child has a beginning tenth-grade reading comprehension level, which will need to be accommodated with higher-level literature and appropriate content for a younger gifted child. This can often be accomplished by using carefully chosen classic literature, which offers more complex language, perhaps of an antiquated style. Literature study should also progress from books likely to encourage a love of reading to those presenting existential dilemmas. The gifted child's abstract reasoning should be challenged if he or she is to be engaged by the work.

Child I's other achievement levels are not as high as reading, but spelling, punctuation, and word usage (Dictation) are quite good, so advanced work in composition will be easy. Calculation is higher than Applied Problems, suggesting very accurate calculation skills but less advanced instruction in math concepts.

Child J, age 8-3

WJ-R Subtest	Standard Score	Percentile Rank	Grade Equivalent
Letter-Word Identification	137	99.0	6.7
Passage Comprehension	147	99.9	11.0
Calculation	194	99.9	7.8
Applied Problems	171	99.9	10.8
Dictation	131	98.0	5.6
Broad Reading	141	99.7	8.1
Broad Math	196	99.9	9.2
Skills	152	99.9	7.3

Child J has remarkable math achievement for an eight-year-old. To be at the high tenth-grade level in math reasoning (Applied Problems), this child had to demonstrate some mastery of higher-level mathematics (algebra and beyond), as well as general mastery of arithmetic. Reading comprehension is at the level of the average high school student beginning his junior year.

Child J's current achievement is two to eight grade levels above third grade. If this child were actually placed in a third-grade classroom, full-grade acceleration would be strongly indicated, if the child concurred with the placement. If so, moving him or her to the fifth grade in the fall (or the fourth if this situation were encountered in the fall of third grade) would be wise. Usually grade acceleration is attempted one year at a time, with frequent review of the child's situation thereafter. If the child had reservations about acceleration, individualization would be essential in the third-grade classroom. Acceleration to a higher grade level in only one subject might also be tried, if the child felt this would be acceptable. This solution would help to meet educational goals in that subject, and would also acquaint the child with the older group to ease a future full-grade skip.

It is difficult for teachers to accommodate students with such varying needs. As gifted children mature, the discrepancy between their actual achievement levels and grade-level expectations increases. Most gifted children can cope with typical kindergarten and, perhaps, first-grade curricula, unless they enter school with very advanced reading. However, it becomes harder for them to find comfort in the regular classroom as they acquire basic skills in reading, math, and writing more quickly than other students. They begin to surge ahead.

Moreover, each child's achievement in the different academic areas may vary; a child may need significant accommodations in one area, but not others. As a result, the teacher responsible for a range of gifted children of about the same age may face huge variability in his or her students' readiness to learn new topics. Some children's achievement may place them in the stratosphere in all academic areas, whereas other students may need only moderate accommodation in one area. Imagine when these needs are encountered by a teacher in a regular classroom, where the gifted students exist in addition to other children with special needs. Knowing that children learn best when taught approximately at their correct level, we see the inherent complication with the typical public school classroom. Most of the children seen at the Gifted Development Center are brought by parents concerned about them being held back and losing motivation to learn. Sometimes, the same complaint is made about a school for the gifted, although less frequently. It occurs in schools that have a more rigid curriculum that all gifted children must pass through, as opposed to a program designed to meet individual needs.

Child K, age 9-11

WJ-R Subtest	Standard Score	Percentile Rank	Grade Equivalent
Letter-Word Identification	121	92.0	7.6
Passage Comprehension	122	93.0	8.3
Calculation	134	99.0	6.7
Applied Problems	140	99.6	10.1
Dictation	107	68.0	5.2
Broad Reading	123	94.0	7.9
Broad Math	142	99.7	7.9

Child K, a likely fourth-grade placement in a typical school, has eighth-grade reading comprehension and beginning tenth-grade abilities in math reasoning (Applied Problems). Child K's math calculation skills (at the sixth-grade level) might benefit from assistance so that they will fully support mathematical reasoning; however, any extra work will need to be enjoyable. More drill and practice is not likely to help. Computer math games or competitions would be fun ways to improve calculation skills. This student, who is stronger in math than reading, is less advanced in spelling and punctuation skills—a common pattern with visual-spatial learners. Spelling can become a strength if a visualization approach is used and the child develops the ability to see "if a word looks right." Attention to the suggestions of a spelling checker also improves spelling over time.

As gifted children continue to mature, we see grade equivalents extending beyond the high school-graduate level (>12.9).

Child L, age 10-3

WJ-R Subtest	Standard Score	Percentile Rank	Grade Equivalent
Letter-Word Identification	134	99.0	10.7
Passage Comprehension	143	99.8	15.6
Calculation	128	97.0	6.7
Applied Problems	135	99.0	10.8
Dictation	115	84.0	6.9
Broad Reading	145	99.9	12.5
Broad Math	136	99.0	8.1

Note that Child L, at age 10, is nearing the college graduate level (grade equivalent 15.6) in Passage (reading) Comprehension. Consider the ramifications of limiting literature study to typical fifth-grade fare. Though content that is both challenging and appropriate for such a child is more difficult to find, it is needed to engage this child. Child L's math reasoning (Applied Problems) is also very high, suggesting the need to move to algebra early. The greater abstraction of higher-level math is needed to maintain interest in mathematics. It is important with such children to avoid too many years of arithmetic, which is usually not tolerated well. Calculation might improve if more advanced arithmetic concepts were presented, and this would better support mathematical reasoning ability. However, most types of advanced arithmetic are included in algebra word problems, which involve percentages, decimals, etc. Most gifted children find them more interesting in the context of algebra and learn them more readily.

Child M, age 10-6

WJ-R Subtest	Standard Score	Percentile Rank	Grade Equivalent
Letter-Word Identification	129	97.0	9.7
Passage Comprehension	151	99.9	16.9
Calculation	149	99.9	8.3
Applied Problems	135	99.0	10.8
Dictation	131	98.0	9.8
Broad Reading	146	99.9	12.9
Broad Math	146	99.9	9.4

Note that this 10½-year-old has reading comprehension at the level of a student graduating from college, as well as math reasoning at the high tenth-grade level. Child M is another strong candidate for grade acceleration as the lowest grade equivalent is three years above typical fifth-grade work.

Child N, age 10-10

WJ-R Subtest	Standard Score	Percentile Rank	Grade Equivalent
Letter-Word Identification	142	99.7	13.6
Passage Comprehension	138	99.0	14.2
Calculation	134	99.0	7.3
Applied Problems	144	99.8	13.1
Dictation	113	80.0	6.9
Broad Reading	150	99.9	14.1
Broad Math	146	99.9	9.9

Child N has both reading and math reasoning (Applied Problems) to be accommodated at the college level (algebra might be undertaken early). Less advanced is Dictation (spelling, punctuation, and word usage) at the high sixth-grade level. Child N should use a computer word processor and pay close attention to suggested spellings the spelling checker provides. Practice with proofreading might be of help, as well, along with a brief review of punctuation and usage rules.

Child O, age 11-2

WJ-R Subtest	Standard Score	Percentile Rank	Grade Equivalent
Letter-Word Identification	99	48.0	5.8
Passage Comprehension	121	92.0	10.0
Calculation	164	99.9	12.2
Applied Problems	143	99.8	13.8
Dictation	93	33.0	4.9
Broad Reading	111	76.0	7.1
Broad Math	164	99.9	13.5

Child O has an interesting score profile with superior reading comprehension and average decoding skills. This pattern in a gifted child can suggest very subtle dyslexia, especially when the other achievement scores are so much higher. Such a child struggles with phonics and the recognition of individual words, and finds spelling very difficult, but compensates immensely with abstract reasoning to glean meaning from context (especially when the reading comprehension test is untimed). However, these children may need accommodations as reading demands increase. They may require more time for reading, limited assignments, or a text reader that audibly *reads* material on a computer. Child O also needs very advanced math instruction, but would likely be placed in the sixth grade in middle school. As many middle schools have limited honors classes to allow for heterogeneous instruction of all students, Child O might experience significant frustration in math (wanting to do more advanced work) and potential difficulty with reading.

Child P, age 13-11

WJ-R Subtest	Standard Score	Percentile Rank	Grade Equivalent
Letter-Word Identification	124	95.0	13.6
Passage Comprehension	139	99.5	16.9
Calculation	155	99.9	16.9
Applied Problems	151	99.9	16.9
Dictation	103	58.0	8.9
Broad Reading	138	99.0	16.2
Broad Math	156	99.9	16.9

At age 13-11, Child P is performing mostly at the level of a college senior, except in spelling and reading sight words. This is the student who needs very high-level instruction, as well as the liberal use of *spell check* when word processing! Likewise, Child Q (Age 14-5), on the following page, is functioning at the level of a college graduate in reading and math reasoning. Again, only Dictation is low, necessitating some extra care checking spelling, punctuation, and word usage.

Child Q, age 14-5

WJ-R Subtest	Standard Score	Percentile Rank	Grade Equivalent
Letter-Word Identification	130	98.0	16.8
Passage Comprehension	143	99.8	16.9
Calculation	120	90.0	12.2
Applied Problems	134	99.0	16.9
Dictation	95	38.0	7.4
Broad Reading	142	99.7	16.9
Broad Math	129	97.0	15.3

At this point, both Child P and Child Q would be most comfortable in high school placements, skipping at least a grade in middle school. High school graduation requires a specific number of credits, but middle school has no such requirement, so acceleration before high school is usually a good choice.

The Need to Learn at the Appropriate Level

Although the achievement levels of these children vary, they all present a substantial challenge for the teacher to teach appropriately in the regular classroom. Each child should be learning at the proper level in each academic area if learning is to be relevant. The advanced reader should be given higher level reading materials and should move beyond consideration of concrete details in literature to a higher level of abstraction. The accelerated math student should be working at a level of current achievement, moving ahead as each new concept is mastered. Even in spelling, the child should be learning to spell words at his or her correct level. Coursework in science and social studies should offer more depth and breadth for these children, which is usually characteristic of studying the same topics at a higher grade level.

Expecting a child to do average work who has progressed considerably beyond that level is unfair and produces negative results. Not only is motivation threatened by the continuous restriction of advancement, but study and organizational skills are not learned when they are not yet necessary to the successful completion of assignments. The child who can remember lecture material well enough to recall it on a test does not learn to take notes. Likewise, the child who can procrastinate until the last moment, quickly complete a project, and get an *A*, does not learn to schedule a long-term assignment over time. The simple learning of a good work ethic is thwarted by the lack of difficult, relevant work. Most gifted students have never learned this lesson: "If at first you don't succeed, try, try again," because nothing has been difficult enough to warrant learning it. Far too many gifted children are crippled by poor study and organizational skills, and have never learned the patience needed to undertake a truly challenging task. When they finally face the level of challenge that requires these skills, it is in an advanced high school class, in college, or in graduate school, where they may or may not be able to handle the work. These are skills any parent of an average child would expect the child to have learned in school; it is fair for parents of the gifted to expect no less.

Instructional Approaches

Teachers who have successfully taught gifted children learn strategies to handle their students' higher-level learning needs, their faster learning pace, and their earlier abstract reasoning. They have explored curriculum compacting with added enrichment, grouping strategies, grade acceleration, subject acceleration, and other approaches designed to accommodate these able learners. Adept at analyzing the learning options available within a school, they have learned to use them flexibly to meet a child's specific needs. Though they have had to abandon many traditional assumptions about what and how a child should be learning at a particular grade level, they have experienced success teaching and motivating these children.

Unless a gifted student is homeschooled, it can be difficult to create a program for a child to be taught at his or her assessed level in every subject, with pacing determined by the child. A homeschooling parent can order materials exactly geared to the child, and can order new ones as needed due to unusual progress. The grade-level teacher in a more typical public or private school, however, is accustomed to teaching many children together at the same level, with similar materials designed for more average children. Therefore, accommodations for a gifted child within a classroom usually involve careful consideration of the existing curriculum to discover which parts will work and which will not, before determining what else will be needed. A gifted student requiring modifications of regular work is likely to have already mastered some of what will be taught, but not all, and can learn new material more quickly.

Curriculum Compacting

Curriculum compacting is a powerful tool for teachers to use when a child needs faster pacing through new material than other children in the class require and/or has already mastered a portion of the curriculum being taught. Susan Winebrenner, in her book *Teaching Gifted Kids in the Regular Classroom* (1992), instructs teachers in the technique of determining what children know before teaching, eliminating already-mastered material, teaching new concepts with less drill and practice, and providing additional enrichment with the time gained. For children who have not encountered the material before, but can learn it more efficiently, she offers suggestions to increase the interest level of the topic being studied. For example, while other students complete a text-book-based unit, the gifted child who learns quickly might read the text independently and focus on a related project that can be shared with the class. Curriculum compacting allows the gifted child to be accommodated within the regular classroom, using topics and materials related to what the rest of the class is learning. However, it frees the gifted child from the lower-level, slower-paced learning that can undermine motivation, and can be very effective when used consistently. Susan Winebrenner notes, "Teaching methods that rely on scope-and-sequence charts or regular and cumulative review are not compatible with how gifted students learn, which is fast and forever" (p. 11).

Advanced Independent Study

When the material the child requires is clearly beyond what his or her classmates are studying, the classroom teacher can make accommodations for the child by creating an independent study program. Although it somewhat isolates a child within the classroom, it allows him or her to remain in close proximity to friends. For the child reluctant to attend class with older students, this can be a welcome solution. Independent study is possible in all subject areas. Students might read different literature than the rest of the class or undertake a research project in an area of interest. Teachers must teach any independent learning and research skills the child may need, however. Although advanced, gifted children are not born with such skills.

The end result of an independent study program must be reasonable. If it involves any accelerated work typical of a higher grade level, it should lead to activities next year that are an appropriate next step. It should not take the child through a portion of the next year's curriculum with the expectation that he or she will simply repeat those concepts next year. What makes gifted children most at risk is their inability to progress as needed in their studies, so acceleration offered at one point without regard to future options is as unwise as ignoring needs now.

Subject Acceleration

Significant advancement can often be more easily accommodated by having the child go to a higher-grade-level classroom for the subject(s) needed. The teacher of this class has already prepared to teach this material and the child can learn with others. Arrangements have to be made to accommodate a student's attendance at the given time, as teachers usually do not teach the same subjects at the same times of day. However, this can usually be accomplished when flexible teachers agree there is a need. In cases where a child has reservations about full-grade acceleration, attending a more advanced class for one subject can be an icebreaker. Once the child makes friends among the older group, the prospect of moving to that grade for all subjects is less daunting. It is important to note that pacing difficulties are likely to reemerge at some point at the higher grade level, as well. After the child settles in with the older children and any *holes* in mastery of previous material have been filled, he or she will likely grasp new concepts more quickly than the other students. The acceleration will not eliminate this need, but will improve the *fit* for the child within the curriculum for the time being.

Mentors and Other Opportunities Outside of School

Instructional strategies for the gifted may also include the use of outside mentors, projects, and other opportunities to broaden a child's study within the classroom. An interest in math or writing might be further supported by a mentor in the community or at a local college, and those experiences might become part of the child's program at school. In this way, the child's passions and advancement in specific areas are supported by the teacher, beyond the boundaries of the classroom. Scientific investigations, shadowing experiences with the mentor, and literary accomplishments all offer possibilities for the child to substitute more meaningful outside work for typical grade-level classwork.

Acceleration vs. Enrichment

Acceleration and *enrichment* warrant discussion here as they relate to instructional approaches. Because many educators are reluctant to make a change in a gifted child's regular curriculum, which may significantly affect the entire curriculum sequence, there is a bias in favor of offering *enrichment* opportunities instead of *accelerative* options. The belief is that it is always beneficial to enrich a child's study, and if that can be done without presenting concepts from the next year's curriculum, the child will benefit. However, *enrichment* unrelated to the child's work or any grade-level curriculum rarely motivates the child. Only *relevant enrichment*, which increases the depth and breadth of the child's study, significantly improves the child's situation in the classroom. If a truly enriched curriculum is offered, it will lead to *acceleration* at some point. This is because curricula are designed to cycle through the same concepts a number of times at different grade levels, adding more depth and breadth as the child matures. So, the curriculum of one grade, now significantly *enriched*, resembles the curriculum of a higher grade, especially in less sequential subjects such as science, social studies and language arts. Southern and Jones (1991) note,

> *In truth, advanced study in any discipline may entail the kinds of activities normally associated with enrichment. Some of these include original investigations, productive and critical thinking in the content area, moral and ethical implications of procedures, and advanced levels of analysis, synthesis, and evaluation.* (p. 22)

There is nothing wrong with offering interesting enrichment opportunities, provided the teacher is always assessing the child's grade-level placement and whether it continues to be appropriate. The concepts of *enrichment* and *acceleration* overlap considerably; however, *acceleration* confers credit for material that is mastered and affirms the right of the child to move on.

The Individual Educational Plan

All of the above instructional approaches imply that planning has taken place for the gifted child's educational year. Since planning is critical to successfully working with any *special needs* child, it is important to complete an Individual Educational Plan (IEP) yearly. The plan should detail the child's specific needs in each subject area, with ways to meet those needs listed. The IEP requires the input of parents, the teacher, and the child to be relevant, since each brings important information to the planning process. It should be reviewed during the year and revised, if necessary. Goals that were set should also be evaluated at the end of the year to provide information for the next year's teacher to use in further planning. Although IEPs for the gifted are rarely mandated by state law, they are, nevertheless, important to create. Even a brief IEP contributes to better accommodations for gifted students, offered consistently throughout the year. Highly and profoundly gifted children placed in full-time schools or programs for the gifted will need IEPs, as well, to plan for needs beyond those of the moderately gifted.

Successful Instructional Assumptions

Good teachers of the gifted bring to their classrooms valuable assumptions about teaching. First, they know to always engage their students through abstract reasoning. They instinctively *bump up* the level of classroom conversations to challenge these wonderful minds. Those familiar with Bloom's Taxonomy (1956) know to encourage the higher level thinking skills of analysis (e.g., categorize, compare, contrast), synthesis (e.g., create, construct, compose), and evaluation over the simple acquisition and parroting back of facts. The model one middle school teacher of the gifted used for literature study specifically directed students to start with the concrete details of each piece and move to an understanding of its universal truths. With such an approach, study is always expansive and supportive of the gifted mind that simultaneously sees many sides of an issue and recognizes different levels of meaning.

Second, these teachers understand that some students will find different, less traditional ways of reaching an answer. Especially in math, we see difficulty among the gifted following typical problem-solving sequences. Successful teachers are more flexible reviewing their students' work and following alternate lines of reasoning. Of course, it is important to teach students logical ways of thinking and to prepare them for future teachers; however, different (correct) approaches need to be respected. In other subjects besides math, it is important to see alternate answers, as well. The essay question on a test should be conceived to generate more than one answer from students—an acceptable answer being one that is well-supported.

Another basic tenet in teaching the gifted is to have naturally high expectations, ignoring what others think "children this age can't do." I recall a new science teacher for an accelerated charter middle school noting that her biology lesson plans, previously used while teaching college freshmen, should be "just about right" for the bright group of middle-schoolers she was expecting to have. Indeed, she went on to sponsor many state science fair winners by supporting unusually high-level research and teaching what looked like high school or college-level, lab-based classes. An English teacher at the same school, who came from teaching high school seniors Honors English in a private school in the Northeast, had similarly high expectations for her middle school students. Although she initially had to admit that her students were good thinkers but not yet good writers, she focused upon how to help them accomplish the goals she felt they could meet. Doing a masterful job of teaching what was most essential and having extremely high expectations in her evaluations of student writing, she proclaimed her finishing eighth-graders "ready for college English courses." Most were.

Related to high expectations, the successful teacher observes no ceilings in the classroom, in terms of questions that can be asked or topics discussed. Discussions are allowed to rise to any level, embracing higher-level observations and never restricting students to grade-level concepts. One teacher liked to divide his class time into three parts: discussing planned topics with the entire class, helping his students who were struggling, and exploring the most difficult material he could find related to the day's topic with his gifted students.

Such teachers tend to serve as advocates for the gifted even when other teachers create roadblocks. Usually strong, independent thinkers, they forge ahead with novel plans and create options that allow gifted students to progress.

A willingness to modify a gifted student's educational plan when the original plan isn't working is another common thread among these teachers. They recognize there are no prescribed methods that always work for gifted students. In every case, the plans made are the best guess by the teacher, parent, and student of what will meet needs. If plans fail, they simply modify them and try something else.

Understanding the special relationship a gifted student may have with the teacher is also important; the student may relate better intellectually to the teacher than classmates, so the quality of the relationship is important. Good teachers of the gifted can be life-changing role models.

Grouping Strategies

Anti-tracking

Although grouping gifted children to provide higher-level, faster-paced instruction is a reasonable approach to save time and effort accommodating them, it is addressed separately here because the concept of grouping arouses considerable controversy. The School Reform Movement of the 1980s and 1990s reacted sharply to the perceived abuses of *tracking* children, which had previously been a common instructional strategy in America's schools. Children had frequently been divided into low, medium and high-ability groups by the end of elementary school, with these placements lasting through junior high and high school, and the classifications being difficult to change. Whereas gifted children usually benefited educationally from this type of grouping, when their curriculum was modified in accordance with their learning needs, the other groups did not always experience favorable results. There was some comfort for the low groups in being grouped for remedial work, but concerns were voiced about their teachers stressing discipline over the teaching of new concepts. It was also felt that middle and low-ability groups needed high-functioning students as role models. The resulting backlash resisted all forms of grouping in favor of teaching children in hetero-geneous groups. We can see that this resistance has extended to not only restricting classes for various ability levels, but also to grouping children within classes (perhaps for reading or math), and to creating schools to address the needs of the gifted.

Although teachers are certainly using ability-grouping strategies in classes today, opinions are mixed as to whether such grouping is ethical. Many schools of education are turning out graduates indoctrinated against ability grouping, or at least with strong views that *instructional grouping* should be short-term and with the groups changing composition frequently. Especially within middle schools, where heterogeneous grouping has been a hallmark of middle school philosophy, there are teachers who feel they would be acting unethically if they created a small cluster group of gifted students within a class and modified the group's curriculum to address student needs. These are generally not teachers with background in gifted education; they are unaware of the tremendous damage that can be done to the gifted by holding them back. Restricting gifted students to typical grade-level content is not perceived to be harmful and many believe that gifted students benefit by teaching others. We have seen some encouraging recent philosophical change among teachers and administrators in middle schools in Colorado and across the United States. Seeing that gifted students are often not excelling in hetero-geneously grouped classes, with a relative absence of honors classes, some are beginning to embrace accelerative options for these students, and to emphasize differentiation within the classroom.

Cooperative Learning

One very prevalent form of grouping deserves mention here. Cooperative learning was an instructional strategy pushed ardently by schools in the early 1990s, and one that is still respected and used by many educators today. The notion is to create small groups of students within the classroom who will have to function together to accomplish shared learning goals and thus learn important lessons about being team players. As adults in the work world must increasingly master team-oriented work environments, cooperative learning was designed to teach students the social skills necessary to accomplish this. Most cooperative learning approaches directed the teacher to group the children heterogeneously; each group would have one high-ability child, one low, and several more average children.

The high-ability child would ostensibly benefit from teaching the others and the others would profit from having a strong role model. Teachers in our school district were actually pushed to increase their overall use of cooperative learning strategies to a large percentage of their instructional time because the approach was felt to be so valuable.

Unfortunately, cooperative learning, as described above, has had negative results with gifted children. Not only are the gifted usually held to grade-level work with this approach, but are forced to be largely teachers and leaders if their groups are to be successful. Many gifted students are intro-verts who find it difficult to be successful leaders in such a situation, so cooperative learning has been a nightmare for some. Moreover, the fact that many teachers assign group grades for cooperative learning projects, to mimic rewards in the outside world, can make this approach traumatic for gifted students who feel they have lost control over their grades.

Fortunately, there are solutions to the problems encountered. Cooperative learning does not have to be practiced with heterogeneous groups. Gifted children do much better when allowed to choose their own groups and, actually, more homogeneous groups mimic real-life work experiences more closely. Teachers can also allow different children in hetero-geneous groups contributions at different levels, extending the potential challenge of the gifted student's work and accommodating struggling students better. And, group grades need not be given.

Research on Grouping

When gifted children are underchallenged in school, parents and supportive teachers often look to homogeneous grouping strategies as a potential solution. If advanced students can be grouped and taught together at the proper level and pace, their education can better meet their needs. However, there are educators today who balk at this notion, sometimes citing *research* to support their views. This occurred in the Boulder Valley School District several years ago, when a past superintendent insisted that "the research" proved grouping would produce dire consequences, armed with only a single study by Jeannie Oakes. While Oakes' work pointed to important concerns about rigid tracking systems, it was relatively unrepresentative of the bulk of research on instructional grouping which generally documents positive gains when advanced students are grouped and instructed appropriately. Because more schools for the gifted, gifted classrooms, and other grouped gifted accommodations are so desperately needed, it is important to be familiar with the research of Dr. Karen Rogers at the University of St. Thomas. Dr. Rogers reviewed all of the studies, not just one. Her work is indispensable to gifted advocates.

Dr. Rogers' 1991 work, *The Relationship of Grouping Practices to the Education of the Gifted and Talented Learner: Research-Based Decision Making*, sought to conduct a meta-evaluative synthesis of the research on grouping, including all research up to that time: over 700 studies on ability grouping, over 300 studies on cooperative learning, and over 300 studies on accelerative options involving forms of regrouping. The executive summary of Rogers' work was distributed through The National Research Center on the Gifted and Talented (NRC G/T), funded by the Javits Act Program, administered by the Office of Educational Research and Improvement, U.S. Department of Education. This summary, a brief and readable document, is discussed below and can be helpful in dealing with grouping issues with school personnel. Rogers' new book, *Re-Forming Gifted Education: Matching the Program to the Child* (2002), updates all of the research on ability grouping, acceleration, and individualization through 1998. This is essential reading for the gifted advocate as it strongly supports the use of grouping strategies for the provision of accelerative and enrichment options for the gifted. Gifted students grouped with similar peers and offered programming modified to meet their learning needs have marked academic achievement gains, as well as moderate increases in attitude. Rogers has also found a lack of research support for mixed-ability cooperative learning.

The research offers interesting conclusions about ability grouping for enrichment. Full-time ability grouping (tracking) for regular instruction makes no discernible difference in the academic achievement of average and low-ability students, but it does produce substantial academic gains for gifted students enrolled full-time in special programs for the gifted and talented. In addition, high-ability student groups have more extensive plans to attend college and are more likely to enroll in college, but the research has not been able to substantiate that this is directly influenced by grouping. Likewise, research has not been able to substantiate a marked difference in the quality of teachers who work with high-ability students or in the instructional strategies and learning times apportioned in such classes.

Ability grouping for enrichment, especially when enrichment is part of a within-class, ability-grouping practice or as a pullout program, produces substantial academic gains in general achievement, critical thinking, and creativity for the gifted and talented learner. It also produces a moderate improvement in attitude toward the subjects in which students are grouped. (In fact, a moderate improvement in attitude toward subject has been found for all ability levels when homogeneously grouped on a full-time basis.) Finally, ability grouping is not synonymous with *tracking*. It may take many forms beneficial to gifted learners, including full-time enrollment in special programs or classrooms for the gifted, regrouping for special subject instruction, cross-grade grouping for specific subjects or for the entire school curriculum, pullout groups for enrichment, and within-class ability grouping, as well as cluster grouping. The major benefit of each grouping strategy for gifted students is its provision of the format for enriching or accelerating the curriculum they are offered. It is unlikely that grouping itself causes academic gains; rather, what goes on in the group does.

The research on cooperative learning for regular instruction of gifted students fails to support its use as a learning tool, when employed in mixed-ability groups. Likewise, there is no research below the college level to support cooperative learning in like-ability groups for gifted students. Although there is some evidence to support sizable academic effects for those forms of cooperative learning that incorporate individual task accountability, little research has been reported that would allow this to be extrapolated to the gifted population. Likewise, although there is some evidence to support sizable affective outcomes for mixed-ability cooperative learning, particularly for the acceptance of culturally diverse and academically handicapped students, no research has been reported which would allow this to be extrapolated to the gifted population.

Research on the effects of grouping for acceleration yields important conclusions for the gifted advocate. Grouping for the acceleration of curriculum for gifted students produces substantial academic gains for the forms of Nongraded Classrooms, Curriculum Compression (Compacting), Grade Telescoping (Rapid Progression at Junior or Senior High), Subject Acceleration, and early admission to college. Advanced Placement programs were found to produce moderate, nearly significant academic gains as well. These forms of acceleration do not appear to have a direct impact on self-esteem, either positively or negatively. It is apparent that a host of other environmental, personalogical, and academic variables are more directly involved with changes in self-esteem.

Because a primary emphasis of The National Research Center on the Gifted and Talented is the dissemination of research results to educators in the field, all researchers are

asked to provide specific recommendations for teachers.
Dr. Rogers offers the following recommendations drawn from
the research syntheses for educators who are considering
various grouping options:

> Guideline One: Students who are academically or
> intellectually gifted and talented should spend the
> majority of their school day with others of similar
> abilities and interests. Both general intellectual
> ability grouping programs (such as School Within a
> School, Gifted Magnet Schools, Full-time Gifted
> Programs, or Gifted Classrooms) and full-time
> grouping for special academic ability (such as Magnet
> Schools) have produced marked academic achieve-
> ment gains as well as moderate increases in attitude
> toward the subjects in which these students are
> grouped.

> Guideline Two: The Cluster grouping of a small
> number of students, either intellectually gifted or
> gifted in a similar academic domain, within an other-
> wise heterogeneously grouped classroom can be
> considered when schools cannot support a full-time
> gifted program (demographically, economically, or
> philosophically). The "Cluster Teacher" must,
> however, be sufficiently trained to work with gifted
> students, must be given adequate preparation time
> and must be willing to devote a proportionate amount
> of classroom time to the direct provision of learning
> experiences for the cluster group.

> Guideline Three: In the absence of full-time gifted
> program enrollment, gifted and talented students
> might be offered specific group instruction across
> grade levels, according to their individual knowledge
> acquisition in school subjects, either in conjunction
> with cluster grouping or in its stead. This "cross

grade grouping" option has been found effective for the gifted and talented in both single subject and full-time programming (i.e., Nongraded Classrooms).

Guideline Four: Students who are gifted and talented should be given experiences involving a variety of appropriate acceleration-based options, which may be offered to gifted students as a group or on an individual basis. It is, of course, important to consider the social and psychological adjustment of each student for whom such options are being considered as well as cognitive capabilities in making the optimal match to the student's needs.

Guideline Five: Students who are gifted and talented should be given experiences which involve various forms of enrichment that extend the regular school curriculum, leading to the more complete development of concepts, principles, and generalizations. This enrichment could be provided within the classroom through numerous curriculum delivery models currently used in the field, or in the form of enrichment pullout programs.

Guideline Six: Mixed-ability Cooperative Learning should be used sparingly for students who are gifted and talented, perhaps only for social skills development programs. Until evidence is accumulated that this form of Cooperative Learning provides academic outcomes similar or superior to the various forms of ability grouping, it is important to continue with the grouping practices that are supported by research.

A Curriculum and Instruction Challenge

This chapter has deliberately not focused on an ideal curriculum for the gifted; that is the domain of curriculum developers and the unlikely dream of most gifted students and their families. Rather, the parent or teacher advocate must find ways to provide for a gifted child's needs, to the degree possible, each year the child attends school. Concerns about scope and sequence, about a seamless flow from one piece of coursework to the next, take a backseat to ensuring opportunities to study at a higher level, to tackle a passionate interest. The more fortunate gifted child usually has a patchwork of educational experiences that, together, are just adequate to maintain interest and motivation, and nurture self-esteem. Rarely do these children enjoy long-term educational planning, advisors within the schools who take responsibility for meeting their unusual needs, consistently high-level coursework, or opportunities to develop strong work ethics and organizational skills. We could provide so much more.

The good news is that gifted students do succeed—and some succeed beautifully—with proper advocacy and reasonable options. The fact that their programs are often odd conglomerations of offerings from diverse sources at various levels does not render them ineffectual. The Intel Science Competition winner who went directly from sixth grade to high school, skipping part of middle school and completing many years of math in a computer-based program, is doing well at MIT. My youngest son skipped third grade, went to an accelerated charter middle school, began high school with essentially junior-level coursework, and graduated (perhaps a year later than would have been best for motivation) at 15. For some, partial homeschooling offers the opportunity to study very advanced subjects at home, while maintaining contact with friends at school. For others, the opportunity to take just one advanced class is enough; the middle-schooler who takes AP Calculus with seniors at the nearby high school may have adequate challenge. Yet, all of these students found options that were tolerable.

Whereas the typical school curriculum supports the majority of learners, curricula that support the gifted may look very different. Ideally, options are chosen to address a child's achievement levels in each subject area, creating a *diagnostic-prescriptive curriculum*, allowing continuous progress in school. When material is mastered, the child moves on. If our students are spending the majority of their days learning new material, then plans for them have been relatively successful. Happily, there seems to be no inherent loss when first-graders are reading at a fourth-grade level or fifth-graders are studying algebra. Those who choose to grade accelerate usually do very well socially, relieved that older classmates laugh at their jokes a bit more readily. Advocacy that results in such opportunities is not fraught with danger at every turn. Gifted children who veer significantly from typical educational paths can succeed magnificently, when the changes in their programs address their unique needs. Unusual placements, older friends, and unlikely course choices all play a possible role in ensuring that the gifted maintain the natural curiosity and love of learning that so characterized them as young children.

Where the gifted student has only the regular grade-level options of public school, the risk is enormous that those offerings will be insufficient. When we restrict an individual's opportunity to stretch and grow, we threaten his or her innermost curiosity about the world and excitement of discovery. We risk damage to the gifted student far greater than any nontraditional education could pose.

Quinn O'Leary...Curriculum and Instruction

I didn't notice my fatigue until, in the space between blinks, I passed out. It was more than simply falling asleep, it was sudden, an almost violent venture, the annoyed flick of

Morpheus' casual hand. I woke two hours later with my mother shaking me. I was going to be late for school again.

The harried monotony of morning preparations, the ritual of brushes and water and carefully sniffed clothing, gave me time to groggily reflect over the evening previous. I had discovered new things, an excellent Internet site on Native American mysticism—really nothing more than the animal-based creationism myths. Coyote was quickly joining other benevolently roguish troublemakers as a personal hero. After devouring everything the site could offer, I deliberately sought out other similar myths; the religion of the Maya and the campfire tales of Hawaii's first settlers were taking root in my fertile imagination.

There was so much more to know, I reflected, as I brushed cursorily at my teeth and rushed out the door, backpack spine-telescopingly heavy with textbooks I had not yet needed to open, had done nothing with save carry for several weeks. The conversations of other, older peers referenced such elusively magical names as Kazinzakis, Thoreau, Joyce, Neitzche and Faulkner. They mentioned with the insousiance of familiarity, worlds beyond my current scope, great orchards of beautiful and unknown wisdom. I envisioned these orchards to be littered with windfalls, small, delectable gems of knowledge that set my mind awhirl with their imagined sweetness.

The unfairness of that struck my reeling mind suddenly. Why did I never find the thrill of discovery in the dense collections of rote recitation currently curving my spine? There was no personal gain, no joy in pounding out hundreds of similar equations, in rereading and analyzing pieces of literature usually enjoyed by children years my junior, stifling in a classroom peopled by bored kids, antagonistic teachers and dry curriculum. Eight worthless hours stolen from my studies and squandered, adding up to a travesty. I spent sleep-hazed years wasting away in the comfortless plastic of a school desk, too angry to enjoy myself, too hopelessly bored to care. That day, like many days both before and after, I didn't make it to class—ontime or at all. I spent my precious school time at the library in the best possible way, self-medicating with a real education.

References

Bloom, B. (Ed.) (1956). *Taxonomy of educational objectives: The classification of educational goals: Handbook I, cognitive domain.* New York: Longmans, Green.

Reis, S. M., Westberg, K. L., Kulikowich, J., Caillard, F., Hebert, T. P., & Plucker, J. A. (1993). *Why not let high ability students start school in January? The curriculum compacting study.* (Research Monograph #93106). Storrs, CT: National Research Center on the Gifted and Talented, University of Connecticut.

Silverman, L. K. (2002). *Upside-down brilliance: The visual-spatial learner.* Denver, CO: DeLeon Publishing.

Southern, W. T. & Jones, E. D. (1991). Academic acceleration: Background and issues. In W. T. Southern & E. D. Jones (Eds.), *The academic acceleration of gifted children* (pp. 1-28). New York: Teacher's College Press.

Start, K. B. (1995). *The relationship of learning pace and ability in concept acquisition.* Paper presented at the Annual Supporting the Emotional Needs of the Gifted (SENG) Conference. San Diego, CA.

Rogers, K. B. (1991). *The relationship of grouping practices to the education of the gifted and talented learner* (Research-Based Decision Making Series). Storrs, CT: National Research Center on the Gifted and Talented, University of Connecticut.

Rogers, K. B. (2002). *Re-forming gifted education: Matching the program to the child.* Scottsdale, AZ: Great Potential Press.

Winebrenner, S. (1992). *Teaching gifted kids in the regular classroom.* Minneapolis, MN: Free Spirit Publishing.

For Further Reading

Bloom, Benjamin. A Google search (http://www.google.com) will produce a number of websites with information about encouraging higher-level thinking skills in the classroom.

Colangelo, N., Assouline, S. G. and Gross, M.U.M. (2004). *A nation deceived: How schools hold back America's brightest students.* Iowa City, IA: The University of Iowa. Available at www.nationdeceived.org (07 Oct. 2004).

ERIC Digest articles on gifted and cluster grouping, curriculum compacting, etc. Available at www.hoagiesgifted.org (07 Oct. 2004).

Gentry, M. L. (1999) (RM99138). *Promoting student achievement and exemplary classroom practices through cluster grouping: A research-based alternative to heterogeneous elementary classrooms.* Storrs, CT: The National Research Center on the Gifted and Talented. http://www.gifted.uconn.edu/gentry.html (23 Feb. 2003).

National Research Center on the Gifted and Talented (NRC/GT) articles on curriculum, program options, and grouping, available at University of Connecticut, Storrs, CT, 860-486-4676, http://www.gifted.uconn.edu/nrcgt.html (23 Feb. 2003).

Reis, S., Burns, D. & Renzulli, J. (1992). *Curriculum compacting.* Mansfield Center, CT: Creative Learning Press, Inc.

Robinson, N. M. & Weimer, L. J. (1991). Selection of candidates for early admission to kindergarten and first grade. In W. T. Southern & E. D. Jones (Eds.), *The academic acceleration of gifted children* (pp. 29-50). New York: Teacher's College Press.

Robinson, A. (1990). Cooperation or exploitation? The argument against cooperative learning for talented students. *Journal for the Education of the Gifted, 14,* 9-27, 31-36.

Southern, W. T. & Jones, E. D. (Eds.)(1991). *The academic acceleration of gifted children.* New York: Teacher's College Press.

Winebrenner, S. (2001). *Teaching gifted kids in the regular classroom.* Minneapolis, MN: Free Spirit Publishing.

Winebrenner, S. & Devlin, B. *Cluster grouping of gifted students: How to provide full-time services on a part-time budget.* (1991) (ERIC Digest; E 538, E 607). Available at www.hoagiesgifted.org (07 Oct. 2004).

Why The Gifted Fail to Achieve

Underachievement:
Preface to Chapters 5 and 6

When a child who is exceptionally bright fails to achieve in school, it can be a bewildering experience. Is something at school very wrong? Have we overestimated the abilities of a beloved child? Is the school program inappropriate for the child? Are there hidden learning disabilities or other deficits that need to be identified and addressed? Are there attentional issues beyond what is normal for the active boy or girl? Or where disabilities have always been apparent, has a child's giftedness been ignored, causing a lack of motivation? Myriad possibilities exist that require further investigation.

We frequently see underachieving gifted children at the Gifted Development Center (GDC) and generally recommend a thorough clinical assessment to sort out the issues, which may involve anything from a very advanced child placed in an underchallenging program to a child with a complex combination of strengths and weaknesses. Just because a child is intellectually gifted doesn't mean that he or she will have any innate protection from deficits. We may find both giftedness and disabilities in the same child or may see families with a profoundly gifted child and one with multiple learning disabilities. Intellectual potential clearly runs in families and we can usually assume similar ability. Learning disabilities often appear in several members, as well, but they may present themselves to greater or lesser degrees in the various individuals within a family.

The fact that teachers have little exposure to training in gifted education is especially problematic when under-achievement is involved. Teachers often have difficulty acknowledging a child's giftedness when the child does not excel at grade-level work. If the child is far more capable than average, wouldn't he or she find typical work easy and do well? Actually, gifted children may be so unmotivated by average work that they perform at a mediocre level, effectively preventing teachers from recognizing their gifts.

Likewise, without training in the education of the gifted, many teachers don't realize children can be *twice exceptional*, having both gifted intellectual potential and deficits. Because these teachers are more thoroughly trained in special education issues, learning disabilities and disorders such as AD/HD, they are more likely to see signs of deficits. However, those deficits can be obscured by the gifted child's ability to compensate or the disabilities can be recognized, obscuring the giftedness. Chapters 5 and 6 explore the reasons for underachievement and their interventions.

5

Underachievement:
When a Child is Too Advanced for the Educational Program

When testing documents gifted abilities with no apparent weaknesses, the cause of underachievement is typically an educational program that doesn't fit the child. The child is in an age-appropriate grade level, being taught according to assumptions about average learners of that age. Yet, he or she knows most or all of the material being taught and could pace more quickly though new concepts. This type of underachievement typically becomes apparent after some time in school. The child has entered school with enthusiasm and an enormous desire to learn. Yet, he or she has encountered, on multiple occasions, pressure to conform to the learning patterns of the majority of students. This situation is compounded year after year by such experiences until the child begins to lose motivation to learn and performance is affected.

Underachievement in Girls

Underachievement usually, but not always, takes different forms in boys and girls. In girls, the extreme sensitivity to the social expectations of others often causes them to "dumb down" and appear to be at the ability level of any group in which they are placed. They are patently aware (often from early elementary school age) that being smart is not *cool* and they make the choice to do what is more acceptable. Their special educational needs, therefore, become invisible to the classroom teacher and their high potential goes unnurtured. Mothers of children found to be gifted at the GDC occasionally embark on new and challenging careers, once they realize the likelihood of their own giftedness. Many *went underground* with their own giftedness, and have not yet begun to reach their full potential.

We frequently recommend that gifted girls (with the help of their parents) actively seek out other gifted girls because there seems to be safety in numbers. When these girls are able to socialize with each other, they gain strength to achieve at higher levels with less embarrassment and to pursue their real interests. We suggest that they read *Reviving Ophelia* (1994) by Mary Pipher and become aware that much of the world will be satisfied if they aspire to far less than they're capable of accomplishing. They need to learn about professional career options and insist on academic preparation that will support their most demanding career choices. Awareness and support help considerably, but parents need to be forever watchful that their daughters will not place too much emphasis on popularity, at the expense of education.

It is important to note here that girls who have chosen not to *dumb down* and underachieve must often lead their own silent rebellion. They have had to choose between being themselves and being acceptable to others, with the choice to be themselves bringing a quiet suffering that they endure in the hope of there being better times ahead. Girls often seem to have a stronger capacity to be patient and delay gratification. They may also have a highly developed ethical sense that prevents them from ignoring their academic responsibilities, even though they may be feeling a terrible sense of rebellion. Better times usually do occur for these girls, eventually, but perhaps not until they find themselves with true peers in AP classes in high school or until they enter college. Some will not feel comfortable in the classroom until graduate school.

Underachievement in Boys

Boys, on the other hand, are more likely to openly rebel against school situations that they perceive to be hurting them. It is usually, but not always, the boys who are acting out in school, failing to turn in assignments, refusing to attend, in danger of being expelled, threatening to drop out, or considering suicide. Schools usually react poorly to these cases, producing a show of authority and a plethora of attendance rules that further alienate the boys and may lead to their leaving school (if they are not forced out).

Most male underachievers have felt alienated for years, but their rebellion is usually strongest in middle and high school. As older elementary students they are usually anxious to attend middle school, with its increased class options, having spent years with grade-level material and few, if any, *gifted* accommodations. Elementary school is clearly not the fun place they originally thought it would be and they are angry. They assume middle school will provide the higher-level coursework they crave. Unfortunately, middle school philosophy in many parts of the country has embraced heterogeneous instruction of all students, with few honors classes offered and pressure to remain with one's age peers. As a result, many gifted students find their middle school experience to be their most frustrating time in school. Their efforts to find work of an appropriate level may be largely ignored, increasing their resistance to school programs.

Building upon these difficulties, high school-age under-achievers may express more intense displeasure. If they failed to be high achievers in middle school, they may not

have access to higher-level high school classes that would
be a better fit for them (high schools may require recommendations from middle school teachers or excellent grades to
place students in these classes). Or, they may have access to
such classes, but refuse to fully engage in work that they
feel is still beneath them. They may address their issues in
more dangerous ways than just failing to attend class or
turn in assignments. Efforts to cope may bring about drug
use, skirmishes with the judicial system, or serious depression and danger of suicide. The gifted underachiever is
suffering not only from the intense pressure of being
different, which itself can bring about the need for counseling
in gifted students, but also the lack of alternatives to the
traditional high school experience. The student has no
acceptable way to refuse to participate in the high school
environment. The punishments for those who rebel are
enormous and threaten to limit options in later life. The
student's belief that he has no way out of an untenable
situation places him at extreme risk. This is the perception
of students considering suicide and it is of uppermost
importance that we provide them with options. No matter
how much a parent may have depended on a student
graduating, making good grades, or going to a good college,
these assumptions are unimportant when balanced with the
life of a young person. Such students do drop out of school,
do experience frightening times, and can, eventually, find
their way with adequate support. We have wondered at the
GDC how some of the students we have seen survived their
situations outside or staying within school. They are to be
commended for their resilience.

Quinn

One such student is Quinn O'Leary, who was later tapped to
write his inner impressions of giftedness for this book.
Graduating from high school at the time of our initial inter-

view, he agreed to share his story for the sake of his "progeny." His story follows as originally written.

Declared a National Merit Semi-Finalist after taking the PSAT, he was unable to become a finalist because student grades are taken into account and his have rarely exceeded B's and C's in high school. As gifted as he is, he has only recently decided to attend college.

Quinn recalls his earliest experience in public school being one of alienation. He didn't like kindergarten, didn't relate to his age peers and didn't get along with his teacher, who seemed boring and trite to him. Moving to a smaller school in first grade, he recalls the school being a "vicious place" with frequent schoolyard fights. Quinn was a sensitive boy who cried easily and would lose his temper and hit other children. He was also a poor fit with the other students, speaking at an adult level quite early and having different interests than they had.

His experience of the school finally improved in grades four through six, when he got along better with teachers. Fourth grade brought his inclusion in a weekly pull-out program for 12 gifted students for in-depth instruction in various areas. One unit studied was the popular Voyage of the Mimi that utilizes a marine excursion to teach concepts in various subject areas. Quinn enjoyed these opportunities very much. Moreover, he recalls with great appreciation and affection the teacher he had for the fifth and sixth grades. She arranged for him to study eighth grade math (algebra), along with two other advanced students. He remembers she would teach him individually, at times, and took a special interest in him.

It is important to note that most gifted underachievers, such as Quinn, have fond memories of a few teachers who supported and challenged them. They are not oblivious to the efforts teachers made. However, most have pitifully few such experiences to report—and many more painful ones. Most are highly sensitive; few, despite occasional bravado, seem to be hardened individuals. They appear to need both a curriculum that is a reasonable fit for their needs and some degree of sincere acceptance from teachers. Sensitive to subtle nuances of communication, they are painfully aware when their teachers find their knowledge annoying, their intelligence threatening, or find them lacking in the qualities typical students are expected to display.

After elementary school, Quinn's educational experiences worsened and he had increased social problems. He recalls fellow students in the seventh grade being cruel and he rated his teachers "terrible." His honors English class was unchallenging and the school stressed only basic reading. He was already an avid reader of literature well above the level emphasized. His classes seemed substandard to him. Although he had two close friends his age, he tended to choose friends four to five years older, which his considerably higher mental age would have allowed. However, he now refers to the older group as clearly "bad people," who engaged in minor acts of shoplifting and received curfew and drug violations.

He escaped getting into serious trouble when his family moved to Colorado during the summer following seventh grade. There, he attended eighth grade in a suburban middle school that was considerably safer and where the students were more accepting. He met another very bright underachiever, Forrest, who got into more trouble than he did, but was, nevertheless, a more kindred spirit. He still found the school to be "academically mediocre," but liked his history class for his teacher's interesting lectures. More "entertaining and engaging," the class provided an environment where he was able to do well. He also thoroughly enjoyed woodshop. Yet, he despised English class and the teacher wasn't fond of him, either. He and Forrest often made a point of wasting class time, only to quickly finish a project in the last 15 minutes that was deserving of an *A* grade. His teacher resented that. Although Quinn had some positive experiences, he concludes the whole experience was "pretty solid drudgery," and he responded with average grades (*B*'s and *C*'s), that were less than average for him.

Quinn recalls his freshman year in high school being similar to middle school. He was disappointed that an honors version of the school's freshman "Core" (a combined class of English, geography and U.S. government) would not be offered, as promised, but the school allowed him to take sophomore "Literature and Composition." Writing was becoming a strength for Quinn. He was able to take geography and U.S. government at a nearby university, instead of his high school. He was placed in a higher-level math class in which he didn't do as well, which was also becoming a pattern. He recalls that his social maturity level was still "not great" and that he was a little overwhelmed by the high school atmosphere, with much older students and an "air of simmering hormones." Quinn concluded that he didn't "enjoy the masses" because they seemed to be avoiding developing personalities. "These are the years when people are supposed to be developing personalities," he insisted. At times, he felt other students were ostracizing *him* for trying to develop one. Yet, he reached a point where he could say, "I got along decently well with everyone as per always. Nobody hated me; a few really liked me." He became involved with sports, participating in wrestling and swimming. He said he wouldn't have pursued a more team-oriented sport, but enjoyed individual sports.

The beginning of Quinn's sophomore year marked a distinct departure. He attended classes for the first three days and decided school was not *fun* anymore. He didn't want summer to be over. Of that time, he now says, "I had a nascent rebelliousness I needed to express." Quinn failed to go to school for the next three weeks, triggering attendance alarms at the high school. His mother was called in and told about his series of *excused* absences (Quinn had phoned in and excused himself while she was at work) and about the punishments that would befall him if his illnesses weren't real (he would, essentially, be kicked out of school). When asked if the absences were, indeed, *excused*, she answered, "Yes," to keep him in school. Quinn still feels terrible about putting his parents in that position.

Continuing to miss classes during his sophomore and junior years, he managed to stop just short of prompting serious disciplinary action, and still maintained mediocre grades. Quinn struggled socially with friends. "I was trying really hard to establish myself as a person. I was violent at times. I wasn't quite mature enough to associate with one particular group on their level at that time." There was "one-upmanship back and forth, cutting remarks, pointed insinuations." Quinn recalls painfully, "The group ostracized me. I felt horribly betrayed."

Quinn's senior year has seen an improvement in his grades, two AP teachers he respects and enjoys, and his recent decision to attend college. He also notes that this is the first year when he has decided to generally hang out with "smart people," the most thoughtful students in the classes he likes. He writes articles for the school newspaper that are always thoughtful, articulate, and, necessarily, a bit out-rageous. He feels he is growing up and finding "a happy medium between insane, wild nastiness and a mellow person." Quinn speaks with admiration and appreciation about his AP English teacher who has challenged his thinking, recognized his tremendous writing talents, and provided support. He talks of perhaps becoming a high school English teacher, himself.

Discussing with Quinn the causes of his underachievement, it was clear that he was intellectually too advanced for his classes throughout his educational career. He was terribly out-of-sync before he was equipped emotionally to handle the mismatch, if anyone ever is. This is common for very gifted children; it can, at first, be confusing, then devastating. His highly sensitive nature made him even more vulnerable.

He suffered deeply whenever his attempts to "develop a personality" didn't meet with the approval of others whose experience of life was more limited than his. Quinn agreed that *will* also played a great part. In some ways, he felt he showed "a blazing lack of will power." Yet in other ways, he said, "Will power's the problem. You're too sure of yourself to say 'I'll do it your way.' " Quinn doesn't want to be a part of "mainstream society" and, indeed, should aspire to be far more.

Quinn should find that life improves as he takes on greater intellectual challenges and continues to associate with more highly gifted true peers. Such peers will be more likely to share his interests, his sensitivity, his strong will, his self-examination, and his ultimate hopefulness about the future. He feels he is friends with a lot of people, but there are "no soul mates, no brothers." Hopefully, his sense of alienation and isolation will fade as he finds lasting friends and a meaningful place for himself in the world.

When asked what type of educational program would have served him better, Quinn said, "Something like the Internet. The simple act of accessing information yields multitudinous results." He enjoys the speed at which information can be accessed because curiosity can be satisfied far more quickly than in the slower-paced classroom. Likewise, information is varied and representative of different points of view and his mind will require no less. Yet, he also admitted he liked the personal, but safe, contact of email and chat rooms. The latter, he added, "provided words on a screen...they can't hurt you...it's a more cerebral way to interact."

Scars of Alienation

Quinn's story is similar to that of other gifted under-achievers we have seen. They all bear scars of alienation that vary somewhat, but may include a distrust of others, a tendency to be critical of teachers, strong will, usually less than stellar study habits (their academic work must be difficult enough for them to require such skills or they will not learn them), a greater willingness to miss classes, the tendency to perform much better for respected teachers, and inconsistent perfectionism (they may apply the highest standards to a particular piece of work they feel is important, then miss another assignment they feel is not). Being both critics of the systems within which they find themselves and individuals with the most abiding love of learning, they commit themselves to the educational process only as much as they are able.

The Effect of High School Attendance Policies

Most underachieving gifted boys also have some resistance to authority, particularly to those administrators who enforce attendance policies in high school. Our local high school gives a student who is five minutes late to class an unexcused absence. The student is not allowed to turn in homework or take tests when unexcused. Four unexcused absences in the same class bring a grade of *F* on the student's permanent record, unless authorities choose to give the student a second chance. In our case, our son Nick was incensed that such rules were created for the expressed purpose of "keeping kids in school," when it was clear they would be encouraging students to leave. In fact, our high school pursued these policies because other schools had found attendance rose a few percentage points with such rules and our school personnel were anxious to improve attendance, too. Yet, such policies seem ineffective with the gifted. Students struggling to find a reason to stay in school are frequently late and, under such circumstances, are easily convinced to simply not go at all. They see no point to a punishment that garners them a second chance to avoid a permanent *F*, when it seems obvious to them that grades should depend on the student's work, not picayune attendance policies. Our son was told he would be given a second chance if he spent 10 hours studying in the vice-principal's office. Under duress, he agreed, yet later concluded, "You know I can't do that." The ambivalence about school, with which he struggled every day, would not be helped by studying for 10 hours in the vice-principal's office. In fact, the punishment made school considerably less attractive to him.

Gifted students at risk of dropping out would be better served by exempting them from such rules (letting their grades reflect their work) and by providing them with additional support to attend school. Assigning them mentors, for example, who would encourage them to come and take an interest in how they're doing, would be a more positive approach and would support their high level of sensitivity better. Nick knew teachers who would have been appropriate, including several who had struggled themselves in high school, even though they were very bright. What was inappropriate was that our school, or any other, would respond to this type of dilemma with a show of force. Ken Seeley, in his chapter "Gifted Students at Risk" in *Counseling the Gifted and Talented* (1993), describes a study of gifted underachievers in which the number one *reason* for dropping out of high school was attendance policies that tended to push students out of school (p. 267).

Closeness to Family

One heartening observation is that many gifted under-achievers remain quite close to their parents during their most difficult times, at least in the majority of gifted families in which authoritarian parenting practices are not used. Gifted children, in general, appear to thrive in homes where issues are discussed together and reasons always given for decisions. Loving, patient support is critical for most and is provided by their equally sensitive parents. Quinn notes that he has always remained close to his parents, despite his

most intense rebellion against school, and it has given him
strength. Our son, likewise, has benefited from a close,
supportive family that felt, ultimately, that it was more
important to support him than the school. Most of the
parents of underachievers that we see at the GDC do not
seem overly indulgent; rather, they look to the deeper issues
of whether the son's (or sometimes daughter's) school
program is actually meeting needs or causing harm. Of
course, parents struggle with these issues because their
children are limiting future options by their rebellion.
However, the young person's well-being is ultimately far
more important and his experiences, with support, can
become a part of a stronger individual in the making.

Viewing Spirit as Strength

Mary Kurcinka, in her book *Raising Your Spirited Child*
(1992), points out that many of the qualities parents find
difficult to deal with in their growing children are the same
qualities that can empower them as adults. Speaking at a
conference on the gifted, sponsored by the GDC in the
summer of 1999, she asked parents to jot down the most
representative traits of their "spirited" children. A long list of
characteristics was generated among the audience to
describe our most challenging offspring: "intense," "bossy,"
"high maintenance," "overly sensitive," and "rebellious."
Kurcinka discussed each trait with an eye toward the
future. The "intense" child may become the "passionate'
adult, whereas the "bossy" child may be the "able leader."
The child viewed as "high maintenance" might turn out to
be the adult with "high standards and expectations"; the
"overly sensitive" child has the capacity to become
enormously receptive to others. The "rebellious" child may
ultimately become the adult "with a vision." Although the
idea of a happy and obedient child is pleasant to all parents,
few of us would choose to create so uninteresting an adult.

The gifted underachiever often has many of these traits and challenges us to help him create something positive from his potential strengths and his negative experiences in school.

Despite apparent lost options, gifted students who survive their underachievement do have futures filled with promise. They are more likely to be late bloomers, but usually do not depart completely from the values learned from their parents. As our son's teacher says, "The apple doesn't usually fall too far from the tree." These students will typically find a way, at some point, to pursue their educations in earnest, or find an acceptable substitute. For example, although Quinn initially lost opportunities to attend colleges with greater prestige, and was even later turned down by the state school from which his mother, father, and sister graduated (a hurtful blow), he did find an acceptable way to distinguish himself. [Read on.] Graduate school would certainly be a likely option for this English major, and he might have considerably more schools to choose from depending upon his performance as an undergraduate.

Our son, Nick, who dropped out of school in his senior year, has more work to do to place himself in a position for quality further education. He easily obtained his G.E.D. and took some community college courses to fill in holes in his high school education, particularly in math and science. Though his efforts to move on with his life are frustrated by the slower pace of instruction in these classes, he is now much more concerned about earning A's and making himself a good prospect for colleges. Moreover, the jobs he has had have shown him both that he is unusually competent and that he needs to get a good education to have access to work he truly finds meaningful. He plans to begin his undergraduate work soon in mechanical engineering.

Some gifted students conclude that traditional classes are never going to work for them, but they have high aspirations, nevertheless. One such man we know has taken an individual approach to his education, teaching himself computer programming and polishing his strong writing skills. Programming is now part of his livelihood, but he has also enjoyed success as a writer and playwright.

The Risk of Dropping Out

Every gifted child who is a poor fit in an educational program is at risk of losing his or her motivation to learn. Some parents realize this, even when their children are fairly young. One woman brought her elementary school-age son to the GDC to be tested in order to gain advice early. He was becoming bored in the classroom and she said, "I'm afraid he'll do exactly what I did—drop out of high school." It is important that all parents of the gifted realize this risk and know that creating an adequate program for a gifted student requires more than trivial changes. Providing "just a little enrichment" is unlikely to satisfy the child's needs, nor is the parent's determination to make a traditional school work for a child necessarily going to be enough.

At the 1999 gifted conference, as I sat ready to participate in a panel discussion about education for the gifted, Linda Silverman brought a woman to the table to speak briefly with me. Her son was miserable in high school and threatening to drop out. As she spoke, tears began to flow about the consequences that were almost too horrible to imagine. Few of us are prepared for such a possibility because we have always known our children had such promise. We have not considered their dropping out of school an option. Yet, when this threat arises, our students are letting us know that they are having serious problems with school and we must listen. Once we accept the fact that a young person will be unable to complete school in the typical manner (and this takes considerable soul-searching), we can begin to consider reasonable options. Moreover, the sooner we can reach that point, the better we can support our children as individuals needing to make a healthy change in their lives. Students in this situation find themselves on very shaky ground. It is not their fault that they are a poor fit in school, yet they feel terribly guilty about it and about disappointing us. Supporting and assisting their decisions helps them to know we respect them enough as individuals to take their concerns seriously.

Be Willing to Accept Options

Parents facing serious underachievement or threats of dropping out of school need to know that there are always options for a student and they need to work actively to find and offer alternatives. A *time-out* from school is always a possibility, as is homeschooling. Or, a student may consider a different school, especially one that offers a more challenging program. For these students, the more *difficult* program will generally be *easier* because it is more engaging. Avoid choosing *easier* class options in the hope of raising poor grades. Such students will usually perform worse. Some gifted students have chosen to simply leave high school early, obtain a G.E.D., and move on to college. In fact, our son's principal noted that his failure to graduate from high school probably wouldn't make all that much difference, except to rule out more prestigious schools initially. He had high SAT scores and could always attend community college for a while. These problems can be fixed and do not have to ruin lives permanently. However, it is essential that changes be addressed when a child is suffering. Failure to do so increases the possibility of suicide. If even a vague threat of suicide has been made, professional help must be sought.

Supporting a Student's Motivation to Learn

Underachievement, although not irreparable, is more easily prevented. The best insurance against its occurrence is an educational program that allows the gifted student to progress continuously in his or her learning. When concepts are grasped, the child moves on to new material. This progression need not be perfect, but it must be at least reasonable. Gifted children most frequently experience learning rate problems; they learn with fewer repetitions and little or no drill and practice. When they are kept to the level of more average classmates and not allowed to move ahead, dissatisfaction occurs. Moreover, when they are grouped with slower children in the hope of facilitating greater improvement for those who struggle, gifted children have no opportunity to learn at their appropriate level. This can seriously undermine motivation to learn. Parents need to monitor and take seriously children's comments about school. Is the child excited about learning at school? Is there satisfaction with work well done or high test grades? Is the child impressed with what the teacher is teaching about a particular topic? These are all healthy signs of children who are well-placed in their school programs. On the other hand, does the child complain of boredom? Does he or she want to move on to harder material but is prevented from doing so? Does the teacher complain, "I wish your son wouldn't talk to the other kids so much when he finishes his own work early"? These are red flags that should be investigated. Children can withstand less-than-perfect circumstances for a while, but should never be asked to endure a truly inappropriate program over a long period of time.

Quinn O'Leary...Underachievement

I first ditched school in third grade. It was a spring morning and by seven, as I trudged to the bus stop, it was already shaping into one of the fine feathery days that seems crafted for outdoor romping, perfectly tailored to any of the gut-twistingly nostalgic notions usually drooped over the memory of that age. It was a morning full of nascent lilacs, sweet apple blossoms, and the crisp scent of dew-wet grass, smells that have always been the most conducive to caprice and carefreeness. Back then, school was hated only because it caused me to miss any number of momentous occasions, from staying up for a sunrise to finishing books as fast as I would have liked. It was disliked, assuredly, but certainly not to the level of extremity it eventually gained. It did not, in short, hurt me overmuch.

I was reading J.R.R. Tolkien's books at the time and I think the memory of the magical world he spread across the pages, the total immersion in a realm of sprites and goblins, of heroic furfooted hobbits in whom I could see myself turned me around. I returned to the house and, latchkey kid that I was, had it all to myself until my parents returned home.

Recollection is fuzzy with the rampant ravages of day-to-day fadings, but I remember that day as one of the finest few weekdays I have spent, scholastic obligation and eventual punishment notwithstanding. A hand cramped with the ancient punishment of scribing my sin a thousand times could not compare to the simple release of a single day's layaway.

My true dalliance with failure came much later, however. Four years after that first fateful absence I discovered the truth about middle school and began hating it in earnest. I expected a collegiate atmosphere, a school full of kids like me working towards their own edification, in diversified, individualized plans of education, different routes for different people.

The first disappointment came in the form of the worthless selection of classes, the self-assured certainty of an administration touting drivel as enrichment. The classes I wanted, that I needed, did not exist. The ones I felt I could perhaps *settle for were bureaucratically placed out of reach, guarded by hateful administrators.*

My memories of the teachers are far from flattering, relics of archaic academia who meted out similar sentences to those who interrupted to ask a question and those who punched a peer. In an advanced language arts class, I was barred from reading my books in favor of the selected tome, an idiot novel of no consequence save as a warning against illiteracy. Still, I finished the book in a fraction the allotted time, hoping that I would be allowed, once my work was finished, to pursue more personally attractive modes of learning.

Such a dream, of course, was a juvenile fancy. I languished in class, routinely having my own books irrevocably confiscated (to be picked up at the end of the day in the office) because I was "inappropriately using class time."

Seven classes a day, roughly eight hours of similar torture one hundred eighty days of the year. An insistence on my own morals, values, voice and ideas earned me the distaste of the faculty as well as my peers. Shunned, hated and with a growing sense of anger, I stalked into high school with a tear in my frustrated eye and a dutifully bowed head.

High school was no turning point, no respite from the unfitting angles of my education, the burgeoning angst that was starting to spill over into my attitude. If I wasn't happy, surely there was something wrong. If I wasn't the only one unhappy, surely it was not my fault. I began to place blame where I saw it necessary, overwhelmingly upon the school.

That blame, however, did not change the low mediocrity of my achievement, nor did it help assuage the stomach-wound pain that came when I saw my parents' reaction to my poor grades or my apparent behavioral problems. Swayed by their arguments, I oscillated between accepting responsibility for my failures and hating my environment, a blend that led to an unparalleled number of unexcused absences from my school. With a school-wide policy of credit loss after the fourth unexempted absence, it was my glib lies, my handiness at forgery and my brilliance at circumventing a system of rules designed by idiots to corral idiots that kept me from ever receiving a NC-Fail grade on a report card.

Such a thing was not necessarily a victory, however. I avoided triggering all but the most sensitive radars to my ditching habit, but my grades suffered tremendously. My rebellion was transmuting mindlessly repetitive homework assignments into a string of zeros spiced with 100% test scores. Usually, my average was somewhere in the upper sixties until a week from semester's end, when I would churn out a hundred pages of retroactive regurgitant and raise it ten percent or so. Only so many teachers would accept this huge dump of long overdue work, however, and I found myself scraping the bottom levels of passing grades.

Meanwhile, I learned to separate the seeds and stems from pot. I learned a half-dozen ways to sneak silently out of and into my house at night, a dozen ways to hide a hangover.

I also learned that colleges don't care whether I am brilliant, that being locked out in the dead of winter is painful, that not only can I not pay for college, but that I cannot even get accepted. I learned, as an unremembered writer once poignantly remarked, a hundred different names for tears.

References

Pipher, M. (1994). *Reviving Ophelia: Saving the selves of adolescent girls*. New York: Putnam.

Seeley, K. (1993). Gifted students at risk. In L. K. Silverman (Ed.), *Counseling the gifted and talented* (pp. 263-275). Denver, CO: Love.

Kurcinka, M. S. (1999, June). *Raising your spirited child*. Keynote presentation at the 20th anniversary conference of the Gifted Development Center, Denver, CO.

For Further Reading

Association for the Education of Gifted Underachieving Students-AEGUS. http://www.aegus.org.futuresite.register.com (22 Feb. 2003).

Kearney, K. (1996, Summer/Fall). Highly gifted children in full inclusion classrooms. *Highly Gifted Children, 12*(4). http://www.hollingworth.org/fullincl.html (22 Feb. 2003).

Kerr, B. A., & Cohn, S. J. (2001). *Smart boys: Talent, manhood, and the search for meaning*. Scottsdale, AZ: Gifted Psychology Press.

Kurcinka, M. S. (1992). *Raising your spirited child: A guide for parents whose child is more intense, sensitive, perceptive, persistent, energetic*. New York: HarperCollins.

Silverman, L. K. (1986). What happens to the gifted girl? In C. J. Maker (Ed.), *Critical issues in gifted education: Vol. 1. Defensible programs for the gifted* (pp. 43-89). Austin, TX: Pro-Ed.

Silverman, L. K. (1993). Social development, leadership, and gender issues. In L. K. Silverman (Ed.), *Counseling the gifted and talented* (pp. 295-307). Denver, CO: Love.

Silverman, L. K. (1995). To be gifted or feminine: The forced choice of adolescence. *Journal of Secondary Gifted Education, 6*, 141-156.

Supplee, P. L. (1990). *Reaching the gifted underachiever: Program strategy and design*. New York: Teachers College Press.

Whitmore, J. (1980). *Giftedness, conflict, and underachievement*. Needham Heights, MA: Allyn & Bacon.

6

Underachievement:
Gifted Children With Learning Disabilities or Other Deficits

The lack of a good fit between the gifted child's advanced learning capacity and the typical school curriculum is sufficient to produce underachievement in students such as Quinn, but there are other bright students whose underachievement is more difficult to understand. Linda Silverman writes in her article, "Invisible Gifts, Invisible Handicaps," that the "most fertile ground for unearthing learning disabled/gifted children is among underachievers" (1989). Comparing the following descriptions of gifted underachievers and of learning disabled/gifted children, she finds intriguing similarities. First, Linda notes that Joanne Whitmore, in her book *Giftedness, Conflict and Underachievement*, lists these traits of gifted underachievers:

- Perfectionistic
- Supersensitive
- Lacks social skills
- Socially isolated
- Has unrealistic self-expectations
- Low in self-esteem
- Hyperactive
- Distractible

- Has psychomotor inefficiency
- Chronically inattentive
- Frustrated by the demands of the classroom
- Fails to complete assignments
- Excessively critical of self and others
- Rebellious against drill and excessive repetition
- Disparaging of the work they are required to do
- Becomes "an expert" in one area and dominates discussions with own expertise

At the same time, Linda Silverman notes that studies of learning disabled/gifted children (cited in parentheses) have produced an identical set of characteristics.

- Perfectionistic (Rosner & Seymour, 1983)
- Supersensitive (Maker, 1977; Pendarvis & Grossi, 1980; Schiff, Kaufman & Kaufman, 1981; Tannenbaum & Baldwin, 1983; Wolf & Gygi, 1981)
- Lacks social skills (Baldwin & Gargiulo, 1983; Osman, 1979)
- Socially isolated (Schiff, Kaufman & Kaufman, 1981)
- Has unrealistic self-expectations (Maker, 1977; Wolf & Gygi, 1981)
- Low in self-esteem (Daniels, 1983; Pendarvis & Grossi, 1980; Schiff, Kaufman & Kaufman, 1981)
- Hyperactive (Tannenbaum & Baldwin, 1983)
- Distractible (Schiff, Kaufman & Kaufman, 1981; Tannenbaum & Baldwin, 1983)
- Has psychomotor inefficiency (Rosner, 1983; Schiff, Kaufman & Kaufman, 1981)
- Chronically Inattentive (Tannenbaum & Baldwin, 1983)
- Frustrated by the demands of the classroom (Tannenbaum & Baldwin, 1983)
- Fails to complete assignments (Tannenbaum & Baldwin, 1983)

- Excessively critical of self and others (Maker, 1977; Tannenbaum & Baldwin, 1983; Wolf & Gygi, 1981)
- Rebellious against drill and excessive repetition (Tannenbaum & Baldwin, 1983)
- Disparaging of the work they are required to do (Tannenbaum & Baldwin, 1983)
- Becomes "an expert" in one area and dominates discussions with own expertise (Rosner & Seymour, 1983; Tannenbaum & Baldwin, 1983)

Linda Silverman points out that the coincidence between these characteristics is less surprising when we realize that both populations have been identified through discrepancies between performance on measures of aptitude and achievement, and thus the groups overlap. However, she feels the significant question is, "When we are looking at a student who won't do the work, how do we know we aren't actually seeing a child who can't do the work?" Adults are often quick to misjudge such students as "lazy," damaging their already fragile self-esteem. Gifted students with learning disabilities may do an excellent job of compensating, thereby keeping their deficits hidden from parents and teachers and receiving no help for them. The result is a loss of performance, sometimes mistaken for more average overall ability. Instead of the child being viewed as twice exceptional, with obvious gifts and noticeable handicaps, only the blend (averaging) of strengths and weaknesses may be apparent.

Learning disabled/gifted children tend to have a characteristic pattern of abilities on Wechsler tests. They generally score high on those subtests most highly correlated with abstract verbal and spatial reasoning ability (Information, Similarities, Vocabulary, Comprehension and Block Design). Yet, they may show large discrepancies between their strengths in these areas and weaknesses in other areas.

What Exactly is a Learning Disability?

For parents who suspect their child's underachievement in school may be related to a subtle disability, it is important to know how *learning disability* is defined. The term connotes some problem that interferes with learning, but it has a more specific definition within school districts. It is typically a deficit that causes the child to achieve at a significantly lower level than his or her ability would predict. In assessment terms, a learning disabled child scores significantly lower in some area of academic achievement than he or she scored on an IQ test. Special education services are available for children exhibiting a specified degree of discrepancy in their areas of weakness. Such services are offered to help remediate the problem and/or teach the child compensatory strategies to deal with it. In addition, classroom accommodations are offered when the child requires modifications to his or her program.

The degree of discrepancy is the most important determinant of the need for services, but states may have rules that limit the participation of gifted children. For example, until several years ago, Colorado had an upper limit on IQ scores, in the 130s. A child with a higher IQ score would have to show a larger discrepancy than other children to be approved for services. The upper limit has now been raised, but such rules can negatively affect gifted children with disabilities. Moreover, even though a gifted child may have a very significant weakness when compared to his or her overall cognitive ability, that weakness may not be as severe on an absolute scale as those of more average children and may go unnoticed. Gifted children are also able to compensate considerably for deficits, minimizing their apparent severity. However, a 1995 clarification of federal law by the Office of Special Education Programs (OSEP) noted that, "each child who is evaluated for a suspected learning disability must be measured against his or her own expected performance, and not against some arbitrary general standard." Nevertheless, we continue to hear of difficulties individual gifted children have experienced in various states.

Some parents have complained that their states do not even recognize the existence of *twice exceptionality*. Special Education departments in their states have interpreted federal law to mean that being both gifted and learning disabled is an impossibility—by definition. Yet, OSEP has made it clear that no exclusions can be made based on intelligence level. While the learning disabilities of gifted children often do not appear severe enough to qualify for services, they may reflect very serious needs requiring accommodation. Without services, the child cannot develop to his or her full potential.

Types of Learning Disabilities

Learning disabilities must be documented as falling into specific acceptable categories for services to be granted. The 1995 clarification of law by OSEP notes that a multidisciplinary team may determine that a child has a specific learning disability if the child does not achieve commensurate with his or her age and ability levels in one or more of the following areas:

- (i) Oral expression;
- (ii) Listening comprehension;
- (iii) Written expression;
- (iv) Basic reading skill;
- (v) Reading comprehension;
- (vi) Mathematics calculation; or
- (vii) Mathematics reasoning.

Learning disabilities are perceptual or communicative disabilities, which prevent a child from receiving reasonable benefit from his or her education. Such difficulties are not primarily the result of visual, hearing, or motor handicaps, limited intellectual capacity or significant identifiable emotional disability, or due to environmental, cultural, or economic disadvantage. For a child to be approved for services the school psychologist must usually document the IQ/achievement discrepancy through testing; show evidence of a difficulty with cognitive and/or language processing (visual processing, long-term retrieval, integrated generalization difficulty, auditory processing, reasoning, short-term memory, visual-motor integration or other); and see significantly impaired achievement in reading skills, reading comprehension, written language expression (e.g., problems in handwriting, spelling, sentence structure, and written organization), or comprehension, application, and retention of math concepts.

A sizeable percentage of children we see at the GDC have subtle learning problems that affect their success in school, but many never receive services. Such problems can reduce scores on IQ tests (not just achievement tests), making the necessary discrepancy between IQ and achievement scores difficult to document with the gifted. In addition, parents would often like to avoid involvement with special education services because of the emphasis on weaknesses and increased difficulty obtaining accommodations for giftedness. However, when they are necessary, we make recommendations to classroom teachers for accommodations to support learning disabilities, once we have emphasized accommodations for giftedness first.

Other Deficits

There are other relative weaknesses/deficits that gifted children sometimes exhibit that may not qualify as *learning disabilities*, but require support, nevertheless. Any physical handicap, for example, deserves accommodations in the classroom and many respond well to assistive technology. Attention-Deficit/Hyperactivity Disorder may also warrant modifications for the student to be successful. These particular difficulties qualify for accommodations in the classroom or workplace through Section 504 of the Rehabilitation Act of 1973. This federal legislation guarantees accommodations that the student or employee needs to be successful over the individual's life span (e.g., assignments to be provided in writing, or the use of a keyboard for writing tasks). It does not provide remediation or instructional services as Special Education provides for children in the public schools.

Whether or not the gifted child is offered services for disabilities within his or her school, it is important for parents to follow up on any concerns they may have about their child. Subtle disabilities in the gifted are so frequently overlooked that these children often suffer for years, criticized for their lack of effort. It is far healthier to identify problems, treat them to the degree possible, and teach compensatory strategies early. This supports healthy self-esteem and the dream of a future with excellent potential.

Exploring the Disabilities of the Gifted

Because IQ tests have diagnostic capabilities, we are able to learn a considerable amount about each child's strengths and weaknesses. When apparent deficits are detected, we recommend specialists for further evaluation. Although many types of weaknesses are possible, those we most frequently diagnose in gifted children are discussed below.

Spatial Strengths and Sequential Weaknesses

One common pattern in the gifted is having spatial strengths and sequential weaknesses. Linda Silverman noted this pattern early at the GDC because we have seen many such children. They are visual-spatial learners with deficits not common to all of the visual-spatial population.

These children are able to copy complex designs with colored blocks, count blocks in pictured stacks where the existence of some must be inferred, and visualize how paper that is folded and cut would look if it were opened. They are usually wonderful abstract reasoners and divergent thinkers, and they understand complex systems. However, they may have difficulty repeating digits in sequence, repeating a sentence, or recalling the days of the week or months of the year in order. They are poor spellers, poor with phonics, resist rote memorization, and perform badly on timed tests. These children score relatively low on the Arithmetic, Digit Span and Coding subtests of the WISC-III, which assess sequencing, as well as other abilities.

Because these children make intuitive leaps, often under-standing more difficult concepts before simple ones, sequential instruction doesn't work well for them. Yet, most teachers are taught to present a simple concept first, then slowly build upon it day by day. Helping this learner who grasps the *whole* or *gestalt* before the individual parts to mesh with a sequential instructional approach can be tricky. These students need a conceptual framework presented first, into which they can place individual facts learned. They also need flexibility from teachers when asked to "show their work," because they may devise their own problem-solving strategies and not see the *steps* involved that the teacher sees.

The learning of such students is paradoxical in that they can often accomplish complex tasks, when they cannot master simple ones. In fact, many parents have said of their children brought to the GDC, "For _____, *what is difficult is easy* and *what is easy is difficult*." Most teachers feel that they must insist a child master easier concepts before proceeding to more difficult ones (e.g., mastering math facts before tackling more complex math reasoning). This often causes extreme frustration for these learners. They need to be taught to their strengths, providing support for weaknesses to the degree possible as they move ahead. Holding them back until they can learn in a typical sequence usually doesn't work.

Auditory Processing Deficits

Many gifted children who have a history of chronic ear infections as young children and some who have parents with auditory weaknesses exhibit auditory processing deficits. Virtually all have had repeated ear infections beginning in their first year, which were treated with antibiotics, and which persisted through the period when they were learning to talk. Those who had tubes implanted in their ears to forestall further infection generally fared better, but many parents were relieved their doctors didn't press for tubes and they were never considered. Unfortunately, the damage seems most apparent where antibiotics were the sole treatment. Many of these children had audiological exams once the infections cleared and their auditory acuity was found to be normal. However, these same children tend to have difficulty with short-term, auditory-sequential memory items and seem to have reduced *listening* capacity. The fact that they were learning to speak and process auditory information while their ears were infected and fluid-filled, seems to have affected their ability to process auditory information.

The physician mother of one of our clients noted a number of cases in her practice in which tubes were implanted in a child's ears and the parents called the next day to say the child had suddenly begun to talk or "was a different child." Research by Lynn Feagans (1986) has found auditory processing deficits in children who had nine or more bouts of otitis media (middle ear infection) before the age of three. In addition, there appears to be a higher incidence of attentional deficits in these children as they mature. IQ tests may not be able to discriminate between auditory processing problems and attentional deficits. The tasks that suggest both when scores are low usually involve short-term auditory memory. A child may fail to do well because of auditory processing issues or because he can't attend to the material well enough to recall it. Sometimes, we need to evaluate both possibilities to clarify the problem. These problems often confuse or invite criticism from others.

One mother recently commented about her son, "As bright as he is, you almost need to tackle him and tattoo instructions on his arm in order to get him to listen to and follow instructions. I can't tell if it is willful disobedience or he doesn't hear or doesn't process. I don't see him as willfully disobedient." The boy's history included both chronic ear infections and a past diagnosis of AD/HD. His mother was right to view him sympathetically as children generally do not choose to be "willfully disobedient." However, after being supported in her concern for him, she admitted she really needed help to make his grandparents understand. "They think he's horrible," she said, as she recounted years of their criticism. The cost of not diagnosing such disabilities in our children is measured in their loss of confidence and self-esteem. We have seen improvement in children with auditory processing problems when auditory memory games have been played at home and, in some cases, when an audiologist has prescribed ear filters to reduce background noise.

Visual Deficits

There is a range of visual processing problems that can cause difficulty on IQ tests. In some cases, children show apparent visual perception problems (they experience visual confusion when trying to copy a design with blocks and may be unable to tell if their copy is correct) or children may have visual tracking problems (their eyes can't follow a printed line in a book or pursue a path in a maze). They may have difficulty scanning and discerning visual detail or they may not easily change focus from far to near. We have observed that children have been helped by vision therapy (vision exercises done for several months under professional supervision). Upon retesting, some of these children scored much higher on the tasks they had originally found difficult on our tests. Also, quite commonly, gifted children may have difficulty attending to visual detail due to farsightedness. The fact that many are early readers may place stress on developing eyes that are often farsighted in young children. Gifted children may be reading more difficult books with small print when their eyes would appreciate large-print *easy readers*. Many are helped temporarily with bifocals to ease the stress of reading. When we see evidence of visual processing weakness in our testing, we frequently refer parents to a behavioral optometrist who is trained to assess how well the visual system is working. This approach is somewhat different than that taken by ophthalmologists who are concerned with the health of the eyes and distance vision. The behavioral optometrist additionally looks at the way the eyes function—team together, adjust their focus from far point to near point and back, track moving objects or lines of print, etc.—and suggests short-term therapy to improve weaker abilities. Athletes often take advantage of such therapy to improve *sports vision*, but it can make a significant difference for children with certain visual processing difficulties.

Consider the case of Diane. A bright, verbal young girl, Diane struggled to read. She was given help with prereading basics, taught to understand the building blocks of language and the rules of phonics. However, it was only after nine months of vision therapy for serious visual tracking problems that Diane was able to read her first billboard while riding in her parents' car. After this therapy, I tested her and she earned a Full Scale IQ score in the 140s. What was amazing was that she was gifted enough to fool many who believed she was reading. Her father realized while trying to do vision exercises with her that some were "impossible" for him. A person who also struggled to read, he shared many of her same visual processing difficulties. Although she improved immensely, her mother reported a problem several years later. Having become quite capable in mathematics, she still struggled on tests. Diane admitted that she couldn't always see written math problems accurately because the numbers *jumped around* and the vertical columns blurred, causing her to miscalculate. She could do the same problems accurately if they were read to her. This is a case where additional vision therapy would likely be warranted, as well as the use of lined paper turned sideways or large graph-paper for calculations, so that the columns stay put. In addition, such a child needs accommodations for tests so that her visual processing problem doesn't undermine her success in math.

Fine-Motor Deficits

Some gifted children struggle with fine-motor difficulties that challenge their ability to manipulate small objects (they struggle to copy block designs and assemble puzzles on the WISC-III) and successfully complete paper and pencil tasks. They can't begin to write as fast as they think and quite a large number will remain frustrated trying to express themselves through their own handwriting. Such children are encouraged to learn keyboarding skills as early as possible because computer word processors will undoubtedly best support their writing. For those who have serious fine-motor disabilities, a computer word processor may even be necessary for all writing in the classroom, or a computer with a voice-activated word processor may be required.

Fine-motor problems cause gifted children the most difficulty in the early grades, when considerable emphasis is being placed on learning to print and write in cursive. Repetitive worksheets used to develop these skills make life difficult for children with fine-motor deficits. Likewise, timed tests become a nightmare. These children regularly struggle to finish their work on time and may develop an avoidance of composition because the physical act of handwriting is so unpleasant. Such children benefit from opportunities to express themselves in other ways. Dictating a composition to a parent or doing an oral presentation, they demonstrate their learning with less frustration. Furthermore, we have suggested keyboard accommodations for even our youngest school-aged clients. Though parents may want to support developing handwriting skills through enjoyable activities (e.g., calligraphy), insisting that children with fine-motor difficulties write extensively by hand is usually counter-productive. These children are fortunate to live in the age of word processors. As they mature somewhat, they will be pressured to type their compositions anyway, so their advanced learning of word processing skills soon becomes an advantage.

In cases where students have significant fine-motor problems that persist as they mature, they may need to take college board or other standardized exams either untimed or with extra time. Or, they may require a scribe or the use of a word processor. Parents need to contact the test publishers for the exact requirements needed to make such exceptions. Typically, a child needs testing documentation of such needs from a licensed or certified psychologist, as well as a history of accommodation in school for the particular problem.

Sensory Integration Dysfunction

Sensory integration is the brain's process of coordinating sensory information and we often see gifted children with deficits in integration. Carol Kranowitz writes in *The Out-of-Sync Child* (p. 23) that the most likely causal factors for Sensory Integration (SI) Dysfunction are a genetic or hereditary predisposition, prenatal circumstances, pre-maturity, birth trauma, or postnatal circumstances (e.g., environmental pollutants, excessive or insufficient stimulation after birth, a lengthy hospitalization or institutionalization, or the lack of normal sensory experiences). SI is often the culprit when children are less coordinated and athletic than their peers, struggle with visual processing issues or handwriting (it may be the cause of the problems described in the previous section), and deal with hypersensitivities to light, sounds, and tactile stimuli. SI Dysfunction may underlie other disorders such as attentional deficits. However, Carol Kranowitz emphasizes, "The red flags of SI Dysfunction are a child's unusual responses to touching and being touched, and/or to moving and being moved" (p.18). These children often suffer from secondary anxiety, as well.

Occupational therapists can provide interventions that bring about vast improvements. The GDC is currently investigating the relationship between children with sensory integration issues and Pitocin administered to their mothers for extended periods of time to induce or accelerate labor. Pitocin was designed to be used for brief periods, perhaps three or four hours, but some of our mothers were given the medication for 24, 36, or even 40 hours, and the incidence of sensory integration problems appears striking. We have some concern that the very hard labor that results from Pitocin, when maintained for long periods of time, may be especially damaging to these children with highly developed central nervous systems and, often, large heads. Parents who note these symptoms are wise to read Jean Ayres' original book on the subject, *Sensory Integration and the Child.* If the symptoms seem a good fit for what parents are observing, a sensory integration evaluation can be done by a pediatric occupational therapist (O.T.). Therapeutic intervention is most effective through age seven, so early assessment is warranted. O.T.s can suggest exercises specifically tailored to an individual child's symptoms. Many of these children also benefit from vision therapy.

Gifted Children With Severe Learning Disabilities

Whereas subtle learning disabilities in an obviously bright child may not be detected because the child compensates well, severe learning disabilities that are easily diagnosed may make giftedness difficult to document in any way. Although families may see the advanced reasoning abilities of these children, only their deficiencies are obvious to teachers, and their early lives may reflect a singular emphasis on remediating their deficits.

Emma

Consider the case of Emma. Emma came to us at age 13, her parents hoping that her intellectual strengths might finally be documented so that they could find an educational program that would adequately challenge her. Emma's deficits were no secret to her family and teachers who had taught her. Her dyslexia made elementary school extremely difficult. She had to learn strategies to discriminate *b*'s from *d*'s, and she could not hear short vowel sounds. When asked to alphabetize, she had to run through the entire alphabet each time. Her spelling was so poor that even after she learned keyboarding skills, spelling checkers were inadequate for her needs. Her spelling did not approximate correct spelling closely enough to cue the software to the appropriate words. Math calculation was also very difficult for her. She had not been able to learn all of her multiplication facts and calculated using the few she knew. She had developed laborious, circuitous strategies to extend what multiplication facts she had internalized, often accompanied by counting on her fingers. Emma was also diagnosed with an auditory memory/sequencing disorder, which made it hard to get teacher instructions straight. With all of these issues, her early education was clearly directed toward her weaknesses. She attended a private school with a strand for students with learning disabilities and attentional deficits, which served her well until the seventh grade, when she was placed in the regular group.

Emma made amazing progress. She learned to read, although she frequently misread words within passages and replaced them with synonyms. Her parents thought this was odd, but came to accept it as just what Emma does. Although her decoding skills were not sophisticated, her understanding of words from context was impressive (reflecting her gifted verbal abstract reasoning ability). She was able to reach a point where her reading was quite good, although she often needed more time to ensure that she could finish her work. She learned to write compositions and to find a way to turn in high quality work with the help of a word processor. She had good math intuition and could perform quite well, within reasonable time limits, given a calculator. Math had become an easy subject for her. She learned to write all assignments down carefully and to ask questions of her teachers whenever she wasn't certain of a detail. In addition, she developed excellent social skills, but had no intimate friends or soul mates.

Tested at age 7 on the WISC-III, Emma earned a Full Scale IQ score of 107, in the average range. The profile of her subtest scores showed the peaks and valleys common with learning disabled children, but her highest scores (Vocabulary and Symbol Search) were in the superior range. There were no gifted-level scores and it was highly unlikely anyone outside of Emma's family would have considered her twice exceptional: both gifted and learning disabled. Yet Emma's brother had earned a 144 on the WISC-III and their parents were highly intelligent individuals in professional positions. In fact, Emma's parents had always viewed her as "at least as intelligent as her brother," but the test did not provide documentation of that.

There were a few others who saw the gifted potential. Emma's verbal ability and social insights always made her ideas worth listening to, and she stood out for this reason.

Some of her teachers and several other adults who got to know her, especially as she got older, did *discover* extraordinary capacities that appeared in various guises. Her fifth grade teacher in the L.D. class, for example, excitedly told her parents that Emma was a "genius," based on work she did on the science projects that year. The task was to build a simple machine out of bits and pieces found around the home or at school. After completing her own project, Emma helped the five other children to build the machines they desired. But it was the speed of her design and the deftness of her construction work, along with her ability to forage through the school collecting the needed pieces almost on the run, which was so striking to the teacher. Emma recalls, ruefully, that her take-charge attitude did not endear her to those classmates, even as they benefited from her help. Other children almost never saw past the dyslexia, the Central Auditory Processing Disorder (CAPD), and the way she dominated the classroom with her need to comment or ask *orienting* questions in compensation. Winning the elementary school (both L.D. and regular stream) speech contest two years running, in grades 5 and 6, was the first official recognition of the excellence of her slowly blooming academic skills.

In seventh grade, Emma moved to the regular strand in her private school. She made good grades, thanks to her compensatory skills and motivation to do her best. She was given extra time for exams and not penalized for her spelling. That year, she won the seventh grade English prize. She was voted the school's community service representative in eighth grade, and awarded the school's gold honor pin, only the second time it was awarded in the school's history. At graduation from the school that year, she won the Science prize and the Mathematics prize. She was co-chair of the graduation exercises, played clarinet in the senior band, and sang in the choir. Yet, she was complaining of boredom. Her parents wondered if retesting at age 13 might document her higher abilities to the extent that a school for the gifted or other challenging program would accept her. Plans were made to bring her to the Gifted Development Center for testing.

Emma was retested on the WISC-III at age 13. Although some of the same highs and lows in her subtest score profile were seen, all of her scores rose dramatically. She earned a Verbal IQ score of 132, in the gifted range, even though her Verbal IQ at age 7 was 112. Likewise, her Performance IQ score of 131 was gifted, compared with a Performance score at age 7 of 102. Her Full Scale IQ score rose from 107 to 134! Moreover, her Verbal Comprehension Index score, based on the verbal subtests most heavily weighted for abstract reasoning ability, was 140, at the 99.6th percentile. This score, we have found, may be the best indicator of students who will perform well in a school for the gifted. Abstract reasoning ability is generally felt to be the most important aspect of intelligence, and verbal reasoning is important for the class discussion and higher level thought schools for the gifted try to incorporate into their programs. Though Emma's scores were very high, she still showed tremendous difficulty with subtests emphasizing short-term, auditory-sequential memory. She earned a low average score repeating digit sequences (low-interest material) and an average score remembering mental math problems presented orally. She also struggled with the mental math calculations on the Arithmetic subtest. Such difficulties brought down her IQ scores, as did the visual confusion she experienced copying one design with blocks. Her difficulty copying angles, at times switching them to face in opposite directions than they were meant to face, mimicked her problem with *b*'s and *d*'s. Yet, she still scored in the gifted range. It would be reasonable to assume that we still have not documented the full range of her ability and that she is likely a very highly gifted individual.

Watching Emma work was impressive. An extravert, she had no qualms about talking herself through both difficult and easy tasks. The act of talking or discussing the problem with herself (testers call this *verbal mediation*) seemed to help. This was a girl who had learned how to compensate to an incredible degree. For example, as she read several math problems, she would begin to read a multiple-digit number starting with the last digit, then correct herself. Taking the Woodcock-Johnson-Revised Tests of Achievement, she struggled to decode words, yet would sound them out deliberately. She read passages haltingly, but well, achieving a college graduate grade equivalent. Her only limit would be the amount of time such reading required. Clearly, she would perform better with books on tape if she had considerable reading to do. Her math calculation placed her at the college graduate level, as well, although the math portions of the test took hours to administer because she could not use a calculator. Math reasoning (Applied Problems) was at the level of a college junior. Writing Samples required Emma to compose sentences according to increasingly specific and descriptive criteria. As spelling was not considered, she scored in the highly gifted range, again at the college graduate level. Her only low score was in Dictation, a test of spelling, punctuation and word usage, where she scored in the low average range (fourth-grade level). Her score of 84 in Dictation contrasts with a score of 154 in Passage (reading) Comprehension!

Emma's parents were delighted that at least gifted-level abilities had been documented because they hoped to enroll her in one of the more challenging local private schools where they lived. Unfortunately, none of the schools to which Emma applied felt they could make accommodations for her, even after they met her and liked her immensely. One school apologetically noted that its teachers simply could not ignore spelling when grading Emma's papers. Fortunately, a public high school with a full-time gifted program was pleased to have her and her latest test scores would be of some benefit to her, after all. Emma was kind enough to share some of her experiences with us for this book. She sent both this early copy and a corrected copy to me; however, I asked that her first version be used so that Emma's challenge with her dyslexia could be better understood.

> When I was little (about four, when I started J.K.) I was told I was slower in class then most kids, but I would ketch up when I was older. My parents weren't to worried because they know I was smart because of my huge vocabulary and my capability to talk to adults like I was an adult. But when it came to grade one I was no learning my A.B.C's and 123's. The teacher reassured my parents once again that I would learn, but my parents were getting a little hesitant and worried. My mother especially was this why since she was the one who would have to drag me from underneath the living room table with me kicking and screaming when I, should say we, did Phonics or any homework. My mother got so distressed that she decided to send me to a specialist to test me for a learning difficulty. I was tested on the Wisk III and other tests and learned that I was very dyslexic. This was in some ways a relief but I wasn't sure what this meant at the time. At the same time it didn't seem to make me fell any more secure, I still was academically last in every thing.
>
> I didn't real know that I was last at the time; all that I know was that I never got the candy for minute math (60 multiplication, adding, subtracting, or/and dividing questions that you needed to do in 60 seconds). Grade one and grade two were not my best years they were mostly filled with frustation, isolation, and

discernment. My parents thought that the [school] I was at was not the right school for me, and deiced to move me to another. The first day I visited I was only meant to stay a half day but I stayed the hole day. This school was ultimately better for me. I learned how to read and spell well enough that spell check gets my spelling about $1/3$ of the time (trust me that is good considering when I when into grade three I couldn't spell 'the"), and I succeed academically too. I was in a small class of 6-7 kids from grade 3-6 with specialized teachers who were highly qualified to teach children with dyslexia.

I loved it at my new school. I would have an activity every day at lunch, was on the honor role every year that I could, won the citizenship award, the speech contest twice, and got the gold and silver honor pins. I have many time consuming little strategies that help me with multiplication, spelling and about any thing else you can think of. When I was in grade 7 English, and won the English award that year. I have to say that my grade 7 English teacher was one of my greatest confidence busters and truly understood me and had the perseverance to look at my work with the 1000 mistakes. In grade 8, I was assessed gifted on the Wisk-III and highly gifted on subtests of the WJ-R. This was an interesting revelation because know I had a new problem: how am I going to get the challenging work that I love that was getting increasingly harder to get? We figured that by dropping French (the augment we used was, "If our daughter took 10 years + to learn English her first language, and still can't spell, how do you expect her to be able to read and spell

French?"), and challenge my self by taking
accelerated Math, Science, and English
courses.

Even though have I have been very successful,
not every academic institutes understands my
learning style. I live in [a large Canadian city]
and all the high-end privet high schools didn't
accept me. I can guarantee you that I got the
politest rejection letters there are in this world,
but for the first time in my life I felt almost
ashamed of my dyslexia even though it was
only for a day or so. I thought that know with
spell check and extra time I was not that hard
to handle. I thought for days why I didn't get in
with an 80+ average in every thing I have done
since grade five it would be dead certain entry.
Instead I will go to a very good public high
school that has a gifted program.

Through out it all I have had a very optimistic
look at life. I guess it's was in my genes to be
happy and to make every thing look as good as
possible. All through my life I have been
challenge, with out that challenge I would have
nothing to work for, so life would be boring. My
advice for any one dyslexia is that no matter
what don't give up because there is always the
computer, calulator, and the good old agenda to
solve all the problems. With these tools we are
equals or supers to those with out dyslexia,
and with time like red wine we only get better.

Although Emma still struggles to express herself in writing,
her speech is highly articulate and completely without
obvious errors in word choice. Word processors with voice
recognition software would seem a logical solution to her

dilemma, yet they still do not record her speech especially well. Her father believes she introduces subtle extra consonant sounds in many words, which human listeners ignore, but the program *hears*. However, frequent changes in technology make this her best hope for the future. As it is, Emma makes use of a text reader that audibly reads her more difficult documents for her. This spares her the time investment required to decipher the material herself. In fact, although she was able to score at the college graduate level on the untimed reading comprehension test administered to her at the GDC, she asked for the report of her evaluation to be emailed to her, as well as hard copies sent, so that she could hear it with her computer text reader.

Working with the gifted, I find that most testers, especially less experienced ones, want to see some evidence of giftedness (scores within the gifted range) within a child's test profile before considering the possibility of gifted intellectual potential. A few want to know that even with deficits, a child can still earn IQ scores in at least the superior range (120^+) if he or she is to be considered *twice exceptional*. Emma is the perfect example that this rule is inappropriate. In truth, these tests that can be relied upon for many purposes can, nevertheless, miss a child's potential when complex and overlapping deficits are at work. In Emma's case, she earned only an average Full Scale IQ score at age seven, with no subtest scores in the gifted range. When considering such a child, it is critical to carefully view all of the background information and the child's test behavior, as well as the test scores. Emma's parents and brother documented a familial history of giftedness and the parents had always felt, "Emma was at least as smart as her brother." Their conclusion about her was clearly the closest estimate of her ability for many years, until her late blooming allowed testing to reveal a more real-istic (if still minimal) estimate. Her father reported that, as the manuscript for this book was being finalized, Emma asked her parents if they ever gave up on her being smart while she was struggling with the early remediation. "No way," her father assured her, adding later, "but we had evidence of her deep wisdom from her spoken output." Still, it is clear Emma has not yet tapped her full potential. With her tireless motivation and irrepressible personality, I suspect she will amaze us all.

Underachievement Due to Attentional Deficits

Parents today worry about the misdiagnosis of Attention-Deficit/Hyperactivity Disorder (AD/HD) and the consequent overuse of stimulant medications in children. However, any consideration of the reasons why a gifted student is an underachiever in school should include an assessment for AD/HD. Increasingly, over the last few years, we have seen children at the GDC whose parents rate them as having a sufficient number of characteristics of AD/HD to be significant for the diagnosis. However, most are quick to note that their children can attend to high-interest material without difficulty. This is actually the pattern encountered in gifted children with AD/HD. Rather than showing consistent attentional inadequacies, the gifted have difficulty attending on demand to low-interest material, but usually have the capacity to *hyperfocus* on high-interest material. We never see gifted children who are unable to attend to a video game for hours. The problems occur with repetitive, low-level material, and are also evident in children's ability to activate their attention (they are fine once they become engaged in an activity, but starting is difficult). We cannot ignore the growing numbers of such children, nor the complexity of the diagnosis.

The current *Diagnostic and Statistical Manual of Mental Disorders* (4th ed.) of the American Psychiatric Association (*DSM-IV*) lists the typical characteristics of Inattention, Hyperactivity, and Impulsivity used to make the diagnosis of Attention-Deficit/Hyperactivity Disorder (a child may exhibit behaviors in one or more of these areas). However, it also offers the caveat that "Inattention in the classroom may also occur when children with high intelligence are placed in **understimulating environments** [*sic*]" (p. 83). Sorting out the relevant issues to make a diagnosis is often difficult. We have seen *some* children's symptoms disappear without medication or other intervention when they are placed in a full-time, highly challenging program for the gifted. Consider the case of Emily.

Emily

Eight-year-old Emily was brought to the GDC by her parents during the summer following second grade. Over the past academic year, she had become increasingly unwilling to attend her public school, had developed long-standing stomach pains of unknown origin, and generally appeared to be underachieving. Her parents had had some testing done when she was five, which indicated that she had an IQ of 142 (well into the gifted range) and would need modifications in her school program to extend the challenge. Unfortunately, the family had relocated and Emily's neighborhood school had provided little.

Emily was initially placed in kindergarten based on her age and size, even though she had previously attended school in another English-speaking country and should have been a third-grade reader at the beginning of the year. Her skills appeared to regress as she tried to fit in with the other students and meet teacher expectations. Likewise, each succeeding year had brought a similar lack of challenge and Emily was no longer displaying her intelligence and eagerness to learn at school. She simply hated school and didn't want to go. Her mother had concluded that the school did not believe gifted children had special needs and Emily had few, if any, options. She was allowed to attend a brief, occasional gifted pull-out program, but her teacher made her make up all regular classwork missed. (Sadly, we have seen a number of children whose teachers are similarly punitive about their participation in such programs.) Emily was seeing a psychologist regarding her physical symptoms, low self-esteem, and underachievement. She told her mother, "I feel like a little possum that's been run over by a truck and, unfortunately, I haven't died."

By bringing Emily to us, her parents hoped to clarify her needs and plan a more appropriate educational experience for her. Her father noted that his two older sons had experienced similar difficulties in school and had dropped out of high school. He was concerned that Emily might follow in their footsteps if solutions were not found.

At the Gifted Development Center, Emily earned a Full Scale IQ score of 132 (gifted range) on the WISC-III, with a Verbal IQ score of 135 (gifted) and a Performance IQ score of 123 (superior). These scores seemed somewhat low in light of her previous testing. Her profile of subtest scores was markedly inconsistent, with dramatic highs and lows ranging from the ceiling level of the test (highly gifted, 99.9[th] percentile) to the average range, more than three standard deviations lower. This is typical of children with learning disabilities, AD/HD or other problems, which can bring down scores and yield an underestimate of intellectual potential. In Emily's case, her verbal reasoning was at or near the ceiling level of the test and her spatial reasoning was high average. Reasoning scores tend to be at about the same level in gifted children when there are no deficits. There was evidence of visual processing problems in Emily's scores, with noticeable visual confusion when attempting to complete some of the items. Problems with the visual system can cause particular difficulty in school in the primary grades, when teachers assign many paper and pencil tasks. A child with fairly subtle visual processing deficits may find it more difficult to do fine-motor activities well and may need more time than is allowed. As we discussed Emily's vision, her mother also told us that Emily was getting headaches reading. Emily, herself, noted a problem when swimming—she couldn't tell how far she was from the end of the pool, so couldn't judge when to turn.

In addition, Emily's profile suggested the possibility of AD/HD and, indeed, her mother had noted that Emily seemed to have a long attention span as a young child, but that was no longer true. In the test session, Emily needed to move through the material quickly to stay interested and was very active. Assembling puzzles, she became a bit boisterous with the pieces, although she was generally very enthusiastic about the testing, enjoying the inherent challenge of the items. Gifted children, even most who have previously been diagnosed with AD/HD, usually show no evidence of distractibility in the one-on-one test session because it is the ideal situation for them. They have the full attention of a supportive adult and are easily engaged with high-interest, novel material. When children such as Emily are distractible, requiring a fast-paced administration and frequent redirection to answer the questions, we take note. Emily had apparent difficulties, further supported by reports of her disorganization at home.

Also of interest were Emily's achievement scores. Having just completed her second-grade year, her reading comprehension score placed her at the equivalent of the tenth-grade level, a fact that shockingly brought home the frustration she must have felt with easy readers and beginning chapter books. In addition, all academic skills were at the fourth-grade level or higher, suggesting a very large discrepancy between what Emily was being taught and what she had already mastered and was ready to learn.

We recommended that Emily be placed in a school or full-day program for the gifted to meet her academic, social and emotional needs better. If that was not available, full-grade acceleration would need to be seriously considered to help Emily maintain her motivation to learn. We felt that she would also need more challenging material in order to improve her attentional focus, although we also provided information and references to educate her parents about AD/HD and allow them to monitor her symptoms. We suggested an evaluation with a behavioral optometrist to assess many aspects of her visual system (not just distance vision) and provide vision therapy, if needed. Emily would need large-print books in the meantime and preferential seating. We suggested help with study and organizational skills (a typical AD/HD challenge) to help her gain better control of her responsibilities.

In Emily's case, her school placement was affecting her physically and emotionally. She had developed stomach-aches and anxiety related to school. The appropriate instructional level, along with supports for her deficits, was necessary for her physical and emotional health.

Unfortunately, the family's requests and our report failed to adequately change Emily's academic program at the local school. She was not allowed to skip a grade and completed third grade with a teacher who felt she was *not* gifted, generally gave her *C*'s, and noted on report cards that Emily "does her best." At the same time, her teacher withheld some materials, resulting in Emily never being advanced. For example, as the students completed a step in learning their multiplication tables, for example the "5's," she would then give them the "6's" and chart each student's progress on the chalkboard. However, Emily was given no materials beyond the "5's" and appeared, on the board, to have the least developed multiplication skills in the class. Although Emily's stomachaches disappeared after second grade, they were replaced with dizzy spells in third grade.

Emily's mother, who by this point was not being spoken to by some employees at the school, located a full-day, *highly gifted* program housed within another regular public school in the district. It was a self-contained class for fourth-through sixth-graders. Children are generally referred by their teachers in their home schools, but Emily's mother described their problem to program administrators and, instead, submitted our report. Emily was accepted to the program because her need was so great, even though it was felt that she might not be *highly gifted*.

We had suggested that Emily be retested in a year, following her likely vision therapy, to gain a better estimate of her abilities. We would retest her on several subtests of the WISC-III to assess visual processing issues and administer the Stanford-Binet L-M to see if her ceiling level verbal reasoning abilities on the WISC-III were actually beyond the limits of that test.

She returned after 14 months, several months into her new gifted program placement, and the results were remarkable. First, she described being thrilled with her new school, the teacher who was so nice to all of the students, and the friends she had made. She said, "We are like a family at that school," and she described how pleased her new friends were when she came back to school after being sick for a few days. Even the boy who always had to be *first* in line got out of line to tell her he was glad she was back!

Second, Emily was a totally focused child during the test session, with no apparent need to rush and a happy, poised demeanor. Her mother was pleased that her change in focus was apparent to us, as well, because there had been no intervention for AD/HD. She noted huge differences at home since the start of the gifted program. Recounting that Emily had always been horribly disorganized, losing materials and even forgetting to get dressed in the mornings once they awakened her, she was now the picture of organization. She couldn't wait to attend school and she placed a high value on her work.

Third, Emily earned a 148 IQ score on the Binet upon retesting, placing her in the *highly gifted* range and documenting a mental age of 14 years, 8 months. She displayed vocabulary, verbal reasoning and spatial reasoning at the Average Adult level. Emily was, indeed, well placed in her program for the highly gifted.

Retesting on three of the WISC-III subtests, Emily scored slightly higher (but not significantly so) on all three, having completed three months of vision therapy. Linda Silverman suggested that she return to the behavioral optometrist for a consideration of additional vision exercises. Ongoing research at the GDC is suggesting that six months of daily exercises is often more effective. In addition, optometrists who pursue higher levels of visual functioning than what would be expected for typical children of a certain age and grade, are more successful with the gifted. Although her scores were only slightly higher, we were pleased to note that Emily experienced significantly less visual confusion when presented with visually complex materials.

Emily's mother struggled to arrange her placement in the gifted class, but the truly frightening problems her daughter experienced have all but evaporated. Emily is a different child now, reminiscent of the little girl who was always exuberant about life and caring of others. Emily now has the opportunity to write frequently, whereas few writing assignments were given in previous years. She has to work to learn, and a strong work ethic is developing. She must learn study and organizational skills to handle the level of her work and she's displaying a newly discovered control of herself and her assignments. Most of all, Emily *fits in* to a degree she has never experienced before. Emily's mother said she recently heard her humming—something she hadn't noticed in years. Emily is so very happy!

The Difficulty of Diagnosing and Treating AD/HD in the Gifted

Sadly, few children we see have the option of a relatively perfect educational placement, so we can only rarely observe the effects of greater challenge on apparent attentional issues. However, we have seen *some* children with serious inattention helped enormously by medication, so we are not prepared to conclude that there is no real AD/HD within the gifted population. In fact, one gifted father, who also struggled from dyslexia as a child, noted recently that his reading disability significantly improved only after he was treated with Ritalin in high school. Treating his attentional difficulties finally enabled him to deal with his reading problems. He still self-medicates with caffeine, as most adults with AD/HD symptomatology do, to maintain focus.

At the same time, we have seen others experience minimal benefits or be unable to tolerate medication. Because virtually all parents are resistant to the idea, medication is rarely our first suggestion. However, we do counsel parents to see an *attentional specialist* and consider that specialist's recommendation for a medication *trial* (to determine response and effectiveness) when the symptoms have been significantly problematic. For example, when the child is beginning to run out of options because he has alienated teachers or been kicked out of schools, is usually a time to consider medication. Or, we have seen some cases in which the child felt desperately out of control and the medication would offer a likely solution to help him regain control of his attention and impulsive behavior. Some of our staff members have noted that within the gifted population we have seen, medication has not been the *magic bullet* that it usually is within the average population. The school psychologists we have working at the GDC, who also work with more average children in schools, have commented that medication alone usually makes a tremendous improvement in the AD/HD symptoms of more average children. But, they feel the gifted don't respond as predictably.

I asked John Ratey, co-author of *Driven to Distraction* with Ned Hallowell, if he had any thoughts about the most common *ADD-like* kid we see at the Gifted Development Center. He's typically male; gifted, or frequently more highly gifted; his organizational skills clearly hurt his schoolwork (he lacks control here); he fits Inattentive type symptoms, without apparent hyperactivity or impulsivity; he did not show signs of AD/HD by age seven, but they appeared over time (the *DSM-IV* indicates that many characteristics should be apparent by this age); and if medication has been tried, it likely has not been especially effective for a variety of reasons.

Ratey observed that the symptoms of children "often appear over time," as opposed to being in place by age six or seven, "as the environment changes and as the demands (external and internal grow)." He added,

> *I am always suspicious of med [medication] trials—usually too much or too little—and not trying the variety of offerings today. It is not always easy to get the right key and sometimes it is not possible to find it—one must be an explorer as a treater and there are not many—I just think that we back off with children as we see them as being too delicate— I think the consequence of ad/hd and failures and frustration are much more a horror for the brain, mind, body—than any possible effects of medication* (J. J. Ratey, personal communication, October 9, 2002).

It is true that few of the children we have seen, who have been prescribed stimulant medication for AD/HD, worked with an attentional specialist. Generally, the child's pediatrician prescribed a dosage that was never altered or tried for long. A specialist in attentional deficits will follow the child carefully for a more extended period, varying dosages, medications, and times the medication is taken to support the child when focus is most critical. We have heard some very positive comments from patients who changed to newer stimulant medications and noted a distinct improvement.

The effect of challenge on the gifted-AD/HD child cannot be overestimated. When the challenge increases, the symptoms are reduced; when the challenge decreases, the symptoms are exacerbated. School personnel generally should *not* make a gifted child's program easier because he or she suffers from attentional deficits. Classroom accommodations for gifted children with AD/HD must first support giftedness with high-level instruction and fast pace. However, other accommodations will be necessary, as well. Help with study and organizational skills is usually essential, providing a quiet place to work without distractions can keep a child on task, allowing the child to move around in the classroom may assist the child in maintaining good control and focus, and offering ways for students and their parents to easily communicate with the teacher to keep track of assignments (details and due dates) can be a lifesaver. Study and organizational skills won't be developed unless the child cannot function without them, so a challenging curriculum helps. We have noticed that it is easier to train a gifted-AD/HD child to focus when the work is really difficult, because they naturally engage.

Teaching the gifted to focus may be particularly critical because they are taking in so much more information than the average individual and must learn to prioritize their thoughts and sensory input in order to accomplish anything of value. An 11-year-old boy I tested recently was aware of every sound within the office and in the adjacent neighborhood during his testing. "You have no idea how much information comes in for me all the time. It's like information overload," he explained. He never lost his focus with the inherently challenging items on the IQ tests administered; however, some attentional issues had been noted by his mother. His attentional capacity would be severely tested with material of low interest that he did not find challenging.

In general, the awareness the gifted have of their environment is more detailed. When they consider issues they see more sides—multiple points of view. At any given moment, the options they must choose from for thought or action can be overwhelming. It is far easier to focus when only one or two choices present themselves. Teaching the gifted at a level and pace that requires sustained focus provides essential practice for them in culling out the most important aspects of their experience and using them in a deliberate, thoughtful exercise of intellectual power. Because we expect relatively little of them in programs developed for average children, many leave high school with poor work habits, inadequate organizational skills, and fluctuating attention and motivation. For these, whether or not we diagnose them as having AD/HD, they must contend with the same ADD-like problems that will have to be addressed at some point.

Supporting the Twice Exceptional to *Bloom*

Learning disabilities and other deficits are no less common in the gifted population than the general population, but they can be more difficult to diagnose. Linda Silverman stresses to all testers at the GDC careful examination of discrepancies of all kinds: between scores on different tests; between performance on various subtests or types of items within a test; between behavior at home and at school; between strong and weak subjects; even between IQ scores of siblings. For example, discrepancies of more than one standard deviation (15-16 points) between the IQ scores of siblings should be investigated. Research with 148 sets of siblings has shown that 36% have IQ scores within 5 points of each other; 61% are within 10 points (Silverman, 1988). The child perceived to be *non-gifted* in a gifted family usually is a gifted child with learning disabilities.

Finding and treating gifted children with learning difficulties can make an enormous difference to the child challenged in this way. The fact that these children can often do advanced work while still struggling with simple concepts is confusing to them, as are the mixed messages they receive about being "bright, but lazy" or simply *disabled* when their parents view them as so much more capable. Every effort should be made to diagnose apparent weaknesses through careful assessment. Where they exist, they should be explained clearly to the child and interventions undertaken.

Twice exceptional children need to be taught first to their strengths and consistently reminded that they are capable. However, in addition to supporting their giftedness, their deficits should be accommodated to the extent necessary for them to thrive and progress. The good news is that the twice exceptional *are* late bloomers. Linda Silverman recalls many examples of students with whom we have worked feeling they were becoming more capable as they matured, noticing the phenomenon at some time between puberty and young adulthood (few did well as young children in elementary school). Many had the sense that they were becoming more intelligent, that their brains were growing, or that they could do things they had not been able to do before. Twice exceptional children will struggle, but they will also improve, become *smarter*, and compensate more effectively. With help, their gifts will become increasingly apparent as their deficits prove to be smaller obstacles.

References

American Psychiatric Association. (1994). *Diagnostic and statistical manual of mental disorders* (4th ed.). Washington, DC: Author.

Ayres, J. (1979). *Sensory integration and the child.* Los Angeles: Western Psychological Services.

Davis, R. (1994). *The gift of dyslexia.* New York: Berkley Publishing Group.

Feagans, L. V. (1986). Otitis media: A model for long-term effects with implications for intervention. In J. Kavanaugh (Ed.), *Otitis media and child development.* Parkton, MD: York Press.

Kranowitz, C. S. (1998). *The out-of-sync child.* New York: The Berkley Publishing Group.

Office of Special Education Programs - OSEP (1995). *Letter to Lillie/Felton.* Wrightslaw. (Letter clarifying policy regarding gifted children with learning disabilities.) http://www.wrightslaw.com/info/elig.sld.osep.felton.htm (22 Feb. 2003).

Silverman, L. K. (1988, October). The second child syndrome. *Mensa Bulletin, 320,* 18-20.

Silverman, L. K. (1989). Invisible gifts, invisible handicaps. *Roeper Review, 12,* 37-42.

For Further Reading

Baum, S. (1984). Meeting the needs of learning disabled gifted students. *Roeper Review, 7*(1), 16-19.

Baum, S. (1991a, Spring). Gifted but learning disabled: A puzzling paradox. *Highly Gifted Children,* 4-6.

Baum, S. (1991b). *To be gifted and learning disabled: From identification to practical intervention strategies.* Mansfield Center, CT: Creative Learning Press.

Davis, R. D. (1994). *The gift of dyslexia.* New York: The Berkley Publishing Group.

ERIC Clearinghouse on Disabilities and Gifted Education (articles on the gifted and gifted/LD). http://www.ericec.org (22 Feb. 2003), http://www.ericec.org/digests.html (22 Feb. 2003), and http://www.ericec.org/gifted/gt-diges.html (22 Feb. 2003).

ERIC Clearinghouse on Disabilities and Gifted Education - ERIC EC. A *Guide to Disability Rights Laws*. http://ericec.org/lawguide.html (22 Feb. 2003).

GT World. GT-Special: *An Electronic Mailing List for the Families of Gifted and Talented Children with Learning Disabilities and other Special Challenges*. (For families of twice exceptional children). http://www.gtworld.org/gtspeclist.html (22 Feb. 2003).

Hallowell, E. & Ratey, J. (1994). *Driven to distraction*. New York: Touchstone.

Hallowell, E. & Ratey, J. (1996). *Answers to distraction*. New York: Bantam Books

Hollingworth, L. S. (1923). *Special talents and defects: Their significance for education*. New York: The Macmillan Company.

Individuals with Disabilities Education Act - IDEA Practices . IDEA '97 Final. (Laws and regulations). http://www.ideapractices.org/law/regulations/index.php (22 Feb. 2003).

Kay, K. (Ed.) (2000). *Uniquely gifted: Identifying and meeting the needs of the twice exceptional student*. Gilsum, NH: Avocus.

Kutner, D. R. (1999). Blurred brilliance: What AD/HD looks like in gifted adults. *Advanced Development*, 8, 87-96.

Learning Disabilities Association of America - LDA. (Information and links to government agencies and support organizations). http://www.ldanatl.org (25 Oct. 2002).

Learning Disabilities Association of America - LDA. *Gifted Students Cannot be Denied Consideration for LD Services*. (LDA link to Dept. of Education regarding accommodations for LD/gifted). http://www.ldanatl.org/bulletins/AC_1_96.html (22 Feb. 2003).

Lovecky, D. V. (1991a, September). The hidden gifted learner: Nonverbal learning disabilities. *Understanding Our Gifted*, 4(1), 3.

Lovecky, D. V. (1991b). Highly gifted children with attention deficit disorder. *Highly Gifted Children*, 7(2), 1-2.

Lovecky, D. V. (1994). Gifted children with attention deficit disorder. *Understanding Our Gifted*, 6(5), 1, 7-10.

Lovecky, D. V. (in press). *Gifted children with attention deficits: Different minds*. London: Jessica Kingsley.

Moon, S. M., Zentall, S. S., Grskovic, J. A., Hall, A., & Stormont, M. (2001). Emotional and social characteristics of boys with AD/HD and giftedness: A comparative case study. *Journal for the Education of the Gifted*, 24, 207-247.

Ratey, J. and Johnson, C. (1998). *Shadow syndromes*. New York: Bantam Books.

Sensory Integration Resource Center. http://www.sinetwork.org (22 Feb. 2003).

Silverman, L. K. (2000). The two-edged sword of compensation: How the gifted cope with learning disabilities. In K. Kay (Ed.), *Uniquely gifted: Identifying and meeting the needs of the twice exceptional student* (Reference edition, pp. 153-165). Gilsum, NH: Avocus.

Silverman, L. K. (2001). Diagnosing and treating visual perceptual issues in gifted children. *Journal of Optometric Vision Development*, 32(3), 153-176.

Silverman, L. K. (2003). Gifted children with learning disabilities. In N. Colangelo & G. A. Davis (Eds.), *Handbook of Gifted Education: Third Edition* (pp. 533-543). Boston: Allyn and Bacon.

Warshaw, Meredith. *Internet resources for gifted/special needs children. Uniquely Gifted*. http://www.uniquelygifted.org/ (22 Feb. 2003).

West, T. G. (1991). *In the mind's eye: Visual thinkers, gifted people with learning disabilities, computer images, and the ironies of creativity*. Buffalo, NY: Prometheus Press.

Whitmore, J. (1980). *Giftedness, conflict and underachievement*. Needham Heights, MA: Allyn and Bacon.

7

Successful Programs For Gifted Students

Seek the Best Options Available

Self-Contained Classrooms or Schools for the Gifted

By far, the most successful option for gifted children is the full-time, self-contained classroom or school for the gifted. We have seen the best academic, social, and emotional development in gifted children placed in such programs. They are designed to accommodate the considerably faster learning pace of the gifted and teachers who teach in them typically have some background in gifted education. If not, they may have experience modifying curriculum to accommodate special education needs or teaching older children with higher level material that they can apply similarly to younger, highly capable children. Ideally, they have been trained in the instructional approaches that best suit the gifted and they are accustomed to more advanced materials and performance expectations.

Schools for the gifted have the luxury of creating curricula specifically for this special population. Taking into account learning rate, learning styles, and other characteristics of gifted students, these schools can increase the depth and breadth of typical study, add topics that would not generally be addressed until children are older, and actually match a program to students. However, because so few schools for the gifted exist, either in the public or private domain, few families have the opportunity to choose between relatively appropriate programs. For most, providing an appropriate curriculum for a gifted student becomes more an issue of working with the school to piece together the best options available, rather than choosing the best ready-made curriculum.

Interestingly, self-contained schools for the gifted are the most cost effective way to educate gifted children in public school. The common notion that we simply can't afford gifted programs only applies to models where the child attends a regular program and gifted *accommodations* are added on. Funds for the regular instruction of students, teacher salaries, and buildings can be spent as easily to place a child in a public school for the gifted as in a regular public school. Self-contained schools for the gifted eliminate the need to hire extra teachers for pull-out programs that extend the regular program. One of the greatest difficulties encountered when attempting to provide appropriate accommodations for the gifted to extend regular programs is that special programs for non-majority populations are always subject to elimination when school funding is limited. The *enrichment* programs and extra teachers are often cut, leaving only the regular school program. Schools for the gifted (some are *schools within schools*) simply utilize regular funding and are not nearly as vulnerable.

Some school districts have created such schools. Yet, many others have not, believing that the heterogeneous grouping of students for instruction is essential for the social development of all students, including the gifted, and to provide high achievers for other students to model. To many, there is an ethical issue, as well. The school reform movement of the 1980s and 1990s sought to remove all aspects of *tracking* from public education and many are reluctant to ability group the gifted. Tracking typically divided children into levels (usually by the end of elementary school) and taught them in separate classes through high school. Whereas tracking usually benefited high ability students, concerns arose for average and lower-track students. So, one extreme form of ability grouping was exchanged for another: heterogeneous grouping. Some hybridization of the two approaches would have been considerably better, especially if the child's flexibility to change levels as needed could have been ensured.

The benefits for gifted students in a full-time gifted program are obvious to those of us who work with them. They are usually challenged sufficiently to maintain their love of learning and develop a solid work ethic. They progress as scholars, learning the study and organizational skills they would not learn if the work were too easy. Socially, they reap the benefits that we take for granted for average children; they are able to find friends with similar interests who understand their jokes. They are more comfortable with mental age peers than chronological, but this placement allows them both. They are not allowed the luxury of always being the best student in the class, who is best with or without much effort. Although it would seem that gifted students in such a setting would become elitist, they generally learn more humility because others are as competent.

We have noted that gifted children in regular classrooms frequently are isolated by other students for being different. When this occurs, such a child develops a defensive posture that slows social development and does not contribute to an openness to others. Gifted children in a school for the gifted *fit in* and it is a psychologically healthy placement for them. They tend to appreciate the differences among their friends and the diversity that makes each friend unique and interesting.

Charter and Magnet Schools

But, what if such a school is not available? Fortunately, there are other options remaining that work. Charter schools, publicly funded schools created by groups in the community who want to meet particular needs, may offer an alternative to more typical curricula. In states where charter schools have been adopted, they have generally done well. They meet a wide variety of needs and, in some cases, are good choices for gifted students. But, because they vary tremendously in philosophy, they must be evaluated carefully with the particular gifted child's needs in mind. One that I helped organize in Boulder, Colorado was created for "students who feel they want or need more challenge" and provided a considerably accelerated curriculum for middle school students anticipating challenging high school programs (i.e., the International Baccalaureate Programme or a high school program with a large number of Advanced Placement courses and possible concurrent enrollment in college).

Likewise, magnet schools that have a particular academic focus (e.g., science, math, computer science, or the arts) and draw top-notch students in those areas may be a good choice, where available. Such programs must be carefully assessed to determine if the level and pace of instruction will be adequate and if placement of students in classes is flexible enough to accommodate a student who has already mastered advanced work.

Homeschooling

Homeschooling is another option that we see increasingly. Although it places enormous demands on parents as teachers, it does provide a ready solution to the problem of how to create a program that's substantially different. Probably more homeschoolers teach their children in the lower grades than the higher, as gifted children quickly

become a challenge to instruct as their knowledge level
rises. But, some homeschooling parents teach their
children through high school and note that their students
increasingly take on the role of autonomous learners. Homeschooling is the best way to achieve a truly unique program
or accommodate an unusually rapid learning rate. There is
help available for parents wishing to do this, including
secular and religious support groups in all states. In
addition, homeschooling parents often combine their efforts
by getting their children together for projects and social
outings. Parents can also arrange partial homeschooling
situations that allow the child to learn some coursework at
home (usually subjects in which the child is most advanced)
and attend school for other work. This is one way to provide
physical education, art and music experiences beyond what
is done at home and allow the child frequent access to
friends at school.

Typical Schools with Grade and Subject Acceleration

Grade and subject acceleration at school provide another
effective alternative to the regular program. Moving up a
child's placement ensures that higher level work will be
provided on a consistent basis, whereas efforts to modify
curriculum for an individual child within a lower level
classroom may be spotty. The child who accelerates is
treated as one of the group and not singled out, and
accelerated students usually relate even better to the older
students who are more likely to be at their mental age and
share interests. Research on acceleration, despite the
warnings one occasionally hears, is quite positive provided
the child approves of the placement. Because gifted children
tend to be introverts, however, they may need opportunities
to visit the older class and time to decide. An escape clause
can be built into the agreement to accelerate, allowing the
child to return to the lower level placement within a month
if he or she is not happy. For children very reluctant to skip

a grade, acceleration in one subject area first can familiarize them with the older students and make the prospect of later full-grade acceleration less daunting.

Private Tutoring and Mentoring

Private tutoring or mentoring (tutoring often has the connotation of helping a child catch up, whereas mentoring implies moving ahead or exploring a wider range) in one or more subject areas is often done, regardless of the child's regular school placement. Local mentors can be found to work with a child in various subject areas: for example, helping the child to extend writing skills, learn a foreign language, or begin algebra early. It is important, however, that the child's school program be modified to reflect the advanced work and higher level of mastery. Children should never be expected to continue to do many hours worth of low-level work in school while they are advancing more appropriately outside of school. Parents engage mentors to support the interests of children who are anxious to move ahead or explore a field, and the school should support the child's efforts, as well. If the school fails to acknowledge this work, it can seriously affect the child's motivation to learn in the classroom.

Computer-Based Instruction, Online and Correspondence Courses

Increasingly, we are seeing another form of accommodation emerge: computer-based instruction. Stanford's EPGY (Education Program for Gifted Youth) offers computer-based math instruction from elementary school through high school that is self-paced. Some science and English courses are offered, as well. The coursework is contained on a CD-ROM for use on a home computer. Tuition is paid and the materials (including textbooks) are sent to the child's home, where the child can progress as quickly as he or she likes (communicating with tutors by email, phone, or instant messaging). This is an option parents may want to consider who feel their child is ready for higher level instruction, but the school refuses. Generally, continuing education credit from Stanford is viewed by schools as reasonable evidence of mastery and the child is then allowed to take more advanced coursework at school. Or, EPGY may become the math instruction that the child whizzes through at a faster pace than the school could provide. One sixth-grade girl we know completed instruction from Algebra I through Calculus in one year. Such a program, if undertaken, should substitute for mathematics at school. The student can do homework at school when that subject is being taught and get instruction at home, when homework for school would normally be done. Johns Hopkins and Duke provide related programs.

Correspondence courses continue to be popular with families of gifted children. For example, the University of Nebraska Independent Study High School offers a full range of courses leading to a high school graduate degree. Some are online courses, where communication and work are transmitted by email, and others are traditional correspondence courses, where materials are mailed to the student and the student corresponds and submits work by mail. The University of Nebraska High School coursework would be appropriate for younger gifted students. Likewise, many colleges will allow advanced younger students access to college-level courses who are high school-aged or younger.

Private and Parochial Schools (not specifically for the gifted)

Private and parochial schools are an option many parents of the gifted consider. They are generally more challenging than regular public school programs, but they need to offer flexible placement in order to fully support gifted students. Parents will encounter a range of different programs available and will need to decide carefully if such a placement will benefit a gifted child. For example, one school well known to us is

Kent Denver. Kent has placed gifted students in their various subjects according to mastery, so that a student could be at various grade levels in different areas. This type of placement works beautifully with the gifted. It allows them to learn new material once previous material is mastered. Another private school we know has a strict grade-level placement, because school personnel are concerned that parents will not like it if some children are acknowledged to be more advanced. Although teachers at this school spend considerable individual time with students in small classes, they insist they do not *individualize*, because that might appear to be offering advantages for some. The principal of this school has also stated, "I don't believe in acceleration and I never will." Such a school can become very oppressive for the advanced student—and parents are paying for it. In addition, some private schools that emphasize high achievement may require considerable homework, more than may be necessary for the learning of a gifted child. Parents need to proceed carefully, ask many questions, and have their children visit if serious consideration seems warranted.

Advanced High School Programs

For gifted high school students, common options include taking the maximum number of Advanced Placement (AP) courses the school offers or attending an International Baccalaureate (IB) program. Advanced Placement courses are typically the highest level courses most high schools offer. They represent the level of work college freshmen could expect to receive and are generally taken by juniors and seniors preparing for AP exams that confer college credit with high enough scores. These courses can be started earlier than usual if the advanced student can place out of entry-level courses (something to be discussed with the principal or guidance counselor). This allows the student more time to take the various advanced courses.

International Baccalaureate (IB) programs technically encompass the junior and senior years of high school, but the schools offering them provide some type of pre-IB preparatory experience for freshmen and sophomores. These pre-IB programs usually ensure higher level freshman and sophomore course offerings which are highly desirable, especially when compared with high schools that offer few honors courses for underclassmen. Earning the IB diploma documents completion of a comprehensive, advanced program with upper-level courses similar to AP level. Since the program is international, an IB diploma is highly regarded around the world.

However, the accelerated American student may want to choose AP classes because AP exams can be taken at any grade level, whereas IB exams may only be taken at the end of the eleventh and twelfth grades. A student ready to take an IB exam early in his or her high school career must wait until later to take it. In contrast, the flexibility of AP testing allowed seventh- and eighth-grade students at a high-challenge local middle school the opportunity to take two AP social science courses, taught by a former AP high school teacher, and take the exit tests. Some of the students earned high enough scores to ensure college credit at most colleges (colleges vary in conferring credit) before they entered high school. In addition, colleges more frequently grant credit for AP courses because they are more familiar with the program.

Concurrent Enrollment in High School and College

Many gifted high school students also choose to take college courses while still in high school (states may pick up some of the tuition through *Post-Secondary Options* acts). If chosen to reflect high school graduation requirements, the college courses then count toward *both* high school gradua-tion and a bachelor's degree. Students may attend local colleges or take college courses online. Most gifted students appreciate such concurrent enrollment as it allows them to compact their high school and college work, and many feel quite comfortable on college campuses. They may enter college with a significant amount of college credit (further augmented by credit earned through AP or IB coursework), usually in the more basic classes required of under-classmen. This allows them to pursue studies in their major area sooner and shortens the time required to earn an undergraduate degree. It may also limit scholarship opportunities open to college freshmen, however, if the student begins full-time college work as a sophomore or junior. Nevertheless, some gifted high school students really need the opportunity to advance and love their early college experiences.

Individualization Within the Regular Heterogeneous Classroom

Probably the most common program option for gifted children, particularly in elementary schools, is individual-ization within the regular classroom. The child is placed normally with age-peers and his or her work is modified where needed to accommodate special learning needs. This allows the teaching of children in heterogeneous groups (which is very important to some), but also recognizes the child's unusual needs. The choice of teacher, specific program options and the consistency of modifications are critical here. Unfortunately, many of the children we see have programs of this sort, with minimal accommodations for special needs. Successful individualization can be difficult for teachers to maintain who also have large classes and students ranging from the mildly delayed (main-streamed into the regular classroom) to the most highly gifted. It requires a teacher who both understands the gifted student's needs and appreciates them. It also requires great ideas for modifying the child's curriculum and a firm resolve to do it consistently. Most of these plans accommodate the child only minimally because they stress teacher resources and are time consuming to maintain. The teachers I have watched succeed beautifully with this method were highly experienced teachers, for whom organizing lesson plans and handling the class are not issues. Furthermore, these are confident individuals, willing to take some risks with a student, despite criticism from other teachers.

Less Successful Options

Irrelevant Enrichment

Although gifted students in America desperately need educational options, some of those currently offered are poor. The gifted need access to higher level material, a faster pace of instruction, accommodation to their learning style, and work that engages their abstract reasoning abilities, but some programs have little to do with this. Julian Stanley (1976), a pioneer in work with mathematically precocious youth at Johns Hopkins, points out that the desire to limit our accommodations to *enrichment* rather than *acceleration* (to avoid affecting the entire grade-level curriculum sequence) can have interesting ramifications. He notes there are four types of enrichment typically employed:
1) *busywork*—e.g., the math class is given the odd problems to do, but the gifted student must do all of the problems because he's smart and can do more work; 2) *irrelevant*—e.g., gifted students are given a leadership class, whether or not that is appropriate for all of them and despite the fact that some non-gifted students might have excellent leader-ship potential; 3) *cultural*—e.g., we might offer gifted students an art appreciation class; it is also irrelevant, but, at least, has some socially redeeming value; and
4) *relevant*—of this last type, Stanley notes that if the enrichment actually increases the depth and breadth of the child's study and is relevant to what he or she is learning,

then it will lead to grade acceleration in the near future. Stanley's point is well taken in that the difference between curriculum at different grade levels on the same subject is usually a difference of depth and breadth. However, it is common to hear people take a stand on enrichment vs. acceleration. "I believe in enrichment, but not acceleration." The two really cannot be separated if the enrichment is of the type most of us envision—the regular work is broadened and more detail is added. Moreover, the simplest instance of giving a child something additional in a classroom can be called *enrichment*, yet not be deserving of merit as a gifted accommodation. Unless relevant enrichment is provided on a consistent basis as part of a planned accommodation for a gifted child, it is likely to be inadequate.

Unfortunately, many gifted programs exist that are quite irrelevant to the child's regular classroom learning. A woman contacted me a couple of years ago, saying that she was a teacher in a gifted pull-out program for elementary and middle school students. Every week, for a few hours, the program provided "thinking skills training" and also taught leadership. She asked how she might improve this program. I asked what contact she had with the students' classroom teachers and could she work more closely with them to modify instruction for these students in the regular classroom? She insisted that there could be no connection; the classroom teachers did not want interference. Yet, what most undermines the motivation of gifted students to learn is the feeling of being trapped in a lock-step system that does not respond to their needs or their accomplishments. What they need most is appropriate daily work, not to be *gifted* only once a week for a few hours. Likewise, we have seen efforts to meet social and emotional needs without any educational accommodations. One middle school, described in a recent newspaper article, was proud of its monthly brown-bag lunches for gifted students that allowed them to commiserate with each other about their frustrations in the classroom. Programs that only minimally address the needs of gifted students are irresponsible.

Acceleration Opportunities Too Small in Scope

Other limitations emerge, as well. Some modifications suggested for the gifted are too small in scope. For example, one "gifted math" group I encountered for fourth-graders was typical of a number of emerging classroom programs that allow students to skip very small amounts of instruction when they can demonstrate mastery of the relevant concepts on tests. These programs are preplanned, without knowledge of the needs of the specific students, to provide an amount of more challenging material acceptable to teachers. But, the amount one can skip doesn't begin to approach the advancement we see in gifted children when we administer achievement tests. A better grouping of gifted math students would occur if the children were all assessed and efforts made to provide appropriate-level instruction for each child, along with the opportunity to move ahead when concepts are mastered. Minimal, preplanned programs offer a false sense of security that the needs of the gifted are being accommodated when the programs actually fall far short of meeting the students' needs.

The notion that the child's accommodation cannot extend beyond grade level is never true. In fact, many gifted children benefit from substantial acceleration. For example, our most mathematically talented students are usually ready to begin algebra several years early, while still in elementary school. Any small holes in their arithmetic mastery can be filled easily in the context of algebra instruction and algebra appeals greatly to their love of abstraction. Teachers are very reluctant to allow this because of the sequential reasoning that all arithmetic must be in place before beginning algebra. Yet, our brightest students in math are hard pressed to endure arithmetic until eighth grade, especially since the number of new math concepts presented in the years just preceding algebra diminishes. Early algebra is a motivator for these students to continue loving math.

The Teacher's Helper

Other accommodations with unreasonable ceilings are also common. For example, using a child as a teacher's helper is sometimes believed to be of great benefit for a gifted child, particularly a well-behaved girl. Sadly, this approach usually ensures that the child will be limited to helping with regular grade-level work and will not have the opportunity to move ahead appropriately. Likewise, pairing the gifted student for a significant amount of instructional time with a child who needs extra help ignores the educational needs of the gifted child. We have seen advanced readers paired with non-readers for extended periods, relieving the teacher of an added instructional burden, but preventing the advanced reader any opportunity to progress. Trying to keep the gifted child *busy* while others catch up cannot be justified; each child has a right to learn primarily new material every day. One Executive Director of Curriculum and Instruction of a local school district recalled having a particularly advanced boy in her classroom years before. He had mastered virtually everything she attempted to teach that year, so was usually to be found reading quietly at his desk. She consoled herself about this situation by thinking that as long as he was reading, he was okay. Although letting this boy read books of his choosing was considerably better than forcing him to do low-level tasks, years of underchallenging work in the classroom take their toll. They have a cumulative effect that, at the very least, undermines the development of good work habits, threatens motivation to learn in school, and may contribute to behaviors that resemble attentional deficits. The child develops habits of mind that free him from the mental drudgery of attending to the low-level material at hand.

The Least Restrictive Environment

Parents of Special Education students have long advocated that their students be taught in the "least restrictive environment." What would that mean for the gifted? It would allow them to be taught at their appropriate level and it would allow for continuous progress; students would be allowed to move ahead once they mastered material. They would not be held to a slower learning pace or made to do drill and practice they did not need. They would be respected as learners, not disapproved of for their failure to be typical. They would have opportunities to interact with true peers who share similar interests and nurture their social development.

Because gifted students differ so much, there is no perfect gifted program that would accommodate them all and provide the ideal education. Schools for the gifted try very hard to create a good match, but such programs usually fit the moderately gifted (IQ 130-144) best because most gifted students are within that range. More highly gifted students need accommodations in gifted schools, as well as regular schools, and flexibility is a key component in an excellent program. Programs in schools for the gifted also vary considerably and the student should be matched with an appropriate program. Some are quite traditional, providing high-level instruction sequenced into somewhat rigid levels most students progress through together. Others are more individualized, with students moving through levels at different rates. They may have traditional classrooms with teachers lecturing to classes, or rooms with sofas, armchairs and small tables where each student is pursuing his week's work individually, meeting with small groups and occasionally the teacher for discussions or projects.

The best curriculum is a rich and varied one that challenges the gifted student's desire to reason and learn in depth. It thoroughly engages the learner and requires real effort without overwhelming him or her. It allows the student to gain self-esteem from meaningful accomplishment. Beyond that, there are many possibilities that we have seen succeed with gifted students.

Some attend private elementary and middle schools for the gifted and earn International Baccalaureate diplomas in high school or attend high schools with a large number of AP classes. Other gifted students are accelerated at one or more points in their public school educations. A forth grade grade boy from Tennessee has been recommended by his school to accelerate directly to high school based upon his IQ and achievement scores. His school includes gifted students in Special Education and wants to provide the least restrictive environment for this very advanced student.

We have seen homeschooled children taking college courses quite early and loving them. Some graduate from high school at nine, 10, or 11 and move on to college work. A few highly gifted students we have known have skipped middle school altogether and moved from elementary school to high school. This is actually quite feasible when the student's middle school offers few, if any, honors courses and the child can progress from being a very advanced student at the end of elementary school, to a high school freshman taking regular level or honors coursework.

There is no body of knowledge that suggests a single model for success with these children. The fortunate gifted child might attend a school for the gifted with a carefully developed curriculum that provides enriched, in-depth material at a faster pace. But, a profoundly gifted child (most likely to suffer in a typical public school environment) might emerge relatively unscathed from high school with a pieced-together conglomeration of efforts made at every level to provide challenge (choosing teachers carefully, occasionally skipping a grade, moving to a more challenging school for a couple of years, placing out of lower level classes in high school, taking college courses concurrently, etc.) What we rarely see is gifted students achieving at a high level and loving school with no accommodations. Some may endure it, but many simply cannot.

Choosing A Program

Prior to School Entrance

Parents preparing a gifted child for school can rest assured that it is always appropriate to support the child's learning at home. There is nothing gained by withholding information from a curious child, in the hope of preventing boredom at school. It is more important for parents to foster their child's curiosity by providing information when it is requested, and letting the child take the lead and pursue knowledge of interest. Parents of the gifted usually try to support their children's interests to the degree possible; however, few push their children into unwanted activities. In fact, the pressure exerted by gifted children on their parents to provide a wide variety of stimulation usually taxes both parental energy and monetary reserves. Yet, parents should feel comfortable offering enrichment activities, opportunities to pursue hobbies and develop talents, and even help to learn specific skills taught in school, if asked. The child who is helped to learn concepts in algebra or geometry, or given any type of requested information, is rewarded for his or her curiosity. The love of learning that is so pronounced in these children from birth should always be supported. Many of the children we see have remarkable stores of knowledge, attesting to the rich sources of information accessible to them. Some learn tremendous amounts from the Discovery and History channels (a good reason to not restrict television too much), others from reading or being read to, others from trips to museums or vacations. They pursue myriad interests and need support in many areas: core academic subjects, athletics, the arts. They are children who want to sample what the world has to offer.

Choosing an Elementary School

When it comes time to send a child to school, deliberately
choosing a school for a gifted child is important. Nowadays,
parents often have a variety of choices, even in public
schools. The neighborhood school is not the only possibility,
although it may be satisfactory. There may also be *schools of
choice* in a school district (magnet or charter schools) that
have a particular emphasis, or schools that parents simply
feel more comfortable in when they meet the staff or find out
about the programs offered. It is often possible to enroll a
child in the school of preference.

A school's principal can be the parents' best long-term ally if
he or she is willing to help place a child with supportive
teachers and/or in the most appropriate classes. In fact,
contacting school principals before a child begins school or
before relocating can be helpful in finding the one who is
most willing to meet a child's needs. A friend of mine
recently moved to the Northwest and contacted a number of
schools to find the best placement for her twice exceptional
son. He was both gifted and had some learning disabilities
and she was naturally concerned about finding an appropriate school. Her calls to principals were surprisingly
revealing; the administrators differed significantly in their
willingness to help plan a program for her son and in their
knowledge of his difficulties and accompanying need for
high levels of challenge. Her search resulted in the choice of
one particular school and the family moved to the appropriate geographic area so that her son could attend that
school.

Teachers may be a factor in the initial choice, as well, and
are a factor every year a child attends school. Teacher
choices may precipitate the move to a different school at
some point or be a factor in grade placement decisions. Even
in a school of preference, whether or not the gifted child is a
good fit in that school depends on the child's chemistry with

each teacher each year. Teachers who are unsupportive of giftedness, inflexible about modifying curriculum, or simply not appreciative of the child should be avoided.

Once children enter school, parents must be careful to ensure that they are learning primarily new material every day and that they are not spending considerable amounts of time on previously mastered material. The child who is fully reading and sounding out words prior to entering first grade should probably skip first, as its main emphasis is reading instruction. Some schools that insist children begin in the age-appropriate grade will accelerate a child within a few weeks once the teacher has had the opportunity to appraise the child's skill levels. Beware of advice to retain a child in the age-appropriate grade simply because social skills do not appear advanced. If the child shows some reluctance to enter into new groups of children without some time to observe and become comfortable, this is typical of the gifted who are primarily introverted. It is not an indication that the child's social skills are too immature for placement at a higher grade level.

As children progress through school, they must be carefully monitored to ensure a continued good fit with the curriculum and instructional pace. Note the child's comments about being bored or having to do things repeatedly. Pay attention to concerns about the work always being "too easy." Note teachers' comments, as well—for example, about a child finishing the work too quickly or talking when work is done (a child is not challenged enough if this occurs). Don't ignore such concerns or assume that it will be character building for a child to learn to be patient and repeatedly wait for others to learn.

Assessment Aids Planning

Have the child tested individually to gain a better idea of his or her abilities, strengths and weaknesses, if this has not been previously done for admission to a gifted program.

Many children are accepted to GT programs based on brief group intelligence tests, which may confirm giftedness, but offer little additional information helpful in making accommodations to the child's school program. Children should also be individually tested if there is reason to believe previous scores are not descriptive of the child or may have changed due to therapeutic interventions. Some obviously gifted children do not score well on group tests and may not be getting accommodations at school that are limited to gifted students. A nine-year-old girl I tested recently earned solidly gifted Verbal, Performance, and Full Scale IQ scores in the 130s on the WISC-III (all in the 98th and 99th percentiles), but had been rejected for the gifted program at school based on her Cognitive Abilities Test (CogAT) scores. On that test, she earned a Verbal score at the 93rd percentile, Quantitative score at the 71st percentile, and Nonverbal score at the 97th percentile. The school considered only the last score high enough, but felt it did not measure giftedness. The girl's mother brought her in for testing based on her personality characteristics. She said that when she read about the personality characteristics of the gifted, she said, "That's my child."

Current achievement levels in academic subject areas are also invaluable in determining whether the level of challenge in each subject area is appropriate. If they are indicative of poor placement (e.g., the child is bored in class and the achievement scores indicate a grade equivalent several years above the child's grade), share the results with the child's teacher or principal, as they undoubtedly relate to the child's frustration. Try to work out solutions to the specific problem encountered. Test results document abilities and skill levels for parents so that they will not be speaking out of intuition or apparent prejudice for their own child.

An Individual Educational Plan (IEP)

Working out a written plan, however simple, is an important goal (see Chapter 11 for sample plans). Whether called an Individualized Educational Plan (IEP), Personalized Learning Plan, or other name, the plan lists modifications to the regular program. (Some schools may be reluctant to call it an IEP, which is special education terminology for a legally-mandated plan provided for the child who meets special education criteria.) Accommodating a child's needs requires a meeting that includes the teacher, the child and the parent. Each can provide needed information that is helpful. Focus on the particular problem and suggest a fix for it. Remember, there are no prescribed solutions—only a general need for higher level material, faster instructional pace, and support of the child's interests.

Solutions that can be put into place with a minimum of effort are most likely to be continued. For example, it is easier to send a child to a higher grade level for math instruction every day than to modify his math program continuously for the rest of the year. Subject acceleration is fairly easy for the two teachers involved. However, the classroom teacher may be able to readily substitute fourth-grade spelling lists for second-grade lists for the advanced speller and this would be a simple modification. Likewise, schools that establish reading groups for different levels of readers within each grade may be able to accommodate the advanced reader. If not, substituting higher level books for assigned texts is often easy for a teacher to do (although it is important to have the related work in a modified reading project engage higher level thinking skills, not just mastery of the concrete details of the book's plot). Special enrichment programs for the gifted in a school will not solve classroom learning issues. They may be enjoyable and offer the opportunity to be with other gifted children, but classroom modifications will be needed, as well. Consider grade acceleration if a child is significantly advanced in all academic areas (individual achievement testing can help determine this) and is comfortable with the idea. Many times children are willing to accelerate because they are so bored and have few close friends anyway.

Middle School Choices

As a child approaches middle school, it is important to check out the various schools and the middle school philosophy in a public school district. Many districts that made the transition from junior high schools to middle schools accepted a series of educational goals for middle level instruction that extend far beyond the choice of grades combined in the building (junior highs usually included grades seven through nine, whereas most middle schools encompass grades six through eight). The ethic of "hetero-geneous grouping of all students for instruction" was accepted by many public middle schools, causing them to eliminate some or all of the honors classes they formerly offered.

Though many are now beginning to make adjustments because gifted children have been underchallenged, it is particularly important to carefully evaluate any middle schools under consideration for a gifted child. The option to take high-level (honors or accelerated) classes must be available at this critical time to support the child's motivation to learn and developing work habits. If there is the option of a public middle school for the gifted or an accelerated middle school, this should be considered. A gifted child needs preparation before entering an advanced high school program, so that he or she will not begin such a program with inadequate study skills or lacking prerequisite courses. At the middle school level, a child can also be placed in higher-grade-level courses, possibly including one or more high school classes, if transportation can be arranged.

High School Programs

At the high school level, again, the choice of school and course options is important, with honors courses, Advanced Placement courses, and International Baccalaureate courses important considerations. Make sure that entry-level courses are needed; if not, try to have a student assigned the next level course. Many schools let advanced students skip the entry-level science course, the freshman English course, and may allow other higher level placements, as well. For example, most students are allowed to take the *next* math class in the sequence offered, even if they are quite advanced coming from a previous school. Counselors often handle these common placement changes; however, the principal is usually needed for more radical advancement.

Principals exert varying degrees of responsibility when it comes to placement and the accommodation of students with unusual needs. For example, in some schools, teachers in the various academic departments make the final decisions about a student's placement in courses. This can work well when the teacher has broad knowledge of the coursework at each level and the appropriate student achievement expected at each level (e.g., the head of the English department at our local high school teaches classes at several levels, including the freshman and AP English classes). Such a teacher can assess the work of an incoming student and make an excellent placement recommendation. However, when the teacher making the placement decision teaches only a class that students frequently wish to skip, very few students may be allowed to move ahead. Choosing a school with a principal who invites parents of gifted students with significant placement issues to see him or her is more likely to produce a positive experience for the student that lasts for the duration of high school. Principals who choose to be involved can make ultimate placement decisions. Such a principal can help plan a student's courses based upon previous work (not grade level), exempt the student from certain course requirements, and offer advice about the best classes for the student to take.

Parents who have successfully guided gifted children through school usually come to prefer *accelerative* options over *enrichment* opportunities unrelated to general learning. As my friend Gerri notes, "Kids get tired of dessert. They just want a real meal." Gifted students usually appreciate the opportunity to move ahead to more difficult work. Also, accelerative options are more dependable in the sense that they represent a step up to higher level material that remains consistent throughout the duration of the class. They are not dependent upon the teacher having extra time to offer special options when he or she is busy with other students. Finally, acceptance of the child's academic progress is a foregone conclusion when the child has successfully completed the advanced class. Noteworthy accomplishment in enrichment projects at the lower level may appear less impressive to later teachers and may not adequately document the need for accelerated work in the next class.

Finding the Perfect Program

The perfect educational program for a gifted child would teach the child at the appropriate level and pace in each subject area, with instructional provisions made for learning style and support of the child's interests. It would also be designed to accommodate the abstract reasoning ability of gifted students, realizing that they are most engaged by activities that require higher level thinking skills. In addition, the program would support the personality characteristics of gifted children, including their sensitivity, intensity, and likely introversion.

The program most likely to meet such needs is the self-contained classroom or school for the gifted. Even if the child has varying abilities in different subject areas, and perhaps is more highly gifted than children the program is designed for, the full-time gifted program comes closest to meeting the academic, social, and emotional needs of gifted students. A flexible, well-run gifted school can modify where needed for individual children, but is virtually always more likely to provide the challenging, advanced work and fast instructional pace gifted children need. Unfortunately, the gifted rarely have access to self-contained gifted programs, either public or private.

For most, a *program* of sorts must be created utilizing options available where the child lives or through computer or correspondence course offerings. Parents invariably become the managers of such programs, in the absence of available long-term guidance from school personnel. It becomes a parental responsibility to determine the child's needs year by year, and an appropriate educational response to them. Possible schools and programs must be checked out, administrators and teachers interviewed, and the child supported to have an active voice in the planning, as well. In this way, a patchwork of educational options can finally emerge to support the gifted child successfully.

Help is available for parents through support groups for gifted families, local and state gifted associations, gifted education consultants, specialists in the assessment of the gifted, internet resources, and some school personnel. Because parents bear such a heavy responsibility for the learning outcomes of their gifted children, it is critical that they educate themselves about their children's needs to the degree possible. Perhaps the most difficult adjustment for parents to make when they have gifted children is to accept that others won't bear the primary responsibility for educating them. Our children's education will not be primarily the domain of the public schools, or even private schools we have carefully chosen. Likewise, it will not be directed by education professionals. Educated parents, advocating for the needs of their gifted students, are the

most likely individuals to understand those needs and
ensure that they are addressed.

Quinn O'Leary...Program Options

*It took me months to realize how good I really had it. It was
not a sudden realization that I liked my teacher or enjoyed
my class. It was a slower, dawning awareness of pleasure,
the subtle, simple glow of general good cheer at random
times throughout the school day—aside, that is, from lunch
and recess.*

*Eventually I wound up adoring both the teacher and the
curriculum so much as to request stridently that I be placed
in her split-grade class again, for sixth grade as well as
fifth. I was the only student, in the few years Mrs. Starry
and I corresponded, who managed to insist strongly enough
to be granted my wish.*

*Mrs. Starry, who often supplanted her name with an "e"
scrawled in after a careless five-point of the variety often
replacing red inked smiles atop a careful student's paper,
was a pale woman with curly dark hair and rather sharp
features. She had been an active thespian throughout her
college years and now, with a classroom of boisterous kids
under her gentle control, she produced casually frequent
classroom plays to the students' delight.*

*Perhaps my remembrances are slightly clouded with
nostalgia, but it seems to me that those two final years of
elementary school were the two finest for several years
before or after.*

*Mrs. Starry had a knack for engaging students at their
particular level, a penchant for drawing the best from
everyone.*

Spelling was dependent upon ability, reading materials chosen by the particular student. My language requirements were traded for public viewing of amateur claymation made at home with a camcorder capable, if clicked rapidly enough, of half-second frames. I participated in a self-initiated pull-out program in math with books borrowed from the junior high school up the street. We learned in units, no lecture save an occasional jest that the projects we submitted were too numerous.

Mrs. Starry was a catalyst of sorts, the type of dynamically irrepressible person that draws groups together and force-forges lasting friendships simply by introducing two people.

It was her gentle insistence and unconcealed exuberance that pulled the three disparate social landscapes of the other fifth and sixth grade classes into a united whole, studying and competing as a single heterogeneously huge group.

By the end of my fifth grade year, incidentally Mrs. Starry's first at the school, she held enough trust and clout with administrators and parents to have her odd ideas not only taken seriously but often accepted. Her unorthodox plan was to spend the last week of school, time usually reserved for finding out how many times a student will put up with cleaning his or her desk, in a cabined camp in the nearby mountains.

The Environmental Field Trip, as the trip was termed, rose as a huge success, an example of iconoclastic education at its best. The week was composed of multitudinous small quirks of intellectual stimulation, from conservation tactics to long, rambling walks.

There, amongst the subtly vanilla-scented Ponderosas of Idaho's hills, I came to understand new things about the nuisance of school. I had never before conceived of it as a place for personal growth, but I have never since forgotten its potential.

References

Stanley, J. C. (1976). The case for extreme educational acceleration of
    intellectually brilliant youths. *Gifted Child Quarterly, 20*(1), 66-75,
    41.

For Further Reading

Full-Time Schools and Full-Time Self-Contained Classrooms for the Gifted

Governors' Schools (State residential high schools for the gifted).
    http://www.ncogs.org/ (22 Feb. 2003).

NAGC Summer and Enrichment Programs and Special Schools for the
    Gifted. http://www.nagc.org/summer/02intro.htm (22 Feb. 2003).

Schools for the Gifted (list). http://www.hoagiesgifted.org/schools.htm
    (22 Feb. 2003).

Grade/Subject Acceleration

Texas Tech University Extended Studies/Texas Tech University School
    District. Offers distance-learning courses and the opportunity to
    test out of grades and courses using the "credit by examination"
    program, K-12, in an accredited public school sponsored by Texas
    Tech University.
    http://www.dce.ttu.edu/TTUiSD/ttues.asp (22 Feb. 2003).

Advanced High School Programs

Advanced Placement (AP) Program Website, including AP course
    descriptions and syllabi.
    http://apcentral.collegeboard.com/program/0,1289,150-0-0-
    0,00.html (22 Feb. 2003).

International Baccalaureate Organization (IBO).
    http://www.ibo.org/ (22 Feb. 2003).

States with Post-Secondary Options Acts- Many states have a state law that allows gifted and academically advanced high school students to take college courses at public expense, including ME, IA, CO, and MN, among others. Check with your state Department of Education consultant in gifted education to find out if your state has such a law.

Computer-Based, Online, and Correspondence

Center for Talent Development Northwestern University. http://www.ctd.northwestern.edu/ (22 Feb. 2003).

Coastside EPGY Alternative. http://armadillosoft.com/epgy/faq.php (22 Feb. 2003).

EPGY (Education Program for Gifted Youth), Ventura Hall, Stanford University, Stanford, CA 94305-4115, (800) 372 EPGY, (650) 329-9920. http://www-epgy.stanford.edu/ (22 Feb. 2003).

Hollingworth Center for Highly Gifted Children (a national support and resource network focused on the needs of highly gifted). http://www.hollingworth.org/ (22 Feb. 2003).

Independent Study High School, University of Nebraska, P.O. Box 839400, Lincoln, NE 68583-9400, (402) 472-4422. http://dcs.unl.edu/ishs/ (22 Feb. 2003).

Internet Academy [K-12], 32020 1st Avenue South, #109, Federal Way, WA 98003-5743, (253) 945-2230. http://www.iacademy.org/ (22 Feb. 2003).

Kentucky Migrant Technology Project. Very low-cost, standards-based, online distance learning courses. http://www.migrant.org/ (22 Feb. 2003).

Northwestern's Learning Links Program. http://www.ctd.north-western.edu/programs/ll/program.html (28 Oct. 2002).

Virtual School for the Gifted. http://www.vsg.edu.au/ (22 Feb. 2003).

Homeschooling

Center for Distance Education (Johns Hopkins-CTY). http://cty.jhu.edu/cde/ (22 Feb. 2003).

Feldman, J. H. (1986). *Nature's gambit: Child prodigies and the development of human potential.* New York: Basic Books.

Free Firewood (free online course resources compiled by Kathi Kearney). http://www.ignitethefire.com/freefirewood.html (22 Feb. 2003).

Free Online High School Courses. http://www.homeschoolersof-maine.org/high_school_&_beyond.htm#Free%20Online%20Courses (22 Feb. 2003).

Gold, L. M. & Zielinski, J. M. (2000). *Homeschool Your Child For Free*. Roseville, CA: Prima Publishing.

Growing Without Schooling. http://www.holtgws.com/ (22 Feb. 2003).

Hollingworth Center for Highly Gifted Children (click on homeschooling). http://www.hollingworth.org/ (22 Feb. 2003).

Home Education Magazine-resources on homeschooling, state laws, etc. http://www.home-ed-magazine.com/ (22 Feb. 2003).

HSLDA Home School Legal Defense Association, P.O. Box 3000, Purcellville, VA 20134-9000 · Phone: (540) 338-5600, Fax: (540) 338-2733, E-mail: info@hslda.org.

Kearney, K. (1984, May/June). At home in Maine: Gifted children and homeschooling. *G/C/T*, May/June, Issue Number 33, 16-19.

Kearney; K. (1989). Homeschooling gifted children. *Understanding Our Gifted*, *1*(3), 1, 12-13, 15-16, 20.

Rivero, L. (2000). *Gifted education comes home: A case for self-directed homeschooling*. Manassas, VA: Gifted Education Press.

Rivero, L. (2002). *Creative homeschooling for gifted children: A resource guide*. Scottsdale, AZ: Great Potential Press

Suzy (no additional name listed), Home schooling- a family affair. http://www.hoagiesgifted.org/home_schooling.htm (22 Feb. 2003).

Wallace, N. (1983). *Better than school*. Burdett, NY: Larson Publications.

Westbridge Academy. http://www.flash.net/~wx3o/westbridge/ (22 Feb. 2003).

Choosing Schools

Silverman, L. K. & Leviton, L. (1991). In search of the perfect program. *Gifted Child Today*, *14*(6), 31-34.

8

Models of Advocacy for Parents

Once we realize that a gifted child needs our help to improve an inadequate educational program, we have to decide what form our advocacy will take. Do we contact the child's teacher and ask for modifications? Or, fearing that the teacher may not be willing or allowed to make the necessary changes, must the principal be approached first? Or, is this an appropriate matter for the counselor because the child is unhappy in school...or the school psychologist because the child's abilities may suggest unusual needs? Is there a gifted and talented coordinator in the building (perhaps a teacher or paraprofessional hired for this purpose) who could help?

When the issues occur in a public school, must we go beyond the level of the individual school to the district level? Does the school district have a gifted and talented coordinator who might be responsible for such cases? Are there other district-level administrators who could lead such an effort? Finally, what do district regulations and state laws say about gifted education that would support such a request? Are there legal ramifications for the school denying accommodations?

Is it helpful to become a member of the school's *gifted committee* or the *school improvement team* or some type of site-based advisory/accountability committee within the child's school (given that most schools today give considerable power to committees consisting of teachers, parents, and school administrators)? What about member-ship in the school district's gifted advisory committee? Could changes be made that benefit not only this student but others, as well? Or, if state laws are inadequate, would legislative efforts be in order? When a child is suffering, where do we place our energy and direct our efforts for change?

Demonstrate a Documented Need

To have any chance of success asking for significant accommodations from school personnel at any level, we must first be able to show a documented need. If the child has already been identified for the school's gifted program, then his or her *giftedness* is not in question, but we need to provide reasons for the accommodations we are seeking. If the child has not been identified for the gifted program, or there is no program, we have more work to do to justify need. Most schools will require the child be identified as a gifted student before considering accommodations. As discussed in Chapter 3, Testing Considerations, the educational evaluation supports our request by documenting a need that other professionals would support. IQ tests provide the basis for entry into the gifted program, or gifted accommodations in general, by justifying the overall need for challenging programming and faster instructional pace. Achievement tests provide the necessary ammunition for requested changes in instructional level.

Schools are proud of their programs and teachers work hard to meet the needs of their students. When parents ask for changes they are, in effect, saying the program or teacher is inadequate. Documentation allows the discussion with school personnel to focus on finding appropriate solutions for the child ("We've discovered our child has these needs...") and helps teachers avoid feelings of personal failure or defensiveness. For parents, it can be difficult enough to approach school personnel about needed changes with such documentation in hand. Few want to be in the position of saying, "Our child is gifted and needs special accommodations." Without documentation, it is difficult to counter the arguments school personnel often make that the standard program is adequate.

Follow the Chain of Command

Assuming the child's giftedness has been documented and there is no question that this child will probably need some accommodations, the next step can begin. Most longtime gifted advocates would advise parents to follow the chain of command, beginning with the person closest to the child: the classroom teacher. When a child is already enrolled and attending a school, this is the best place to start when inadequacies in the school program are apparent and we have information about what is needed.

Arrange a Conference with the Teacher

In such situations, it is usually best to arrange a conference with the teacher to discuss concerns. Many times, the teacher is somewhat unaware of the extent of the child's abilities and lacks training in how to deal with them. It is essential that such meetings be as upbeat, honest, respectful of the teacher, and oriented to finding "joint" solutions as possible. It is best not to go to the school in anger, not to demand specifics, and not to imply that this is entirely the teacher's problem—the parents have no responsibility. Parents need to be reasonable partners of the teacher in the education of this child. In most cases, the teacher is concerned about the child and is willing to try some varied instructional approaches.

Test results give us a starting point. For example, they can provide information about a child's advanced math capabilities and a recommendation from the tester that the child needs accelerated work can initiate a discussion about how to provide that. Or, achievement test scores that show a second-grader is reading at the seventh-grade level can spark consideration of literature options and whether it would be better to have the child attend a higher-grade-level reading group.

Parents can also provide anecdotal data about what the child is doing at home. Does a first-grader have a chemistry lab in the basement and an already large store of knowledge in science? Or, has a third-grader already published poetry? Some parents have created portfolios of their children's advanced work, which can be invaluable when trying to convince teachers of a need for higher level instruction.

Bring an Expert

Where appropriate, it can be helpful to bring an expert along. We at the GDC have been asked many times to attend meetings at the school or to speak with a teacher or principal on the phone locally or long distance. Sometimes parents even bring a teacher to the post-test conference. The *expert* can usually discuss the child's needs with the teacher easily, whereas parents find this to be more difficult. I find it easier to advocate for children with whom I've worked than my own. Parents of the gifted are painfully sensitive to the perception that they are *elitist* and asking for accommodations for an advantaged child. Likewise, they are often perceived as *just parents* by school personnel, regardless of their expertise in gifted education issues, and experts have some advantage presenting the necessary arguments on the child's behalf. (I have used my colleagues at the GDC in school meetings about my own children for this reason.)

Create an IEP

Ideally, some kind of Individual Educational Plan (IEP) would be devised for the child as a result of meetings with the teacher. It need not be lengthy or complicated, but it should address the basic needs of the child. An IEP usually includes modifications in every subject area where something different is needed. If the child is advanced in math and science, the IEP should include modifications in the teaching of math and science. English and social studies can be left alone and not included in the IEP. Perhaps accommodations are needed in only one subject area—or all of them. The IEP is the plan that corrects the deficiencies of the regular program. The IEP may also include some *extras*. Perhaps the child will work with a mentor in some area of interest or participate in other activities outside of the classroom. These kinds of accommodations are added to support passions, develop talents, and encourage interests not directly related to classroom instruction. If the teacher is willing to devise a plan, it is best to include the child in the planning process. However, this should be done only when it is clear the teacher is willing to consider modifications. The child should not be involved in a rancorous meeting with a teacher who is unwilling to consider any changes.

Obtaining an IEP that attempts to meet the child's needs for that year, in a reasonable way, is a very positive accomplishment. However, all parties need to view it as a best guess for what will benefit the child. If something is not working, the plan should be revisited. Parents need to let the teacher have flexibility to try things and flexibility to fail. There are no certain ways of ensuring success with these children, but a positive plan developed by all parties is a wonderful start.

Meet With the Principal

If, on the other hand, parents approach a teacher and receive an absolute refusal to consider modifications, or the teacher has been generally reluctant to make agreed-upon changes over several months, it is time to contact the principal. Principals vary in their willingness to support parents when there is parent-teacher friction. The best principals will try to make everyone happy, either working for a compromise or considering the child's placement with another teacher. Although principals today tend not to rule with an iron hand (site-based committees and teachers retain considerable power) they are the most powerful individuals within their schools and have the most influence. If a principal is willing to accommodate a child's needs, he or she often knows about many options within the school. For example, the principal may be able to choose a teacher who has strengths and interests compatible with those of the child. Where a principal is willing to get involved, the child has an important ally.

Counselors, School Psychologists, and G/T Coordinators

Counselors and school psychologists tend to be less influential than teachers and principals. They can offer input, but usually do not make binding decisions about what will happen in the classroom. Likewise, building G/T coordinators can usually only offer some enrichment opportunities, brief pull-out options, or ideas for teachers, but cannot determine classroom modifications.

Involving District Personnel

If the teacher and principal have shown no support for accommodations for the child, district personnel can be contacted. We have seen cases of teachers stubbornly asserting that a child has no special needs and of principals backing them up. Some principals will blatantly admit that they are uncomfortable with giftedness and some will assert that all children are gifted, effectively blocking most accommodations. The school districts we have dealt with all acknowledge responsibility for gifted students, but are usually reluctant to bring any considerable, immediate pressure to bear on a principal reluctant to comply. A number of such complaints might make a difference in the results of the next periodic evaluation the principal undergoes. However, district involvement is not likely to be swift and decisive. Only where strict laws apply outlining services for the gifted can immediate help be obtained. School districts do not want lawsuits. Unfortunately, for most of us residing in states with *softer* mandates, district administrators will not solve our immediate problems.

District personnel can often help us in another way, however. Usually privy to what is going on in the various schools in the district, they can suggest school choices. They know which principals support gifted children, which ones have a background in gifted education, which are more flexible, and which are likely to accommodate parents in this situation. They can inform us of special program options and provide test scores from various schools. They know where the math teacher works who has taught the district's best mathematicians. When parents have a serious need, district personnel often have some ideas, if approached in a positive, problem-solving manner.

Pursue Committee Membership When You Have Extra Time

Some parents have sought membership in school committees, hoping to support changes in their child's classroom via changes in school policy. Although the need for schools across the country to better accommodate gifted students is immense, membership tends to produce small improvements in policy, if any, which are often abandoned once the individuals who propose the changes leave the committee. Furthermore, committee decisions are rarely binding; they usually address goals, but have no real clout. Making a difference in this way, though a noble cause, should be pursued only with "extra time," when the needs of our children in the classroom have basically been met.

I spent a considerable amount of time on committees, but I consider my time within the school district best spent helping to organize a charter school. Committee work was time consuming, filled with the frustration of never having a real mandate for gifted education, and seemed to produce so little. For example, I served on a middle school talented and gifted committee that seemed to meet simply to exchange ideas. I had been asked to attend by the principal and said "yes" because the school's gifted accommodations were so poor. On one occasion, I spoke about the need to engage the abstract reasoning ability of gifted children when teaching them. I was quickly told by the principal that this was impossible because the majority of middle school students had not matured sufficiently for their abstract reasoning ability to be in place. When I asked, "But what about the children who can reason abstractly?" I was given a blank look. They were committed to hands-on instruction, concrete learning, and an avoidance of abstraction.

One small committee success I recall was being on an elementary *school improvement team* and proposing a school goal to modify curriculum in one subject area within the classroom for each identified gifted student. The goal was approved because it was combined with a similar goal for developmentally disabled students, and educators at the time liked the idea of heterogeneous classrooms where students had unusual needs met through *individualization*. The committee also passed a third achievement goal that year for all students. An advantage of the goal for the gifted was that teachers had to make a plan to enrich or accelerate curriculum by October 1st of each year, effectively forcing some planning for each gifted child. The next year, the committee agreed to extend the goal to "all academic areas necessary" and the resulting procedure made a difference for a few years. Teachers filled out brief IEPs for each gifted child by October 1st. Interestingly, there was considerable resistance from the teachers the first year because there were three goals passed and the teachers expected only one. We were asking too much of them. Yet, it was clear one school goal relating only to gifted children would never have been passed. Unfortunately, the process was finally stopped for lack of support in the building.

In the past 15 years, I have seen our public school district begin three different district-level gifted committees in succession. Each was charged with the responsibility of defining *giftedness*, determining the needs of the gifted, and finding ways schools could meet these needs. Each committee took considerable time to create a body of work, which was largely recreated by the next group. When I worked with the second of the three committees, our efforts resulted in large notebooks of *good ideas* sent to each school. G/T services in our district remain largely voluntary, vary considerably with each school, and are subject mostly to mandates to identify and count the students. What was most clear from that work was the feeling of frustration parents had. Some came to our meetings saying that they had chosen our district because of what they had read about our programs for the gifted. "But, now that we're here, there is just nothing!" many said. Like my older colleagues at the GDC, I've tempered my optimism that things will change significantly, short of a massive change in laws at the state level.

Even when committee work produces some measurable improvement for a group of gifted students, it rarely affects a specific child's classroom situation and is best pursued by parent advocates who have already solved their children's current educational issues. Many of the most successful advocates dealing with state laws have grown children and are now able to commit the time necessary.

When Do We Give Up?

When the classroom situation remains inadequate, the teacher is defensive, the child is unhappy, the principal offers no reasonable alternatives, and no district help seems forthcoming, it is best to try to find another placement for the child. It is at this point that our own natural need to fight injustice and to insist that the school meet its ethical (and possibly legal) responsibility to educate a gifted child adequately must be set aside. Why? Because resistant teachers rarely respond appropriately when pressure is applied and sensitive gifted children are easily damaged. Parents encountering such a situation must act first to protect the child. Such was the case with Joshua.

Joshua's parents contacted the GDC because their nine-year-old son had refused to go to school and had been at home for the past month. The family had relocated to a neighboring state for the purpose of placing Joshua in a public *Extended Learning* program that would ostensibly meet his needs as a gifted student. What Joshua found, however, was a program with extensive drill and practice (which he did not require to learn) and homework that took him three to four hours a night to complete. The program seemed to his parents to have gifted and high achieving students and a teacher oriented to the students working very hard. Joshua had been moved to the fourth grade from second and had earned virtually all A's in the first half of the year. However, in January, he had had enough and refused to attend.

A sensitive, sometimes anxious boy, he had gone from loving school to being school phobic. Joshua had a history of chronic ear infections, as well as asthma and allergies, and hypersensitive hearing. A child who refused to go to movies without ear protection, he was a member of a large, noisy class with a teacher who yelled frequently when students misbehaved. She had difficulty controlling classroom behavior and seemed pushed to the limit. There was also some sense that she didn't enjoy teaching children this young, having formerly taught a higher grade level. Furthermore, Joshua struggled with handwriting and was slower than others completing paper-and-pencil tasks (no doubt adding to his homework time). He had difficulty working in the noisy classroom and, at times, missed recesses finishing written work.

When Joshua arrived for the testing, which had been arranged to clarify his needs, he seemed anxious, but was soon smiling and very talkative. As several subjects were broached, he spoke in a happy, animated manner. However, when asked about school, Joshua's anxiety increased dramatically. He began to stutter as he spoke about his teacher yelling frequently, his class becoming unruly, the noisiness of the room, and his difficulty getting work done in that environment. Only as we became involved in other activities did Joshua appear calmer.

Joshua's parents had tried to talk with the school about modifying their son's program. He did not need all of the drill and practice and would have benefited greatly from reduced writing assignments, emphasizing quality over quantity. He needed a quiet place to work and they had asked if he could go to the library if he became overstimulated. All requests had been initially denied before Joshua was brought to the GDC. The teacher seemed defensive in regard to him. Both the school and a private psychologist who had worked with Joshua were waiting for our recommendations before deciding what to do.

We felt that Joshua needed a full-time gifted program, with a small class size and a plan to accommodate his sensory integration deficits and giftedness. Under no circumstances should he return to his previous classroom because it was overstimulating and extremely stressful for him. Because there was no classroom appropriate for his full-time placement, we suggested a home-based teacher for half of each day (school districts will sometimes provide these), with part-time placement in another, gentler teacher's classroom to enable Joshua to interact with his friends (several important friendships had been made with other gifted boys and Joshua missed his friends terribly). He needed considerably less drill and repetition and would be able to complete most academic work in half the day. Because he was very advanced in math, we suggested a computer-based math instruction program from a university (EPGY) that could be done with the help of the home-based teacher. We felt that if Joshua became overstimulated and anxious at school (common in children with sensory integration issues), he should be allowed to go to the library. He was a responsible boy who would use his time wisely. Writing done on a word processor and headphones to reduce noise were suggested, as well as relaxation techniques.

When Joshua's parents returned with our recommendations, school personnel refused to provide a home-based teacher and offered to put Joshua back into the same classroom with an IEP. His parents were worried about this offer and called to ask our opinion. Given Joshua's extreme anxiety about his school situation and the fact that the teacher was stressed herself and had been resistant to accommodations, this was not a situation we could recommend. Instead, we suggested further negotiations with the school for other options, and we recommended connecting with an expert in the homeschooling of gifted children, until another placement could be found.

Joshua's parents acted appropriately when they allowed him to stay at home and they sought outside help. They had even noted his increasing calmness after time at home following a stressful climax of tension in the classroom. Their fears about his returning to his previous classroom were absolutely justified. Though we would like a simple solution to present itself in such situations, capitulating to the school's plan was not that solution. We have seen children so damaged by their school experiences that counseling and considerable time were necessary to help them. When parents pull a child out of school suddenly, they are usually correct about the need to do so.

Interviewing Principals and Choosing a School

This section is offered with a father from Texas in mind. Living in a small town with his wife and two gifted children, he was concerned about having no schools for the gifted and no gifted program options as he saw them for his children. Realizing his dilemma, I immediately began to explain how he might address his children's lack of challenge in school— how he might visit the schools in his area, meet principals and talk about how his children's needs might be met in each school, in order to choose the best placement for them. He looked at me and said, "You might be able to do that, but I wouldn't know where to start." This is for all the parents who feel the same way.

It is often difficult to modify poor school situations, but we can take a proactive approach to the education of the gifted. Even though most communities lack full-time, self-contained schools for the gifted, many have excellent, flexible teachers and some programs that stand a better chance of being good placements for gifted students. Across the country, there is movement within public school districts to offer *schools of choice*: alternative schools, magnet schools, and charter schools. Often the neighborhood school is not the only choice for parents now, but even neighborhood schools are trying to develop unique programs to compete with attractive alternatives. Our school district publishes a guide to school choices with a brief summary about each school's focus and offerings. Parents can request several choices for the coming year by a deadline in February and be advised of admission possibilities. Though many schools impose a lottery system because requests outnumber openings, the opportunity for real choice should not be ignored. We have noted at the GDC that it is generally easier to find a more appropriate teacher or school for a child than to effect substantial change in the child's current inadequate program.

If any school appears attractive, it is important to meet with school personnel and learn more about it. When principals are willing to meet or speak on the phone about accommodating an unusual child, that is a very good sign that they value the differential needs of the gifted. Principals vary enormously in their knowledge of giftedness, appreciation of learning differences, willingness to suggest teachers and appropriate options, and flexibility. Such conversations are very revealing. Does the principal automatically begin thinking of ways to meet the child's needs in his or her school? Is there willingness to set aside usual policy in placing a child? Many gifted students need work that is accelerated beyond what typical students their age are offered. Will the principal allow placement at the level of the child's mastery?

In middle schools, can the student study at various grade levels as needed or must he or she stay with age peers in block-scheduled classes? In high schools, can the gifted student skip the entry-level course for freshmen or start with Advanced Placement courses in an academic subject area where he or she is particularly advanced? Can a child visit the program, either the classroom of the most appropriate elementary teacher (in the principal's view), or, in middle or high school, classes in favorite subject areas? The budding high school scientist may want to visit the school's best teachers of chemistry, biology and physics, whereas the advanced writer may want to view AP English. Given such options, with student input, parents can choose the most flexible, supportive program for the particular gifted child and have a better chance (nothing's perfect) of a successful placement.

Homeschooling

When there appear to be no options within the local schools, or the options are simply unacceptable, an increasing number of families are turning to homeschooling. Once the approach taken to educate many of our most gifted learners, homeschooling is especially suited to children with unusual needs. Not only can the subjects be chosen that a child will study and the appropriate level offered, but instructional pace can be adjusted for the learner, an almost impossible element to modify within typical schools. Although the prospect seems daunting to many, homeschooling offers freedom available nowhere else.

The GDC is associated with one of the country's most knowledgeable resources in the homeschooling of gifted children: Kathi Kearney. Kathi tells us that homeschooling is growing at a phenomenal rate as public schools continue to offer less-than-optimal support for gifted learning needs. She notes that there are generally two homeschooling organizations in every state: a secular group and a Christian group. State organizations are further affiliated with numerous support groups. Parents considering the prospect of homeschooling are wise to contact these groups, which offer both support and information about resources available in the area. The groups are knowledgeable about state laws and are usually superior to local school district offices in interpreting them.

Kathi Kearney is a wealth of information herself on available resources, including free coursework available online (she helped compile many of the resources presented in this book). A longtime tester and educator, she is practiced in developing curricula, although she agrees some gifted children can lay waste to the best planned curricula, as they master concepts much more quickly than anticipated. She is also knowledgeable about learning styles and can suggest ways to teach children that will be most effective, using their testing information (Kathi is the consummate tester of gifted children). Parents can find her articles, annotated bibliographies, and resource lists on various websites: The Hollingworth Center for Highly Gifted Children (a support group she started); Hoagies' Gifted; PG-CyberSource, and The Gifted Development Center (see pp. 399, 401).

Homeschooling offers ultimate choice. The parents of one large homeschooled family created for each of their children a "grand plan." Designed to meet the needs of each child, the plan contained specific goals that needed to be met, but within a timeframe chosen by each child. The children completed these at various times, ranging from a fairly typical number of years in school to very few. The students in the family determined their own rate of acceleration.

Kathi's overall understanding of gifted curriculum and instruction allows her to see education in very atypical ways and to consider possibilities that have not occurred to most. She tells the story of an eight-year-old girl with whom she worked, who quickly accelerated in elementary school and was frustrated in her efforts to learn what she wanted. The little girl hoped to learn French, which was not offered at her elementary school. So, her mother, a college student, suggested she could study the language on her own or take a high school correspondence course (through the University of Nebraska Independent Study High School). Though the girl was willing to do either of these things, she asked if it wouldn't be better to take the course with other people so that she could speak with them in French. Why couldn't she go with her mother to college and take a course there? This initiated a discussion about the difference between courses at different levels, and the girl's mother explained that courses at higher levels progressed more quickly. The little girl pondered this and concluded that if all of the beginning French courses started at the same level, but progressed at different rates, then why couldn't she take one that progressed quickly? In the end, the college her mother attended allowed her to take beginning French and she did well. This launched a whole series of college courses that the little girl loved.

Because many of the GDC's clients have become disenchanted with school by the time we see them, I asked Kathi if homeschooling could still be a reasonable alternative for them. Can children become too jaded to be homeschooled successfully? She noted that it is not uncommon for families beginning homeschooling to need a period of "deschooling" before they can actually begin. As the term suggests, some of these children need an extended vacation from school and the situations that were oppressive for them, before they can regain an appreciation for education. They need time to rekindle the natural curiosity they were born with and to rediscover the love of learning that allows them to pursue studies in depth. Such was the case for the son of one mother we know.

Jean, a mother of three, stands out as an advocate because she has consistently relied on her own instincts, research, and homeschooling efforts to meet the needs of her children. When her eldest child, a son, was experiencing boredom and stress at school, the school offered to evaluate him. Administration of the WISC-III yielded a Full Scale IQ score of 124; however, his mother questioned this score. She had received considerable information and support from other parents of gifted children on the Internet, and used this to correctly diagnose the higher ability we were later able to document with his evaluation at the GDC. In fact, Jean correctly assumed her children were all highly gifted and suffering from AD/HD. When she received no support from anyone in her area, she packed the kids into the car and drove them to the GDC in Colorado to have them all tested. We absolutely agreed with her diagnoses and were able to help with additional suggestions.

Jean and her husband had removed their son from school after first grade, before he was tested with us at age 9,

realizing that it was not going to be a successful placement
for him. Jean continues today to be a happy homeschooling
mom of her three children, but admits that a period of
deschooling was necessary for her eldest. He was "too
sensitive for that environment (overwhelmed, distracted,
upset by other kids' actions and inabilities)." His love of
learning was disappearing and he developed nervous habits,
tics, and stomachaches. Since his removal from school,
these had stopped and he had become curious again.
Because the boy was positive for AD/HD, exhibiting both
symptoms of Inattention and Hyperactivity/Impulsivity,
homeschooling was ideal because his mother could make
sure he was spending most of his time with new, novel
material and progressing quickly. He had the opportunity to
move ahead as soon as he mastered concepts. This minimizes attentional deficits by emphasizing high-interest
material that is more engaging.

Because her son earned a Stanford-Binet Intelligence
Scale—Form L-M IQ score of 152, radical acceleration would
be appropriate. We were able to confirm with his achievement scores in the 150s, as well, that he was being
challenged appropriately in his homeschooling program.

Choices in Advocacy

When a gifted child faces an unacceptable classroom
situation, parents need to act to solve the problem.
Sometimes the best choice is to work with the school and
current teacher to provide accommodations; sometimes it is
to move to another classroom, grade, or entirely different
school; and sometimes it is best to remove a child from
school. Parents should trust themselves to assess the level
of need, but always know that the cumulative effect of a
child not having his or her needs met over a long period of
time is negative. There is no benefit to teaching a child to
graciously accept being held back.

Most parents choose to keep their gifted children in school, and it is often possible to support a reasonable education there. One couple comes to mind as excellent advocates for their daughters. Joyce and John first learned to advocate for their autistic daughter, whom they realized would not have a reasonable education, regardless of the support of law, without their involvement. Having educated themselves as fully as possible about her needs and learned about advocating successfully for her, they were then needed to advocate for their younger, highly gifted daughter. They have learned some interesting lessons.

First, they have realized the need to become experts about their daughters' situations. They have had them assessed and learned what they could from professionals. They participate in support groups and read the latest books available. Second, they understand that teachers also need help in learning about autism and high levels of giftedness. However, they feel teacher in-services are not especially effective. John notes that teachers need access to information and expert advice, but that they also need to "buy in." He believes that teachers appreciate help more when the expert can meet with the teacher, and the teacher can then formulate ideas for working with the child.

John and Joyce have had to ask for many things from their schools, but they have also been helpful members of their schools' communities, willing to volunteer their time and energy when needed. They have made every effort to approach school personnel with courtesy and patience, knowing that some of their requests may require some *processing time*. I attended a meeting of teachers, the principal, and counselor with them to discuss the grade acceleration of their daughter. They asked me to explain testing results and provide more general information, as needed. While the meeting produced the expected concerns by the staff about the child's social development being hampered, Joyce and John's kind, reasonable approach allowed school personnel, who were also kind and reasonable people, to consider the issues without prejudice and decide what would be best for the child. While some teachers still had reservations, a plan was made to allow the girl to visit an accelerated classroom and have contact with the counselor about her experience.

Joyce and John's daughter formally accelerated, found skipping a grade a relative non-issue (as it usually is for children who are bored and asking for more challenge), and is happier in her new classroom. Especially satisfying to her recently was an advanced rocks and minerals project that involved crystal structures she both grew and constructed with Zometools®. Special support was provided by her new teacher for this project. He even invited several younger gifted children, who had an interest in crystals, to his classroom to see her models.

For Further Reading

Hoagies' Gifted Education Page (click on advocacy).
     http://www.hoagiesgifted.com/advocacy.htm (19 Feb. 2003).

LaBonte, K, & Russell, C. (1999, Spring/Summer). Preparing for and
     holding an effective school meeting, *Highly Gifted Children, 12*(4).

Lloyd, M. P. The tea and terrorist society: Parent advocacy at the
     district level. *Highly Gifted Children, 12*(3), The Hollingworth
     Center. http://www.ditd.org/floater.php?location=31
     (19 Feb. 2003).

Neville, C. (1997, Spring). Portfolio: An effective way to present your
     child to the school. *Highly Gifted Children, 11*(1).

9

Teachers of the Gifted

What are the qualities that define a wonderful teacher of the gifted? The parent seeking to ensure a good classroom placement for a gifted child naturally hopes to find the teacher who will see the child's strengths and nurture them in a way that allows for true growth. Likewise, the teacher who wants to truly support a gifted student hopes to find strategies that aid in planning and programming, dealing with social and emotional issues, and interacting with parents and fellow teachers to meet needs. Many of the children profiled in this book have had negative experiences with teachers at some point, yet wonderful teachers of the gifted do inspire such children and change their lives profoundly. What qualities raise a teacher's competence in dealing with gifted educational needs?

Particularly in the case of the elementary school teacher, who generally has the child for all academic subjects, the teacher is a pivotal individual in the child's life for a full school year. But, even in middle and high schools, where a student has multiple teachers, finding the teachers who have high academic standards and support advanced students is important to the gifted student's continued motivation to learn. At all levels of education, the gifted child is a special needs student, unlikely to be adequately educated with the typical curriculum, and is dependent on the choice of teacher for accommodations not usually mandated by law. Having a teacher who values teaching the gifted student and knows how to accomplish it successfully is critical. Teachers have different personalities, backgrounds, and strengths; some are known to be kind and supportive, others are especially effective with children who struggle. What kind of teacher best supports the gifted child? Profiled below are a group of excellent teachers for the gifted, who offer their experience and insights to us about how best to teach gifted students.

Lin Greene: Teaching Gifted Elementary Students

Youthful and spirited, Lin Greene's presence belies her 31 years of experience as an elementary school educator. In 1994, we co-authored an article in *Understanding Our Gifted* ("Challenging Ben") about individualizing a second grade curriculum for a profoundly gifted child. Lin had an impressive record of meeting the needs of a variety of children in her classrooms, and models of individualizing for the gifted within a heterogeneous classroom were desperately needed. She continued to work her special brand of magic with second graders until a year ago, when she retired from the public schools. She strongly believes in empowering children to set goals for themselves and become independent learners.

Make a Written Plan

Lin Greene feels a good first step to take to accommodate a gifted child in her classroom is to make a written plan. The plan, however brief, requires careful consideration of the child's learning needs at the beginning of the year and throughout the time spent in her class. Superior to simply making multiple, unrelated efforts to enrich, the plan acknowledges that a child will come into the classroom with certain knowledge in every subject and will need to make appropriate progress during the year in all academic areas. Lin believes it is important to start early. Ideally, the teacher should sit down with the parents even before school starts. The parents have unique knowledge of their child and can share with the teacher what the child's strengths are (e.g., advanced reading or math skills, or high-level knowledge and interest in science), as well as discuss areas in need of improvement (e.g., organizational skills such as *follow through*, slowness or difficulty with handwriting, poor knowledge of math facts, or a significant learning disability).

Next, Lin Greene suggests that the group meet a month later to finalize the plan. By this time, the teacher has also had time to assess strengths and weaknesses and get better acquainted with the child. In addition, the teacher now knows the options to be offered during the year within the school that may not have been finalized prior to the start of school. For example, the Toastmasters may be willing to provide a weekly opportunity for students to learn the fine art of public speaking, or a retired math teacher may have agreed to serve as a mentor.

Once the needs and options are clear, the parents and teacher should agree to an overall plan for the year, but meet quarterly to review it. Things can change. An initial plan can prove less interesting to the child, or a program they thought would be available may not have materialized. The quarterly meetings allow the teacher to "stay on the same page with the parent." Lin found that some parents would come in and talk with her, but others felt they were intruding or simply didn't have the time. "Please schedule it," she advises. Then, everyone knows what the child is doing and how it is being done. She also agrees that it is important to include the child, if possible, especially if he or she is verbal. A gifted kindergartener might find this difficult, but most gifted second-graders can add important information to the planning process that adults cannot provide.

Look for an Advanced Placement in a Subject of Strength

"One thing I like to do is see if another class besides the general classroom will fit the gifted child," Lin Greene advises. Perhaps the child can be placed in a higher grade level for math or participate in a more advanced reading group. Is the child mature enough to handle leaving the classroom and coming back in? Since many plans are best implemented with the child going alone from the home class-room to another, teachers don't want to lose the child going or coming. At seven years of age, that's important. Yet most gifted second-graders view such an opportunity as a welcome challenge and handle the responsibility beautifully, even learning to know when it's time to leave without being reminded.

Next, make compromises with the other teacher. Lin always believed it was especially helpful to let higher-grade-level teachers know she was available to help if one of their children needed remediation. She could offer to take such a child into her classroom for additional help. This would allow her to help a teacher whom she might, at another time, need to ask to take an accelerated child. Likewise, Lin was always willing to take accelerated younger children into her class. However, she admits this was not a normal occur-rence for many teachers. Because the teacher is ultimately responsible for every child in the classroom, whether a child leaves or not, taking on one more can seem daunting. "You already have 30 children, now you have 31," Lin explains, and the receiving teacher must accept two additional parents and another teacher checking on how she or he is doing with the child. This may be more than the teacher feels she can do. However, Lin concludes that such placements are worth pursuing. "You have to make the compromises if you're the teacher sending the child. But I think it's good for the child's morale. They will put up with a lot if they feel that their needs are being met."

Once placement in another classroom has been arranged, Lin Greene, as the general homeroom teacher, considers what she needs to teach the child in preparation for the new classroom placement. Whether it is cursive, multiplication facts, long division, or regrouping, Lin wants to ensure that the child knows all entry-level tasks that the other teacher's class already knows. "You can teach those tasks to a gifted child quickly. Of course," Lin admits, "there is no extra time to do this." It must be done during the lunch hour or recess, and the gifted student may be running up at inopportune moments asking for another long multiplication problem during social studies. However, Lin concludes, "Be flexible enough to do that because it's going to be so helpful to them."

She feels it's important to help a gifted child to feel good about where he or she is going and the results that are happening—how the student is moving along—because so many of the problems occur when gifted students see themselves stagnating, unable to use any of the talents that they have. "If you can make that happen right away...usually a gifted child has one area—math, reading, writing—that you can facilitate the extension of, right away in September. It's not something you have to spend weeks on—they can go immediately."

What Level of Advanced Work Does the Child Need?

Lin Greene admits that it was helpful to her in making placement decisions to have taught all of the elementary grades, one to six, during her career. She knew the academic levels of children beginning each grade and adds that those were quite different from the levels at which students finish the year. In general, she feels a gifted second-grader can fit into a third-grade class or, if he or she is quite advanced, a fourth-grade class at the beginning of the year. The first few months of each school year include considerable review; this can be helpful for the very advanced accelerating student to ensure coverage of previous material. Lin adds that gifted students are usually more than willing to do any additional work needed. "They're even anxious to take home homework...if it's on their level."

Consider Additional Opportunities

After initial accelerated placements are made, Lin Greene advises looking for any appropriate programs that may become available: Science Fair, Toastmasters, a mentor, etc. "Have your antennas up for anything said in a staff meeting that might be helpful to your child." Perhaps there is an elderly person who is willing to donate time mentoring a child in geography. "You have to be the first to sign the paper. If you don't, your child misses out." With such opportunities, a teacher has to be thinking about all of the children in the classroom.

Social and Emotional Issues

Unfortunately, Lin adds, many teachers feel gifted children don't need any help. They are "already above where everybody else is at the start. They're already there." Yet, Lin insists that if teachers merely give them more of the same, "It's just death for a gifted child...They may start to act out, if they tend toward that anyway, or proclaim loudly how 'bored' they are. This can make the other children wonder about the classroom activity they had thought was fun."

Lin believes that teachers may also not realize how much gifted children want to be accepted by the kids in the room. These are the children they went to kindergarten with. "This is their class." The gifted child sometimes wants to run around and do silly things on the playground, but then also likes to work on long division!

Lin adds, "The class itself wants to know that this child is working, too, because they feel they are always working. For them, everything is hard...to the gifted child, hardly anything is hard." Unless the teacher teaches at the appropriate level for that gifted child, nothing will be challenging. It is the teacher's responsibility to make the gifted child struggle, think, have homework, and be expected to really work in class. The class wants to know this will happen, too. Lin feels this is where the teacher's expertise in devising appropriate accommodations is particularly helpful.

Providing direct instruction to the gifted child in what to say to others is beneficial, as well. For example, Lin teaches gifted students that when classmates ask for help, they should ask questions instead of simply giving answers. "Don't assume these children know what to say because they talk to the teacher on an adult level," she cautions, "because their emotions and social skills are not at that level." Train them in what to do when they come back from the upper level classroom. What do they do with that wonderful thing they've made? Classmates may be jealous if they rush to share their experiences. Lin believes in teaching gifted children to come in appropriately—acting respectful. She advises them not to share their creations immediately as they come in the door, but to know there will be a time to share. Gifted kids are good at telling time and waiting. Right after lunch is a great time to share; they can count on it every day. In fact, Lin encourages them to share on a regular basis; otherwise, the other children may think they just went to play! It is also a time to acknowledge what the gifted child has accomplished. "Second-graders like to see a page of note taking or long division. Wow!" Everyone benefits from the sharing of praise.

The Regular Classroom vs. The Gifted Program

Lin cautions that some children have been told at home that everything in the regular classroom will just have to be endured; it will be "boring" and they're not supposed to like it, but things will be better once the "gifted program" starts. "That's where the conference at the beginning really helps.

A positive attitude from the parent is vital to a successful year," she says. Parents have little idea of what will happen in the gifted program or what a minimal role (in most schools) it is likely to play in their child's programming. Most of the time, it's the last thing the school will get started in the year. The reality is that most gifted children spend the majority of their time in the regular classroom, with only minimal accommodations through the gifted program. Moreover, the gifted program is highly dependent on current funding and rarely provides any continuity of educational goals for the child from one year to another. The primary responsibility for gifted accommodations almost always falls to the regular classroom teacher.

Identifying the Gifted

Lin Greene also warns that initial identification for the gifted program doesn't happen quickly; parents shouldn't expect it until the end of the first semester or later. "By the time they test them, it's spring! If you've been there more than one year, you know you can't wait." Asking the assistance of a more experienced teacher can be beneficial in finding children who have not yet been identified, including some who have not been brought to the teacher's attention by parents. Lin likes to get a sample of their writing, see what comments they make, and what their thought processes are. "If they're thinking that many steps beyond the normal seven-year-old, let's see what they can really do!" she advises. Give them an assignment that will reveal what they can do; see if they'll pick up on it. An experienced teacher learns the most from informal, ongoing assessment within the classroom. However, Lin cautions, "...if the child is used to always having to fit in and you ask for them to write a couple of sentences, that may be all that they write." There's also the gifted child who won't write anything. The gifted may have difficulty determining the level at which to respond, perceiving that their best work is not what is being requested. "Assessment at the beginning of the year is tricky at best, but well worth the extra effort," Lin concludes.

Teaching Research Skills and Independent Learning

Once the needs of gifted children have been identified and programming has been decided, other skills that support their learning can be developed. For example, "Gifted children can really get their teeth into research," notes Lin. Gifted second-graders can actually search out information, not just regurgitate it. Before the Internet, one had to know how to do things in alphabetical order to look things up in encyclopedias. Gifted students already know alphabetical order. It is easy to teach them how to use the encyclopedia to research information. "Here's where you can really integrate the child's work with what's happening in the general classroom." Allow them to go to the library by themselves, look up something by themselves, and then come back with a written product. If given small amounts of instruction, they can do it. They love it. "They are learning about the Aurora Borealis—you weren't even going to expand on it, except to say these are the Northern Lights...they look like ribbons of color in the sky." The gifted child takes notes on note cards and teaches the class about the Aurora Borealis with passion! This not only teaches the research skills which gifted students enjoy being taught, but also goal setting and independent learning. "I want everybody in my class to be independent to whatever level that is... For some it's to use the tape dispenser, or stapler because they're not allowed to use it at home." The gifted child can do so much more. "When a child shares his cards, artwork, and sits in the chair where the teacher sits, it shows that he/she is respected by the teacher and has something to offer that they need to listen to—just like everybody else." The feelings and expectations the teacher has for this child are an essential part of a successful student-teacher relationship. If the teacher feels this is just

another child in his or her harried workload, the child will
not work up to potential.

Knowledge of Curriculum at Other Grade Levels

Teaching a range of grades, though unwelcome at the time,
proved invaluable in Lin Greene's work with gifted students.
After training and doing her student teaching in first grade,
she was forced to teach all elementary grades through sixth
before settling more permanently into second grade.
Although she was reluctant to move from one grade level to
another because "There was no rhyme or reason to it...you
were the last one coming in, so you got to move," she believes
the experience gave her a better understanding of where kids
normally are at different grade levels and a greater willingness to let a child accelerate when appropriate. Lin believes
such a decision is much more difficult for the teacher who
has taught only one grade level for many years. Assessing the
child's placement realistically and preparing the child for a
grade skip are truly daunting for some teachers.

Using Parent Volunteers

Helpful to both the gifted child and the ones at the other
end of the scale, were the parent volunteers in Lin's classrooms. They were not counters of papers, or folder stuffers,
or just party helpers; they actually were trained by Lin to
work with the children. "I had some really wonderful
volunteers—but not a huge plethora of them. A lot of them
went on to be very good at, for instance, creative writing."
She would train them to do the small creative writing
groups, focusing on what to say and how to elicit good
questions from the children, rather than criticism. "How did
you come up with that great idea?" the aides would ask, and
they would teach the children to be able to come up with
those types of questions to ask of the child sharing his or
her work. That would free up the teacher. Lin planned for
the aides to be the ones who would go around and kneel

down and help the child who was stuck. She taught them how to "unstick" the child; then, just before the child would be ready for the aide to do the work, the volunteer would move on to help someone else. "I trained them to be little clones of Lin. That was helpful to the gifted child, too."

Should Gifted and Struggling Students be Paired for Instruction?

Asked about the frequent practice of pairing gifted students with struggling students, Lin recalls that approach not working very well in her classroom. First, it could be a problem because gifted children are held to grade-level work. Second, when the two students were from the same class-room, she felt the struggling student had to deal with the dilemma of, "I live with you and you're better than I am, and it's embarrassing." She avoided such pairings within the classroom, but found that occasionally having a child come from another classroom to help on the computer, for example, usually worked very well. "They weren't a part of your classroom, so they were like little teachers and no one was uncomfortable. They could be helpful and didn't put anybody down." When the "Fifth-grade Buddies" would come for an activity, Lin made sure that gifted children were paired together, too. "That made for extra special bonding."

Accommodating Classroom Learning Rates

How did learning rate affect instruction in the classroom? Lin recalls that only about one third of the students needed significant repetition at her school. The gifted would master new concepts right away. "Then you had to risk them being bored because they already had it, for the average child who almost knew the concept, but was going to lose it right away if it was not reviewed. Some children would not ever learn the task and you had to move on. That was hard." She further notes, "That's why grouping in math is so important." When a teacher is not meeting the needs teaching to the entire heterogeneous group, then instruction has to be done differently. She once trained her students to move in thirds in math to three centers in the classroom, each providing different elements of math instruction: manipulative, time with the teacher, and guided practice. As the students came to her center, she provided remediation, practice, or enrichment. It became much easier when her entire team worked together providing *leveled instruction*. "One teacher took the top 18 of our 100 second-graders. They would stay within the math strand being taught, but expand into areas way beyond the rest of the grade level. It was a tremendous help for all the above average and gifted students, as well as those needing extra help in just the basic skills."

The Strong-Willed Teacher

Asked if good teachers of the gifted need to be fairly strong-willed, confident people, Lin agreed. "That's true; you have to be a little out-of-sync yourself, I think. Most teachers are not like that." She recalled her frustration with teachers who would refuse to take a child for one subject if there were scheduling difficulties. "If I was trying to get them to take a child who was higher in reading and have them read with their class, it would just be incredible that they couldn't make any allowances. I like my schedule, too, but I've taken kids from first grade into my room." How much is scheduling and how much is resistance? "More is just resistance, not a scheduling problem. It happened more than you would like," Lin adds. What does a teacher do when the higher-grade-level teacher refuses to take an advanced child? "Luckily, I was in a large enough school that if one teacher said no, I could go and ask another one at the same grade level," Lin notes. "They also knew if the child was coming from me, I was still going to be responsible for the child's behavior and make sure rules were obeyed. However, it was an honor to be going to another classroom, so of course, my gifted child would want to behave!"

Lin believes excellent teachers of the gifted, or of any special needs children, must be willing to buck the system. "You don't get help for children who are out-of-sync by following the normal path. When you want to get a child out of Special Ed and they've always been in Special Ed, you have to be willing to stake your reputation on that." Lin feels teachers should be willing to say, "I think he could handle the Toastmaster's group," or, "She deserves to be in the Spelling Bee. She can't be the winner because that's the way the rules are, but she's a great speller and deserves to be there." Lin observes that most teachers are more passive than that, and admits that the unusual request for a child's accommodation "sometimes doesn't make you very popular."

One place for teachers to be strong advocates is in team meetings to plan programs for gifted students. Known by various titles (our school has the Child Resource Team), such teams of teachers meet with a child's parents for the purpose of deciding future plans for the child at school. Many more of these meetings involve children with disabilities; team meetings are rarely called to consider a gifted child. Lin notes, "I've seen many children's lives helped or hindered by those meetings. You never get together before those meetings to hear what everybody's viewpoint is." Having the child's teacher be a solid advocate is very important, especially since most teachers are not accustomed to offering unusual options to gifted students (e.g., grade acceleration) and may be resistant. If even more help is needed, an outside expert can be called. The Gifted Development Center often sends personnel to meetings in our area to assist parents and supportive teachers, when requested. The large teacher team often lacks knowledge about gifted children, which an expert can provide.

Besides being a staunch advocate for gifted students, what other characteristics contribute to being a good teacher for these children? Lin feels some teachers are better at working with gifted students than others, and personality styles should mesh. Assistance in placing a gifted child can be very helpful if a principal or other administrator is willing to consider a choice based on the child's needs and personality (different gifted children may be optimally placed with different teachers). For example, Lin notes that while some teachers are better at coddling, she feels she was not. "I wasn't the nursemaid, or grandmotherly type. Both the gifted child and Special Ed child were challenged in my room. They knew they would have to stretch. And that's a good thing!"

Advice to Parents

Asked what advice Lin could offer parents, she says enthusiastically, "Come in with the positive attitude that the teacher might have something to offer." She admits, "If they come in with no respect for what you've taught or what you might know, it's just human nature...you close your doors to them." Also, it is best NOT to have too specific a program in mind. "When my parents came in with an open mind and a willingness to work with the teacher for the combined benefit of the child, that was the optimum situation. I knew it was going to be a great year."

Advice to Teachers

Lin also advises teachers to keep an open mind "because that gifted child has a parent that has been dealing with this challenge from the day they started public school. That parent is going to come with a set of 'givens' also." Lin reminds teachers that just because parents may have had rather poor experiences in other classrooms, "That doesn't mean they won't have a good experience in yours. Start by being as understanding as you can; if the parent is also open then it is just wonderful."

Asked how to improve gifted education within the public schools, Lin feels teachers should be paid for being terrific at what they do. Typically, the only benefit they receive is "harder kids the next year." Lin sees virtually nothing in the system to reward teachers, especially as compared with private-sector jobs that offer financial incentives for hard work, merit-based salary increases, and bonuses. In addition, she feels teachers need more training in gifted education and the experience of teaching at various grade levels to fully understand and guide out-of-sync students through the educational sequence.

Lin has enjoyed her work with gifted students through the years, watching them progress in their studies and conceptualize in interesting ways. She still recalls the little second-grade boy who said, "You mean when you tell me to do something, I'm supposed to do it? Is that how it works?"

"I said, 'Yes!'" Lin laughs nostalgically.

Sharon Sikora: Teaching the Gifted Middle-Schooler

Dr. Sharon Sikora is a science teacher at Summit Middle School, a charter school for students seeking a more challenging educational environment (profiled in the charter schools chapter). Having a Ph.D. in biochemistry, and being a parent of gifted children herself, Sharon was anxious to apply her knowledge and teaching experience with college students to high ability middle-schoolers. She described her current challenge dealing with an influx of lower-ability students drawn to the school by high state test scores, and the problems even willing teachers face maintaining programs for gifted students. She also discussed her role in creating a curriculum rigorous enough to withstand the pressures of state assessments with ease, and shared her general views on working with gifted students.

Challenged by the Range of Student Ability

Sharon Sikora's small school of 250 students, which will increase in size to 300 this coming year, has been challenged by a dramatically changing student body in its six years of operation. Although the self-selecting school honestly advertises its accelerated curriculum (which overlaps with typical high school offerings) and the high expectations it has of its students, many families have chosen the school simply for its high test scores. This has created a difficult situation for students and teachers alike. Some students coming to the school find the work far *too* hard and finally leave for placements in more traditional middle school programs. Others struggle but stay, requiring teachers to extend their program downward and increase their teaching skills to include a very different population of learner than initially sought to attend.

Summit has maintained its commitment to the high-end learner by continuing to place children where they need to be and offer unusually high-level coursework where needed. For example, math classes extend through Geometry and Algebra II/Trigonometry, and two students last year took a university correspondence course in Pre-Calculus. There are two levels of English offered that are considered to be high school level, and science students often place into the tenth-grade Pre-IB (International Baccalaureate) science class at a neighboring high school after completing Summit. However, Sharon notes that in the first two years of the school's operation, 60% of Summit students placed into that higher level, tenth-grade Pre-IB class, with 40% placing into the ninth-grade Pre-IB class. Today, about one third place into the tenth-grade Pre-IB class, one third into the ninth-grade Pre-IB class, and one third into regular ninth-grade physical science. Sharon Sikora explains,

> *It is frightening to me because I work well with the high-end kids. Now I have students who can't read well, who can't sit still, who can't*

*see beyond the surface of information, and
aren't critical thinkers—they're not at that point
yet—so I'm guiding them to reach that point
instead of really fine-tuning and developing
critical thinkers, where the other kids are
almost there. From my perspective, it's made
me a better teacher, but my preference is really
taking these kids, who are neglected because
they are so high-end, and providing opportunities for them to grow and expand—for them to
be nurtured—because I think the system often
teaches to the middle of the road. Or, when you
have a lot of low-end kids, it teaches to those
low-end kids because you can't lose them. It's
often not fair to those upper-end kids.*

Sharon points out that the school has a huge waiting list of
students who desperately need an accelerated program they
can't find elsewhere. The Summit program was designed to
meet these unmet needs, but when students who would be
better placed at other schools take the few places available
at Summit, the school can less effectively fulfill its mission.
Stretching extensively to meet the needs of all Summit
students, Sikora feels she still can support the gifted
student, "but I wouldn't want to see it go any further," she
notes. At what point does the range of ability in the classroom preclude adequately teaching the high-end student?

Must Today's Teachers Teach to State Tests?

Sharon Sikora was recently involved, after helping to create
a successful standards-based curriculum at Summit, in a
curriculum project to aid other schools concerned about
their performance on state tests. Unlike some educators,
who feel the pressure of the state tests forces teachers to
abandon quality curricula in favor of "teaching to the test,"
Sharon believes the process can lead to an excellent,

rigorous curriculum that negates the need for excessive test preparation. "We created a process so we can go to a school and help them take the national and state standards, interpret them so that they're standards for their own school, and then create benchmarks so that that happens." How do the benchmarks fit into a scope and sequence for a course? "We created templates and examples for every one of our disciplines, in the core subjects: English, each of the individual languages, science, social studies and math," Sharon explains. "We showed them examples set up in each subject of a scope and sequence that was standards-based and benchmark-based...and then this whole process of the template." Summit teachers went from school to school, did workshops with the teachers, and showed them how to turn what they were doing into a standards-based education.

Sharon Sikora is not adverse to the state tests, which often worry gifted advocates because overadherence to grade-level material may rule out accelerative opportunities. "If you have a very rigorous curriculum, you're meeting those state standards," she asserts.

> *Even though there's a pull and a shove and you just want to say, 'I'm going to take those standards and that's all I'm going to teach— that's how I'm going to get my kids though these tests,'...the bottom line is the standards are still so very vague that if your curriculum is rigorous and standards-based, your kids are going to be fine.*

Sharon understands that teachers may want to focus solely upon the standards (perhaps teaching each for three weeks) because their survival as teachers and the survival of their schools is at issue. Their job security depends upon it. However, she insists that educators can learn to trust their programs. "The issue is that you're teaching well and following a rigorous standards-based curriculum," and adds,

"The cross-check is as much with the kids as with your curriculum. Is your curriculum hitting these standards and when?...and do you know that you're hitting all of them?" Sharon does not believe that such tests are an infringement that force educators to teach to the test and "not be true to ourselves and our mission."

Sharon Sikora feels Summit was "incredibly lucky" because Amanda Avallone, an English teacher who had just finished her Masters degree in curriculum, took a lead role in creating a standards-based curriculum for Summit before most schools in the rest of the state attempted it. "That's the bottom line," Sharon explains, "the reason we were successful was because we had done that." Asked for examples of the standards, Sharon noted that in science the first standard is that students know the scientific process. The benchmarks in that standard might include how to write a proper conclusion, create a hypothesis, distinguish between a hypothesis and a conclusion in a problem statement, and know how to collect data (read a thermometer, know that having more data is better than having less data). Sharon concludes, "So that's standard 1. How do you hit that?" Considering the school's science projects, the curriculum "hits" all of that, but Sharon notes,

> We've actually carefully taken apart the sixth-
> grade curriculum so there are different things
> students work on; they work on writing a
> hypothesis and collecting basic data (and get
> hints of this), and then we reinforce it in
> seventh grade and add on further data collec-
> tion and data analysis. In eighth grade, I break
> the news to them that there really is a stan-
> dard way you write a conclusion. You've taken
> that standard and broken it apart into three
> years and given them little doses of it along the
> way. The beauty of it is that students are
> writing a hypothesis and learning how to do

that in sixth grade, which is one of the first
things they do. They do that again in seventh
grade; they probably cover it 20 times. The
curriculum is rigorous.

Sharon Sikora cautions that teachers must be somewhat critical of the curriculum they're teaching. Some of the books and handouts, for example, only hint about actually writing a hypothesis. The teacher has to lay this foundation, then build upon it through the years spent with the student.

Sharon continues, "The question is how do you teach them that scientific process? Must it be covered just in biology or chemistry?" She insists it can be taught in many ways: with goldfish breeding in cold water; determining whether or not a substance is going to create bubbles when it's testing different minerals; through the use of a plate techtonics model; through chemistry experiments; or studying physics and the motion of a matchbox car on an inclined plane. "The bottom line is you're going to hit this concept in every single discipline." She adds that the other standards in science are very specific to earth science or biology or chemistry or physical science. They are very content driven, so it is essential to make sure students are being taught the content.

Sharon emphasizes, however, that the mandated curriculum need not be taught at the typical pace, year by year, to meet state and federal standards. Since the inception of the Summit program, the typical science content of three years in middle school has been taught in the first two years. "We hit all of those standards in sixth and seventh grade." This has remained the case, even as the student body has changed. She feels the program still works well because third year instruction at Summit can either address the need for remediation or allow the student to progress to high school work. "If we know kids got *C*'s and *D*'s along the way and didn't quite get that [content mastery], they go into our

Advanced Topics class...If they got A's or B's, they can go on to Chem/Physics because they've mastered the middle school curriculum," she explains. She adds that teachers can make this determination by grades or by other assessments, which, up to now, haven't worked as well as grades. "We're still working on fine tuning that." Summit's approach to varying the pace of instruction for different students has met both the varying needs of learners and produced high state test scores. Summit eighth-graders scored at the 97th percentile in science, the 87th percentile in math, and the 92nd percentile in English, utilizing this approach.

"The high schools have finally come to accept our kids," Sharon is pleased to report. One way in which teachers can support advanced students is by advocating for their appropriate placement at their next school. Students will face considerable pressure to take the courses that most students in their same grade take. When their former teachers make a special effort to ensure these students are placed appropriately in higher level courses, it's tremendously helpful. If the receiving school agrees to a more advanced placement, the student avoids repeating work already mastered, maintains higher motivation to learn, and has time to schedule more of the most advanced courses offered. Many students will also choose to take college courses concurrently, particularly because they can usually earn both college credit and credit toward their high school diplomas.

Teachers usually encounter some resistance initially when they recommend more advanced placements at the receiving school. However, as that school gains experience that the recommendations it is receiving are appropriate, the process begins to go more smoothly. "Boulder High decided they would really like to have our kids for their AP scholars program. Boulder High sent us a cake thanking all the faculty," Sharon states. High schools realize at some point that recruiting advanced students helps them to offer their highest level classes, for which there might, otherwise, be insufficient demand. Advanced students who have skipped entry-level courses have more time left during their high school careers to take such classes.

Approaches to Teaching the Gifted

Maintain High Standards

Asked about her general views on teaching the gifted, Sharon Sikora first describes the necessity of having high standards for gifted students. "Make it very clear what you want them to do and assist them in achieving that goal," she says. Sharon routinely expects her middle school students to handle college-like, lab-based classes in which a high level of understanding by the students is expected. Even with this rigor, she cautions, "Don't put a ceiling on! Who knows how high they can go?" Allow students to explore high-end knowledge and be surprised! She adds, "a little bit of mystery is a good thing," when the teacher has not taught higher level material that the student can discover independently.

Learn to Trust

Second, Sharon advises, "If the area of their greatest interest is not your expertise, you must learn to trust." She explains that a teacher can find the right mentor for a student, seek out the community that the student needs or the books that will be required—that's easy. However, the teacher must then trust what the student shares as his or her resultant learning. "You trust that the information they've given you is correct." Of course, the teacher can still look at the student's analytical processing. "As a science teacher, you know when the critical thinking isn't quite right and it's not flowing right and they're jumping to conclusions—it doesn't matter whether it's biology or chemistry or geology or astronomy," Sharon notes. "I've recently had many students whose interests were not in my field and I've had great success with them—if I treat them as if they are the experts and they're teaching me." She helps them fill in the holes or gaps in their knowledge by asking questions and recognizing where those gaps are. "Trust that they're the experts and that they've done good work and that they're willing to work," she insists. She adds that it's important for the teacher to take on the role of a student and say, "You teach me because this is something that I don't know much about." She explains, "It is a great opportunity for them to communicate what they know…and for the two of you to become colleagues, instead of this teacher/student relationship."

Ensure a Strong Content Background

Third, Sharon Sikora believes strong content background is critical to a teacher of the gifted. "I've met some amazing teachers, but none of those amazing teachers in science have only a bachelor's degree; they all have at least a master's," she says. Noting that this is a particular need when working with the gifted, she admits it is also "tricky," because some teachers with higher degrees don't know how to communicate—how to teach. "You do need your teacher training; there are tricks and there are things you have to know," adds Sharon. She also believes, "You don't personally develop your critical thinking until you've done some strong research on your own and then you learn how to think." Sharon's students have won an unusual number of awards, at the highest levels, in science competitions. She is particularly adept at supporting their research. "I think you have to write a thesis—do some research that takes at least a year—to grasp that," she insists. "In English and Social Studies, our most successful teachers have higher degrees, as well." She concludes, "For that really high-end kid, you have to have spent some time in your discipline that is very integral to your being in order to be able to translate that to the students and teach them in the right way."

Allow Any Question

Fourth, Sharon Sikora believes "It's critical in the classroom that you allow any question to happen." She advises teachers to be supportive and admit if they don't know something. "There's a certain amount of respect that the gifted student understands when you say, 'I don't know the answer to that; we can find out.' " With the gifted, it is not so much the issue of a teacher admitting that he or she doesn't know something. It is the teacher letting the student know that it is okay to not know everything—perfectionism should not apply to knowledge. "Here they respect you in the classroom and realize you're not perfect, which lightens up their load. The other thing that happens is that they see you as a colleague," Sharon explains. She strongly believes that gifted students are seeking out colleagues among their teachers. "They want someone who's on their level, who can be at their level, and they see at their level; even the age thing doesn't matter." She adds, "Intellectually, you're their colleague because you don't know everything and, therefore, they can learn from you." With such respect, she believes the student and teacher can then "link arms and go forward." The understanding between them becomes, "I'm going to guide you sometimes and you're going to guide me sometimes. I have more knowledge right now than you do, but I don't have all the knowledge. We can pursue intellec- tual endeavors together." With her most gifted and talented kids, Sharon feels she is still viewed as their teacher and respected, but there is a colleague relationship and "that's what promotes their learning more than anything else."

Interestingly, she believes her less capable students value such a relationship less. "There are some students you don't want to be colleagues with. They are not usually the high-end kids. They need a different relationship." She explains that these students are more comfortable having her play a traditional teacher role, dispensing information to them.

Unfortunately, Sharon believes colleague relationships are not always an option for the gifted with other teachers. She wonders if teachers who are insecure with their knowledge aren't the most resistant. Citing her own difficulties teaching meteorology, she admits, "I'm so insecure that I have to come across as, 'That's the way it is.' " Especially in middle schools, teachers are asked to teach things they're not necessarily comfortable with. They don't have extra time for outside learning and there's no professional development to help them. "That's where the discomfort comes in," Sharon notes. "When a teacher's uncomfortable, the kids pick up on it right away and you get, 'I hate science, I hate....' " Yet, she adds, "When you have a teacher who truly loves what they're doing, that love is really contagious. When you're really passionate about what you're teaching, you can say, 'I don't know the answer to that...I've never thought about that before.' "

When a high-end question is asked in the classroom, for which there is an answer, Sharon Sikora will virtually always take the time to answer that question in class. She believes this is critical, even if the other students have totally lost the thought and don't understand why it was an important question. Sharon explains,

> *At that point in time, I've lost 90% of my class, but I will stop everything I'm doing and answer that good question. For the 10% of the kids who were following along, they feel really good about this; they're getting an answer and they're thinking. It promotes their thinking at a very nice, high level. For the student who asked the question, it's validated his thought processes. He feels good that this was considered*

an important question. For the 90% of kids
you've lost, they realize that there are questions
out there that they can't imagine.

Sharon recalls that her own son actually had an experience this year where he asked one of those questions and the teacher said, "That's too high level for this class. You're going to have to hold on to that question and wait a couple years."

"That is the worst possible thing you can do to these kids!" she exclaims. "They're not going to hold onto it for those years and, suddenly, in that class they're going to stop thinking at a high level because why should they think at a high level? Their high-level thinking isn't even acknowledged."

Sometimes the questions are so complex that they need to be carefully considered before an answer can be given or a class discussion facilitated. Sharon will say, "Let's talk about that after class even if I have to write you a pass. I need to really process that. Let me continue with my lesson, and then we'll talk about it." She makes sure to address the question with the student who asked it that day. Sometimes other questions seem too "off base" for classroom discussion. "You have to weigh whether or not it will be too disruptive to go off on that tangent." Even with questions deemed unsuitable for class discussion, Sharon feels it is important to explain that gently to the student after class. Gifted students tend to be introverts who are easily embarrassed in public.

Ask Open-Ended Questions

Sharon Sikora feels teachers should ask their share of good questions, as well. "Have a lot of open-ended questions on labs and tests—oh, tests are key," she advises. There is the tendency for all teachers to give exams with a lot of multiple-choice items because they are very easy to grade. "It cuts your time in half," Sharon admits. "The other tendency, especially in chemistry, is not to give partial credit for where their thoughts are...not to give problems where you actually have to see their thought processes." She notes that when only the final answer counts, a multiple-choice mentality prevails. Sharon believes tests should generate a lot of discussion ("This is where you went wrong. Do you see where you went wrong?") and contain questions where partial credit is given for correct thought processes. "I still give maybe 8 points worth of multiple-choice items because the whole world is set up for multiple choice. If I don't give multiple choice, it tends to hurt them later on," she explains. Sharon also insists that about 10% of the test questions cover something students have never seen before. "They've seen it, but in another form," she clarifies. Unfortunately, this sometimes draws the ire of both students and parents. "I've been called to the principal's office a few times!" Sharon admits, "and I stand on my ground." She explains,

> *Science is new. It's applying your way of thinking to totally new situations. And that's something that gifted students just love! They are able to see the connection. That goes to their hearts and souls. If you only make it 10% of the test, and you give partial credit if they've sort of gotten there, they see where science is going and understand how the nature of science changes. A lot of teachers won't do that because it takes so much time.*

Finally, Sharon Sikora likes to flexibly meet the needs of her individual students as they arise. For example, "I had a great group of girls this year," she recalls with a smile. "Outstanding, brilliant women. Four gifted young women worked together this year on a project." She explained that each was a past Science Fair winner or had some contact with advanced scientific work through their families. "I put these four together," she states; "I was very manipulative."

Sharon didn't encourage another Science Fair entry because the girls had placed at the state level before, had the basis of scientific inquiry down, and really needed to do Science Fair next in high school, when awards and scholarships would be at stake. Sharon wanted them to consider a team project because, despite the girls' gifted abilities, each needed to learn to work with a group. She suggested the Bayer NSF Competition, a team community innovation project, so they could learn to work together. Sharon provided support as the girls found their way to a highly scientific project. "Outstanding work," she proudly recalls, noting that the girls were regional finalists, won a subscription to Discover Magazine for a year, and were given a beautiful trophy. "There are times to look at the individuals. What are you going to do with them?" she asks. "The district has come to respect so much the work that we're doing," she admits proudly. "One girl on the team, now heading on to high school, was given the chance to do her senior science research project as a sophomore." In four out of the six years Summit has competed in science competitions, its students have placed at the state, regional or national levels.

Richard Borinsky: Challenging Gifted High School Students

Rich Borinsky is an experienced, highly talented teacher, renowned in our school district for his many years of successful teaching of Advanced Placement Biology (usually taught to high school seniors), regular Biology (usually a tenth-grade course), and various related courses of interest. A teacher who always manages to prepare a higher percentage of students to earn 5's on the AP exams, he has achieved a level to which any teacher could aspire. Rich notes that most of his students in his AP classes are not gifted; he would classify most as high achievers who really care about their grades and work very hard. However, he always draws some gifted students (whom he notes don't have to work hard; they "get it the first time") to his classes and is perceived by the gifted students as a teacher who can challenge even the brightest among them. "I don't put limits on their learning," he explains, "I allow them to get there in a lot of different ways."

Noting that all teachers seem to have students with whom they work best, Rich admits, "I've always had success with the student in the gifted range." He does not attribute his success as a teacher to hard work or practice, believing primarily that "teachers are born." However, he does believe that it is helpful for teachers to never be satisfied with the jobs they are doing. A teacher who has the talent can become better. There is always room for improvement.

Challenges of Instructional Grouping

Richard Borinsky began teaching in 1972 when his high school was quite different from what it is today. He recalls that the school, located in a primarily middle class area of reasonably well-educated individuals, many in high-tech fields, was primarily a prep school at that time. The school utilized a college schedule in science, biology, and history that included one-hour lectures two days per week, as well as lab and recitation (both three days per week). Special Education students at that time were isolated in their own program. Students in the college-prep track were virtually all taking biology; it was a fairly homogeneous group. "We didn't have students who couldn't read in biology or who couldn't speak English."

The School Reform Movement brought an emphasis on the heterogeneous grouping of students, beginning with efforts to mainstream Special Education students. These students, whose parents lobbied strongly for their placement into *least restrictive* educational environments, began to be placed into regular biology classes. The Science Topics class, a more basic option, was phased out. Biology became a class for every student at the high school. Yet, Rich notes, the ability ranges became so diverse, it became difficult to be effective.

After many years of teaching within this structure, the science department at his high school is making changes for next year. "We are now going to separate by ability." Next year, his high school will offer two classes of Honors Biology, six to eight classes of regular Biology and two classes of Basic Biology (for students who have significant learning disabilities). Rich is viewing the Honors Biology class as a Pre-AP class. He feels it would be helpful to give students contact with the more abstract concepts earlier. Gifted students typically catch on quickly, but others often need more time with this material. However, Rich believes he might actually be able to take such a group of bright students at the ninth-grade level and prepare them for an AP test! (This was done at a challenging middle school in the Denver area with two AP social studies courses. Some of the students scored high enough to earn college credit before entering high school.) Rich feels that more advanced classes for freshmen and sophomores should be available. Like many schools that offer AP courses, his high school has fewer advanced courses for underclassmen. He would prefer to offer them, as International Baccalaureate (IB) programs do to prepare students for high-level coursework later. IB programs typically have a series of more challenging, honors level, Pre-IB courses for younger students.

Although three levels of introductory biology have been approved for next year, Rich Borinsky expresses some frustration. "If we had had to have two, the honors would have been scrapped and the basic and regular would have been offered," he states. "As a society, we do a great job with learning disabilities. We don't do a very good job with the other end of the spectrum. We don't have much pity for them." He adds that we spend more money printing pamphlets about what we're doing for the gifted than offering meaningful services.

Rich also has concern that the needs of some gifted students are obscured by their failure to be high achievers. The student who fails to achieve at a high level may not be granted access to opportunities that do exist for higher level work and may not appear to need services for the gifted. "Many kids are very, very bright, but don't fit into the mold we have for students. Some won't do homework, or are not organized enough to do well." They miss turning in some assignments—so they're not doing very well for a grade—but they're learning the material.

On Grading

Ultimately, Rich Borinsky wants his students' overall learning of the material to determine a final grade. Because Advanced Placement and International Baccalaureate classes both involve *exit testing*, where a test is given at the end of the class covering all of the material taught, the student's ultimate learning can be measured at the end of the class to an even greater degree than final exams usually measure content mastery. Rich routinely allows students who earn a 5, the top grade on the Advanced Placement Biology test, an *A* in his class, regardless of grades up to that point. "My goal is to put the emphasis on the learning and not the grade...you have to make them accountable for the work they turn in but, in the end, they either know it or they don't...the goal of the class is to learn enough to do well on that exam." Rich likes the fact that the exam is externally evaluated; he cannot affect his students' grades in any way. Doing well on the exam is a powerful indicator that his students have successfully learned the necessary material in biology, even if they've struggled to maintain high grades along the way or have failed to turn in all assignments. Sometimes concepts that weren't fully understood when first tested, become relevant and meaningful to the student later in the year. Scoring high on the AP exam documents that his students, by May of the year in which they take the course, have reached a high-level understanding of the content. "If they do that, then they've accomplished the goal of the class."

Instruction—Empower Independent Learning

"I'm not a person who stands up in front of a room and lectures. I don't think I do that very well. I'm probably average," Rich Borinsky insists. "I think I need to explain some things to them, but I need to find out what it is that they need explained." Rich assumes he will have a variety of students "who know things in different ways and some of them know it a lot better than others and are able to explain it maybe a lot better than I am." Because he also believes that "kids relate to kids probably better than teachers relate to kids," he tries to structure the class to allow a lot of interaction between students. Most work is done in small groups of the students' choosing. "I give them things that they're able to talk about in class." He feels that the small group structure, with each group of students being more homogeneous, can best meet the learning needs of individuals. "I'm a student," he says. "I take a lot of classes. If I find myself in a classroom and I already know the material the professor is talking about, I want to go beyond that, ask questions, or it's very boring." The small groups allow for greater interaction about the course content at the level of the individuals in the group. He tries to minimize lecturing and maximize opportunities to talk to each other and solve a problem. "I try to go beyond the text—incorporate things that are relevant to the text and get them to think about things—use a lot of resources," Rich explains. He also uses critical thinking approaches to ferret out misconceptions, knowing that students can easily parrot back information, but need to understand it thoroughly.

As a result, the class is quite variable. It's not the same every day. Rich notes that some teachers have their entire year planned at the beginning; however, the structure of his class does not allow such long-term planning. "I know exactly what I'm going to be doing on a day-to-day basis, but not next week. Teaching is very difficult for me. I don't know how things will play out from week to week. I may have to work late at night to prepare." Allowing more flexibility for students to pursue ideas requires more continuous planning and last-minute preparation, as adjustments must be ongoing. "My weaknesses may be good for gifted kids," he admits, as the flexibility allows for meeting their unusual needs. "I've never taught AP the same way twice, although I've given out some of the same documents. It's difficult to be that way. It has its disadvantages." In fact, every year brings concern that all topics won't be covered in time for the test and a flurry of activity ensues as the AP test approaches. "I've made videotapes for students to ensure they know something we don't have time to cover in class. It's another part of giving them responsibility." AP Biology involves a huge amount of content—more than is typically taught at the college freshman level, where instructors often leave out anatomy and physiology to meet time constraints. However, the necessary preparation must be done for the AP test. The level to which Richard Borinsky's students are always prepared is a testament to his high standards and annual accomplishment.

"One of the things I'm doing is I'm giving up a lot of control," Rich says of empowering his students to learn more independently. "I realize that some of the students are going to be smarter than I am," he states. "That doesn't threaten me, it intrigues me. I don't have a problem with that at all. I just happen to know more biology than they know so I can still teach them something. I can help guide their enthusiastic questions."

"I'm willing to give up control in a lot of different ways," Rich Borinsky explains. "I let the students determine a lot of that class." He routinely allows students to decide when they will be tested; if tests on two subject areas are needed, do they

want to take them on the same day or different days? He
also gives take-home exams to save class time, trusting
students to complete the tests without outside help.
Sometimes, he even provides students with the answers to
check themselves. Frequently, he has found that open-book
tests produce the best learning. "They're in the class for
their own benefit, not for my benefit," he insists. "If they
want to cheat, they're not going to get much out of it."
Students routinely grade their own exams and other
students' exams, and seem to learn a lot from that. "I like to
take work that's exceptional and share that work with other
students. I photocopy papers or essays that are exceptional,"
Rich adds.

"I look at it as I'm a student, too. I'm a part of their group.
I try to become a part of the group as much as possible,"
Rich explains. He treats his students as peers and fellow
learners. "I'm trying to tell them whether they did well or
didn't do well, and if they didn't do well enough, what they
need to do to get where they need to be." Every day, Rich
Borinsky approaches his students as he would other
responsible adults. "Here's what we're going to do today.
Here's what we need to do. How are we going to do this?
Here's my idea of what this concept means. What's your
idea?" The result is considerable discussion in class that
flows back and forth. "I'm throwing things out, telling them
a little bit, and getting feedback—then having them share
their own ideas with students in their groups," he explains.
Rich also offers special support by trusting students with
high quality equipment. "When we do labs, I give them the
lab and let them do what they need to do with the lab,
trying to use computers and high-tech equipment as much
as we can because they're usually fascinated with it.
I reserve a lot of my best stuff for them and they appreciate
that and do a better job." Special pipettes, Spec 20s, and
interface software for the computer that allows students to
see digitally what's going on in an experiment in terms of
various measurements are all appreciated by Borinsky's AP

students. "One of the best things that I do is to challenge students to solve problems, not to take control of the class."

Another point of emphasis in Rich's classes is "Why are you here?" He explains, "It's really a difficult point to try to get across because every class they've ever taken, they've taken for external reasons—not for their own benefit unless it was a photography class or something really fun." He feels most students have never taken an academic class for fun—and for self-benefit. Rich Borinsky believes in constant reinforcement of this principle in his classes: "Why are you here? If you're only reading this once, are you getting enough out of it?" Demonstrating his own curiosity and overt passion for his subject, and supporting his students as respected peers wanting to learn, Rich shifts the responsibility for learning to his students. They progress from an external locus of control, in which they passively expect to be entertained and taught, to an internal locus of control, where they actively pursue their own learning.

Resist Authoritarianism

How does treating high school students as responsible adult peers co-exist with increasingly authoritarian high school rules? "This is the antithesis of that," Rich Borinsky admits. "Yes, I have to violate rules myself to do that. The first day I got bagels and cream cheese (students are not supposed to eat in class). I view them as peers. I have to kind of tiptoe around the administration." Students are supposed to come to class after the AP test, but Rich doesn't require it. He violates rules to do his highly popular AP study weekend— allowing students to drive up to the mountains in their own cars. The chaperoned students study and take practice tests, sometimes while in the hot tub of a mountain condo or enjoying dinner together. "In this class, they know they have accomplished something and they can feel good about themselves," he believes. He also contends they have to have humor. "They appreciate it and feel more relaxed." Rich occasionally gives such silly assignments as "Write a love story about photosynthesis."

Maintain High Expectations

The expectation is always there that Rich Borinsky's students are going to learn the material to a very high degree. "Mastery learning is something I'm very interested in," he notes. "Not just to get a *B* on something and let it go. They need to know the material at the end." Although he knows students often won't fully comprehend the material when first tested on it, he expects them to understand it by the end of the course. "You keep coming back to it in different contexts and they see the relevancy of it. At the end they know it. That's all I care about. I'm not too concerned as we go along if students don't get something." One thing that Rich does that particularly aids gifted learners is that he gives them considerable practice with multiple-choice tests, which constitute a substantial portion of the AP Biology exam. Because the gifted see many possibilities, they may make the questions more complex than the test author had in mind and see several possible answers. Rich has experienced this problem with gifted students and helps them to focus their answers more appropriately through sample tests. They overcome this difficulty once they become familiar with the tests and learn what knowledge is being assessed.

Ensure A Strong Content Background

Rich Borinsky believes another key to being a good teacher for gifted students is really knowing the subject well. The teacher's content background is an essential element. "You have to think well on your feet and direct their energy. If you have a surface level [of knowledge], they figure that out right away and they will totally write you off. It's critical to have a tremendous background. You can't overemphasize that." A seasoned veteran, Rich continuously takes classes and does "workshop after workshop after workshop." He states, "Everything you take from a workshop, you have to modify and make your own...Too much of the same thing and boredom occurs." Not only does his background prepare him for his most advanced students, but it also allows him to model being a lifelong learner who is always curious to answer new questions. Gifted students usually have great respect for teachers who are both exceptionally competent and open to new ideas. "I've always been interested in improving myself...my background has broadened considerably." Rich worries because "It's difficult to find people with a rich background in biology...right out of college they have a narrow background that needs to be broadened; I see teachers who need to learn so much and it doesn't happen overnight."

Care About Students

Rich Borinsky insists he deserves no credit for his students' high level of learning. To him, the students' accomplishment is their own, and he always feels he could be doing a better job. His students know he cares about what they're doing and Rich believes interacting with them is crucial. He recalls attending one workshop in which he was told that at least 80 percent of the reason a student would learn is because of the relationship with his or her teacher. "It's more important than all other reasons together. If you have a positive relationship with students, they're much more likely to want to do things than if you don't," Rich explains. "By giving up responsibility and creating an environment, I'm establishing positive relationships. I'm encouraging them to learn in their own way, at their own pace, and go as far as they can. So kids will go really far, way beyond." He's willing to go with them. Rich Borinsky notes that there are always a lot of why questions. "I find myself saying 'I don't know' a lot. They ask great questions. If you don't say 'I don't know,' you are going to get killed. They know when you're bluffing; they can smell it." Sometimes, Rich admits, he feels inadequate because he says, "I don't know" 15 or 20 times. But, he focuses on how he and his students can try to find out. "There are resources which are great." He adds that another very typical trait of gifted kids is the kind of questions they ask. They ask more abstract questions: for example, "Would the laws that apply to a certain biological process still apply in space?" Kids who are high achievers don't ask those questions.

"When we get to some things that are really esoteric—abstract—the fun is in differentiating themselves because they do know that. I'm always making them feel special." Rich believes there's nothing wrong with being elite because you know something that very few people know, and he is quick to praise his students for the accomplishment. "Go home and tell your parents about it. If they won't listen, tell your little sister or brother...or a pet," he tells them, certain that their knowledge is worthwhile and should be shared. But, laughing, he also tells them their knowledge and high-level interest in biology is "going to ruin your life." He warns, "The people you hang around with now, who may be interested in how many home runs somebody hit, you're going to become less interested in." With a smile, he cautions, "You're going to want to talk about the light/dark reactions of photosynthesis or how electrons are cycled between photosynthesis and respiration. Your girlfriend or boyfriend is not going to want to hear about this. So whatever your relationship is now, it's going to be trashed."

Passionate About Biology

Rich is passionate about biology. He remembers memorizing one book in a series of children's books his parents bought him—it was the book on science. "When I got to biology in high school, I thought, 'This is just so interesting.' " Rich says there are "hooks" all along the way in biology, fascinating things that make one want to learn more. "It may seem like it would not be interesting, but it is if you know how to frame it," this teacher insists. "I was really interested in ecology when I first started. As I've continued to learn, I've realized every single part of biology is interesting." He says of his students, "Probably they think it's bizarre that you're so interested in something, but if you weren't, they wouldn't be."

Elizabeth Maxwell: Reflections on Gifted Education

The Associate Director of the Gifted Development Center, Betty Maxwell is an accomplished teacher, reading specialist, counselor, and purveyor of wisdom about the gifted. A teacher for 18 years, she taught the fourth, fifth, and sixth grades in a gifted school, as well as second grade, fifth- and sixth-grade language arts, and high school English in more typical schools. She also served as a resource room teacher for grades five through eight.

Betty earned her Master's degree in gifted education, an experience that she feels significantly added to her expertise as a teacher of the gifted. Because she already had some background in learning disabilities from her experience as a resource room teacher, her Master's work helped her realize how she could combine instruction for students with both giftedness and learning disabilities—the twice exceptional. It also helped her to see certain qualities as essential to a good teacher of the gifted.

The Gifted Teacher's Best Characteristics

Appreciate Their Gifts

Betty believes that the ability to appreciate a gifted child is paramount. "Most children aren't able to open up to teachers who don't see them...who don't recognize who they are and what they do," she explains. The teacher must possess a general good will toward high intellect. "So much of the time, children are getting false feedback, that they are wrong in some way. They shouldn't raise their hands so much, should talk less, and need to be patient," she notes. "They are square pegs in round holes." Any teacher who recognizes a child's unusual grasp of things has to recognize giftedness, support it, and have good will toward the gifted.

She also feels teachers need to have at least superior intelligence themselves, as well as imagination, creativity, and humor to appreciate the needs of their students. A larger percentage of gifted children are intuitive, as well, according to Jung's scale. It's helpful for a teacher of the gifted to have that intuitive orientation to be sensitive to the emotional climate within the classroom.

Facilitate Learning

Betty adds, "It's really well known that gifted teachers need to be facilitators, not lecturers. They need to be promoting thinking and discovery on the part of their students; they must encourage questioning." In fact, the art of questioning and follow-up questioning is of crucial importance. The best teachers of the gifted view it as their obligation to ask questions that are provocative—that lead people to thinking.

Empower Students

Gifted teachers need to empower, rather than place limits. They should be delighted with the student's abilities and help the child expand them. "To do this they must have a sincere enthusiasm for ideas, creativity, for what gifted children are revealing, for the opportunity to explore and expand beyond the usual parameters of the class," Betty Maxwell explains.

Don't Tolerate "Meanness"

Just as Stuart Little proclaimed he didn't like "meanness,"
gifted children need a classroom environment that is kind
and supportive, not snide, derogatory and hurtful, Betty
cautions. Where the classroom or playground is out of
control and children are allowed to routinely treat others
roughly, unkindly, or in a bullying fashion, the gifted child
is especially anxious and responds extremely poorly. Where
the teacher is unkind to students, there is not only a lack of
trust that the teacher will keep children safe, but also a
sense of injustice that the teacher is violating the ethical
demands of his or her position. Gifted children can be highly
tolerant of a range of situations when the atmosphere is
"kind." "I've seen gifted students be really patient with
slower students if the teacher was positive and supportive;
they liked that kind of handling of the situation," Betty
Maxwell recalls. Related to this, they don't like strictness
and harshness, when gentler guidance is all they need. "You
need to be very positive," Betty notes, reinforcing their
progress through praise.

Teach Research and Interview Skills

They do want a teacher who is thoroughly knowledgeable,"
Maxwell insists, adding, "That's a huge stretch in an
elementary school. They're likely to be asking quantum
physics questions that go beyond the expertise of most
teachers." However, she reminds teachers to always "be a
facilitator and help them read or interview others who have
those answers." Gifted students' need for information can be
so insatiable that teachers must teach them to be
resourceful. What resources should they turn to? "Give
them practice in how to ask questions to get the most
answers," she advises. Teach them how to interview,
conduct polls, and speak to someone engagingly. They must
learn to find things on the Internet, use computers, and

locate resources in the library. Gifted students require a set of skills, often not taught in the regular classroom, to become independent learners.

Be Sensitive to Affective Needs

The good teacher of the gifted also needs to have some innate counseling skills, be a good listener, and read signs of when someone needs to talk, Betty recommends. The affective side of giftedness requires support just as much as the cognitive. "The teacher needs to create a class where there are a lot of independent projects going on so there's time to take someone aside to talk, or be willing to put in extra hours so they're available to talk," she advises.

Address "Being in the Gifted Class"

Betty Maxwell believes a major problem is that many gifted children are put into a gifted program with no explicit talk about why they're there. The teacher needs to allow them to discuss what it feels like in this special class situation, being pulled out of their regular class, etc. Part of the teaching time needs to deal with emotional issues. Students should begin the year with a discussion of what it means to be gifted. "They need to talk about the ability to learn rapidly, move faster, ask more questions, how annoying that can be to others in the class, and why there's a real need to have separate classes," she suggests. "Discuss how to deal with taunting from classmates and self-consciousness."

Involve Students in Self-Evaluation

Betty also believes it is important to involve students in self-evaluation of some sort; student input should be a part of looking at projects and grades. "Along with that comes a more level playing field—you're in more of a partnership with gifted children," she says. "The teacher needs to be getting their input, helping them understand themselves,

and meeting their needs, but not in a position of command."
The best gifted teachers, she believes, involve their classes in
problems that arise. They use brainstorming techniques to
work the problems out within the group (although emotional
problems need to be dealt with individually).

Be Flexible; Allow Instructional Plans to Change

Betty Maxwell advises teachers to be extremely flexible.
"Plans often get changed because kids will zoom through
plans that you've made that you think will take more time,
or there's a tremendous dislike of the approach, or something else comes up," she explains. "Go with the flow—the
moment; do the same thing in a different way," she
comforts. This can be particularly disheartening to the
inexperienced teacher who puts tremendous effort into a
project or unit, only to see it succeed minimally. It can be
difficult to try again. However, knowing this is an expected
pitfall can help teachers to prepare.

Help Students Stretch

"Aim high," Betty encourages, noting that gifted children
perform so much better when asked to stretch. "Bring into
the classroom some very real, high-level philosophical
problems to solve," she explains. "Raise the bar high."

Be A Rebel

Betty notes, as other teachers have told us, that many
excellent teachers of the gifted are rebels. She feels they are
more original thinkers and frequently question authority
themselves. They like to promote thinking for oneself in their
students. Simply by that orientation, they understand the
gifted student's divergent thinking, resistance to authority,
and need for choice. This also gives them an edge when
other teachers disagree with their methods. Accommodating
the gifted requires significant modifications in educational

programming. These teachers are less afraid to make those changes.

Make Homework Meaningful

Betty Maxwell sees several areas of concern for gifted students in the typical approaches schools take. The first is with homework. Usually assigned to assist less capable children who need additional practice to master concepts, it typically makes little sense for the gifted. "Gifted kids get concepts almost immediately, so their homework is almost always busywork. They are smart enough to realize it doesn't do them any good," she states.

Betty believes most are patient and tolerant of homework in the primary and upper elementary grades, but in the sixth through ninth grades, many become extremely reluctant to continue doing homework. "It doesn't make good pedagogical sense for them to do the same homework as other students. It's just an exacerbation of the usual problem they face in the regular classroom—just a frustration for them." She feels that they face the dual burden of wasting their time in class and having no time outside of the classroom if they're stuck writing down things they already know. "I think it builds resentment toward the schools," she insists. If homework consisted of novel ways of applying what they learn, she thinks their attitude toward homework would change. "Continued pressure to do it even when the students are getting high test grades, and making their grade contingent upon doing homework, is creating dropouts from school and a lot of underachievers." Betty states.

She further believes, "There's some kind of unconscious perception that homework may not be actually teaching kids things and yet there is a drive to preserve it." She believes homework has become more of a moral issue—of building character—than of ensuring content mastery. "You learn how to do this thing that's difficult for you; but, it's difficult in a bad sense. Difficult because it's mindless," she asserts.

"Teaching kids to do things that are mindless doesn't build character. The kids with the best character and integrity will rebel against this," Betty believes. Therefore, this strong stance about homework may be driving some of our best students, of character and integrity, away from school. They won't play the game. "I feel it's criminal the way we're really pushing some of our best students out of school," she concludes.

Betty Maxwell reminds us that "It isn't that these kids don't want to work. They don't want to be held back and treated unintelligently." We need to engage their minds at all levels. "They're willing to learn, but not jump through hoops. They have a need for that inner direction of learning. That's the spark," she notes. Many who find little meaning in regular high school courses are willing to take college or advanced online coursework concurrently. The work ceases to be a burden when the level is correct.

Resist Authoritarianism At School

Betty feels another approach schools take that is at odds with the gifted student's needs is authoritarian rules for behavior and attendance. Especially as children mature and move on to middle school and high school, strict rules and a plethora of consequences begin to overwhelm even our most responsible gifted students. Schools are managing a lot of high-spirited youth, clamping down with rules, dress codes, and ways of being that cause gifted students to rebel.

Not easily directed by others, some do better not going to high school, but to any college campus course or online course because people are not telling them what to do and how to do it. They want more choice. It's difficult in a regular classroom to give some students more choice than others, although that would suit varying individual needs. Betty Maxwell believes there is a growing tension in high schools between students asserting autonomy and administrations clamping down. Teenagers have power, drive cars, earn money at their own jobs. There is an increasing mismatch with the sense of freedom they have and a lot of rules in high school. "The more rules, the more rebellion...the less they're willing to follow the direction and the rules of the schools," she concludes.

In particular, Betty believes "Attendance rules really don't work well." She feels they enable adults to assert their authority over children and teenagers; however, they're really nonproductive at keeping kids in school. What students need most is "band, art, and a few good teachers," she insists. Unfortunately, "Most of those rules are there because school is unattractive to a lot of kids," she adds. Where schools have the rules, implicit in them is the notion that the classes are unattractive. She recalls that attendance rules used to be for the purpose of forcing fathers and mothers to send kids to school rather than make them work on the farm. "Truancy had teeth in it, too, for the same reasons," she states. "Gifted kids need their own set of rules."

Understand the Characteristics of Giftedness

Surveying her teaching career and educational preparation for it, Betty is most grateful to her Master's program for giving her a far greater understanding of the characteristics of the gifted. Before that, she had served on a school committee to set up a gifted program that sought to arrange mentors for gifted students. She recalls, "We created wonderful projects and expected the kids to love them, but it didn't always work." Her graduate work made her aware that gifted students need more choices; they need more input to be passionate. Her studies made her more comfortable with their emotionality, intensity, theatricality, and curiosity—those natural characteristics of giftedness. "I had a better sense of why some curricula worked better for them," she states.

Dabrowski's *Overexcitabilities*

In addition, "Exposure to Dabrowski's Theory of Positive Disintegration helped me see the intensity and sensitivity as very positive things," Betty explains. Kazimierz Dabrowski was a Polish psychiatrist, psychologist, poet, and musician. As a therapist to high ability individuals, he noted that his patients had *overexcitabilities*, as well as a persistent internal need to evolve as persons. Dabrowski believed such intensity and sensitivity enhance the self-actualization process and are part of very important potential. These intensities add to the individual's potential for growth. Maxwell believes that Dabrowski's work "honors emotionality and emotional development...honors the struggle that dealing with oneself can entail...honors positive maladjustment when your conscience exceeds the values of those around you. He honored that struggle in general," Betty clarifies. "You really see a lot of those characteristics, especially the *overexcitabilities*, in the makeup of gifted children. They do form deep attachments, are sensitive, intense, have very high highs and very low lows, an amazing imagination, etc." Supporting and nurturing such characteristics helps gifted children to fulfill their moral as well as their cognitive promise.

Following her teaching career, Betty Maxwell went on to complete training in psychosynthesis counseling and psychoeducational evaluation. She has worked at the Gifted Development Center in her current capacity (consulting, counseling, testing and making educational recommendations for gifted children) since 1989. Gently articulate, she remains a formidable champion of the gifted, of their rebellion, of their right to resist what is hurting them, decry authority for authority's sake, refuse homework that is pointless, and jump through hoops to prove personal value that is inherent. Betty believes education must never seek to break a student's will, but work in concert with it, empowering the individual and nurturing what is most important.

Quinn O'Leary...Teachers of the Gifted

When I walked into the classroom for the first time, it seemed no different than any of the others in the eldest wing of the school. Its institutional cinderblock construction was sheathed by cheap plastic carpet and papered with the idiot avunculism of inspirational posters. It was populated by a herd of cheaply built desks, showing the scars of years of use, and headed by a withered woman with the corners of her mouth drawn down slightly.

When asked to describe the room, I did so in the purple, florid prose of the cheapest pulp novels of a generation past, lashing everything present. The dingy, sad construction became menacing, the small windows unconsciously and invisibly barred. The buzz-saw vibrations that melt into buildings after years of the subconscious torture of youth reverberated strongly in my mind and on the page. The short page's worth of unrefined bile was returned a week later with a few impartial slashes of corrective red and a short, glowing praise of my ability and descriptiveness.

By the time I received that first telling assignment back, however, I had already realized how very different from my description this classroom was. Through the two years I had the pleasure of attending it, the room's shoddiness and disorganization became less distressing and more homey, closer to my ideal. The pent-up anguish of other rooms was here seen only as the mild, happy frustration of true intellectual challenge, of the actual education so rare in my scholastic experiences.

The teacher's name was Sharon Babb, and she remains in my memories like a mythical creature, timeless and

*dangerous, the distilled learning and wisdom of untold eons
at her disposal. Hunkering atop her hoard of treasured
knowledge, tolerant of and nurturing to the puppyish
intellect of her students but managing somehow to convey
the threatening consequence of her disappointment, she
loomed like a dragon over her impersonal, surrogate hatch-
lings. Unlike a mystical lizard, however, Mrs. Babb gave her
hoard to her students, more than willing to share. She
required the best a student had to offer, unsubtly disdaining
any idea she felt was beneath its originator. She forced
knowledge upon her students like an overzealous grandmother cooking huge meals for visiting children, offering so
much nourishment that I often stumbled away from class
with a head groggily full of new language. While time
whiled its lazy way through other classes, in Mrs. Babb's it
hectically rebounded like a super-ball in a bathroom,
always gone too quickly.*

*The atmosphere fostered by this woman's leadership was
one of flitting intellectual stimulation. Arguments arose and
laughter abounded, but the stories discussed and the pages
penned were alive with the crackling energy of newly
discovered academic excitement. The flow from one author
to another, from one linguistic style, period, philosophy and
medium to the next was unbroken, full of soft, frayed
tributaries, shaking hands with other branches. The lacy
interconnectedness of all education became more and more
clear under her expert illumination.*

*This glowing, encompassing flow, covering what it could
reach and hinting at all that it couldn't, brought back what
it was like to immerse myself in a library for days, leaving
to eat and sleep but otherwise with a book always in hand,
the musty smell of binding glue and the subtle scents of the
last person to borrow it ghosting its pages.*

*Few other teachers have taught me as much in their chosen
subject and none have come close to the tutelage I received
in the myriad facets of language. Mrs. Babb prodded the*

books of the proverbial greats to the forefront of the herd clamoring for my perusal, showed me how I want to develop myself as a scholar, as a writer and, almost incidentally, as a teacher.

10

Charter Schools

When local educational options for the gifted are limited or virtually nonexistent, the creation of a charter school is a possibility many states now offer. Charter schools are public schools, not private, that receive similar funding as regular district schools. They are created by citizens in the community who perceive a need for a certain type of school to meet the educational needs of a certain type of student. They may be oriented to disadvantaged students or any of a number of categories of students with a special need. Or, they may simply reflect a concern within the community for higher educational standards or greater adherence to traditional curricula.

Not for the fainthearted, charter school organization is best attempted by parents who are relatively desperate ("We won't send another of our children to that middle school!"), determined to see the process through ("We have no other options"), and have a good idea of what kind of school is needed (this part is important). The process is lengthy and arduous; often fraught with conflict between organizers, with the local school district, and, inevitably, some members of the community; and full of twists and turns from the time the application is submitted to the time the school opens. I often felt it was a lesson in learning about and dealing with new obstacles as we crossed the minefield of application requirements, district regulations, and state laws. A positive aspect, however, is that charter school applications always include a tenet that the children of the organizers will be accepted to the school (without this, no one would do the work necessary). Moreover, to see a school that embodies the hopes and dreams of people working together over a long period of time, and to watch students and parents love it, is unbelievably satisfying.

The school I helped organize was the first charter school approved within the Boulder Valley School District in Boulder, Colorado. Opening in the fall of 1996, the school now enjoys a modicum of stability and an abundance of respect. It is a middle school in the sense of being for students in grades 6 through 8; however, it differs consider-ably from typical middle school philosophy. For those who might want to consider the formation of a charter school, here is how it came to be.

Creating a School from the Ground Up

The Call to Arms

As it happened in other communities across the nation, the popularity of middle schools spread to Boulder Valley and the school district began the process of changing its junior high schools into middle schools. A friend wryly commented that the choice of middle school philosophies had a lot to do with which high-priced consultant a school district hired first; not all middle schools are alike. In the case of Boulder, Colorado the school board approved a list of "Middle School Essentials" that would change middle level education considerably. Not only would the grades change from grades 7 through 9 in junior highs to grades 6 through 8 in the new middle schools, but efforts would be made to group students within grade levels (our middle school had several "pods" per grade) and keep them together with the same teachers to provide a more supportive environment and the opportunity to team teach interdisciplinary courses in block-scheduled time periods. To maintain these close-knit, supportive groupings, students would be taught in hetero-geneous classrooms, *"regardless of ability, needs, and interests."* (This wording was actually used.) In order to keep students together, they could not be taking classes at different levels. The new middle school approach was supposed to provide a protective bridge between elementary school and high school. Junior highs, modeled after high school programs, were perceived as wanting in their ability to adequately support the younger students. Because Boulder is a highly educated community with a large gifted population, the resulting virtual abandonment of honors classes (math was spared in most but not all schools) was of concern to many, although another large cadre of community members felt the highly egalitarian Middle School Essentials were appropriate. In short, this vocal community was divided.

At the same time, a new International Baccalaureate (IB) program was beginning at a local high school. A group of parents at the middle school next door had realistic concerns that, just at the time when their students might need additional high-level preparation to enter the new IB program, district restrictions against honors classes would hinder efforts to provide that.

Support for gifted education was at an all-time low, as well, for the superintendent who fully supported the Middle School Essentials had closed the gifted and talented office. Parents of the gifted were concerned because honors classes had not fully met their children's needs *before*, and the situation would become considerably more grave without them.

Because I was co-chairing the district's gifted and talented advisory committee and volunteering in the IB program, I was invited to meetings the parents had requested at the

middle school to discuss preparing students to enter IB.
From the outset, teachers and administrators at the school
were extremely defensive, even though the conversations
focused mainly upon adding additional high-level work in
English (the school already had an excellent math teacher,
renowned for his advanced program). Not only did school
personnel take issue with the parents' perception that there
was a need to augment the program, but they were insulted
that parents would question their teaching. They, after all,
were the "education professionals." Unfortunately, this
disturbing theme presented itself several times in meetings
the parents tried to keep pleasant and was probably a
strong call to arms for the parents.

The end result was that this middle school's absolute refusal
to consider changes in their program led directly to the
creation of a charter school—an option they never would
have chosen. Recalling those meetings, it seems fairly clear
that the wonderful school that resulted might never have
been created if the middle school's personnel had made even
minimal changes in their English program. For the sake of
many students today, it is fortuitous that they did not.

The Organizing Committee

The first meeting of the "organizing committee" found a
group of parents, none of whom had ever created a school,
together in the same room just after Christmas. They had
the shared view that middle school programs needed to be
more challenging to prepare students for advanced high
school work (IB programs and Advanced Placement classes)
and the hope of creating a school that would open in the
fall. Faced with a restrictive district middle school policy, all
of the members had been frustrated in their efforts to
achieve meaningful change. Of greatest concern was the
danger of students losing their motivation to learn with an
insufficiently challenging curriculum. Specific concerns were
varied: restriction of honors classes to math only, or being

eliminated altogether in some schools; overreliance on heterogeneous cooperative learning strategies with group grades; teachers teaching outside of their areas of specialization to facilitate blocked schedules and interdisciplinary work; an overemphasis on efforts to make students feel good about themselves, when at the same time good students were being socially ostracized; and too much time spent coloring and learning in a *hands-on* fashion without adequate higher level discussion and critical thinking. Fourteen individuals signed the original application. They were a highly educated group; 10 had advanced degrees and virtually all had gifted children (several had profoundly gifted students). Their expertise included backgrounds in the natural sciences (meteorology, chemistry, geology, physics), computer science, mathematics, psychology, child development, social work, education, and law (two attorneys proved to be very helpful). Some were excellent writers. Because the course of application for this school was so arduous, a second charter application was filed, with the organizing committee having grown to over 30 individuals. Their varied backgrounds and willingness to contribute time and multitudinous efforts were significant strengths of the school.

Our school district provided the option of a school becoming a "focus" school, or a local school that follows district educational guidelines but has a particular focus to distinguish its program. The organizing committee was divided as to whether it wanted to create a focus or charter school. A focus school, as a regular district school, would alienate district personnel less and would make a statement that the organizing committee was trying to "play well with others." However, a charter school would have the power to waive many district rules and have considerably more autonomy. Although the group was clearly divided on this issue, application deadlines for each type of school figured in. There was a chance that we would be late for the focus school application deadline, so the decision was made to apply for both. If the focus school application was approved, the charter plan would be withdrawn. If the focus school application was turned down or could not be considered, the charter school application would then be considered. By state law, the local school board had to rule on charter school applications within 60 days of submission.

Writing the Application

The group worked quickly to make crucial decisions and submit this dual application. Committees were formed to handle the application writing, advertise the school, lead public information meetings, and find a potential site. It was decided to base the curriculum on what we knew of the International Baccalaureate Middle Years Programme (international spelling), which was just being released after initial trials in a number of schools around the world. Meetings were held to describe the goals of the program and to obtain letters of interest signed by students and their parents. By February 21st, a tired but determined group of individuals submitted a lengthy application, with sections keyed to the necessary state and district requirements for a *focus school* and a *charter school*. The school district fairly quickly turned down the focus school proposal on the basis that there was not sufficient time to create the program by fall. This activated the charter application, rendering further consideration of the school as a charter. Enough antagonism had developed by this point between the local school district and the organizing committee to make virtually all of the committee's members happy to be taking the more autonomous charter route.

Unfortunately, the Boulder Valley School Board turned down the charter application, as well, forcing us to appeal the decision with the State Board of Education and eliminating any possibility of the school opening its doors in the fall. We would have to wait another year. Thanks to a determined lawyer on the committee, who prepared and argued our case without charge, the State Board sided with our organizing committee, complimenting us on an outstanding application and requiring the Boulder Valley Schools to try to accommodate the program.

Site Challenges

Of critical concern was a site for the new school. Because capital funding was not available for charter schools at that time in Colorado, the organizing committee was having a difficult time finding potential space with the high lease rates in Boulder. The school district was reluctant to site the new school in one of its buildings with available space, so a potentially good program had no place to go. The State Board of Education placed pressure on the local school board to find space. The result was placement of the new charter school, as a school within a school, within the middle school that first refused to augment its curriculum. Because of its declining enrollment in recent years, this school had some extra space; it could offer some class-rooms, gym space, use of the auditorium, and the cafeteria. The additional needed classroom space would be provided by portable classroom buildings erected for that purpose. Another portable would provide space for an office.

As these decisions dragged on, the substance of the school's curriculum became an issue. As we obtained materials from the IB Middle Years Programme, it became apparent that the program, at that time anyway, consisted mostly of goals but little developed content. We liked what we saw in the sciences, but materials were sketchy in the other subject areas and we simply had too little to work with.

Choosing Curriculum

The committee selected a curriculum subcommittee to generate ideas for the full committee to consider. Of greatest help were teachers from other schools who had developed advanced programs in various academic areas and were willing to talk to us. After some time, we gained confidence in our ability to discern what would basically be needed. We knew we did not want to create a detailed curriculum—none of us had the necessary expertise. Yet, our children had been damaged too much by inadequate programs to leave that entirely to chance. The result was an agreement that we would establish basic parameters for the coursework we wanted to offer and expect quality teachers to do the rest.

The school opened the following fall. An adaptation of an article I wrote about the program for Kaleidoscope, a publication of the Colorado Association of the Gifted and Talented, describes the early formulation of the program, which has continued to undergo changes since its inception.

Summit Middle School in 1997

Boulder Valley's first charter school is giving us hope and options for all to copy in challenging the gifted middle level student. Summit Middle School, which opened in the fall of 1996, began offering students an ability-grouped assortment of higher level classes and the results are stunning. Students are delighted with the work and relieved to be in an environment where being smart is not a curse and friends with similar interests are easy to find.

The large parent organizing committee shared a common history of advocacy for challenging educational programs. The group began by waiving the district's Middle Level Education Essentials, which mandated heterogeneous grouping of a full range of students for instruction and restricted honors classes. They utilized the independence of a charter school to create a hiring plan for teachers, and waived the requirement that teachers be hired from the district's union pool. Teacher certification was waived as a mandate, as long as teachers had adequate expertise to apply for "alternative" state certification. It was decided not to create a school for the gifted, but a self-selecting school "for students who feel they want or need more challenge." Then began the enormous challenge of creating a diagnostic-prescriptive curriculum for the range of students the school expected to attract. To the degree possible, it also had to meet or exceed the district curriculum, conform adequately to district and state content standards, and provide a reasonable bridge from elementary schools in the area to a nearby International Baccalaureate or other advanced high school programs.

There was early agreement that the curriculum would have a balanced emphasis on content and critical thinking skills. It would be based on the assumption that Summit students can reason abstractly and need this level of challenge to maintain their motivation to learn. Middle school literature has stressed that a majority of students have not yet reached a level where they can reason abstractly (Tomlinson, 1992); therefore, most middle schools believe that hands-on approaches for concrete learners must be used for all students in a heterogeneously structured environment. In contrast, Summit would emphasize meeting individual needs based on level, pace, learning style and disability.

Many types of curricula were investigated: the International Baccalaureate Middle Years Programme, curricula from schools for the gifted and magnet schools in the Denver metropolitan area, and other middle schools with higher challenge offerings in a particular subject area. Teachers who had developed innovative programs for high ability students were invited to curriculum meetings.

General parameters were set for the classes to be offered; teachers would be asked to create the details of course syllabi. It was agreed to offer more than three year-long courses (typically four to five) in each subject area to allow placement of students at different points in a flexible sequence. The courses reflected fairly traditional content areas to blend with high school work and facilitate transfers. Summit classes at the high end overlapped with high school offerings.

Courses were defined in five core subject areas: English, science, math, social studies, and foreign language. The first year, four literature-based English courses were offered differing primarily by reading level. Courses were based upon the excellent challenge language arts program developed by Gerri Masson and Kathy Barry at Prairie Middle School in Cherry Creek. Students were directed in the study of quality pieces of literature, generally classics, at the pace of approximately one per month. They discussed the literature in depth within the classroom, moving from consideration of the concrete aspects of each piece to universal themes, providing a high level of abstraction. They wrote an essay with each piece, as well as completed creative writing assignments, "visual," and oral presentations. Each assignment offered a number of choices and students were allowed to present an alternative idea for approval. Direct instruction in grammar and essay writing were an integral part of the program, with modification for students testing out of these units. The heavy writing emphasis, high level of abstraction, multiple types of assignments to address different learning styles, enjoyable creative aspects and books of more appropriate reading level were felt to meet the needs of this range of students.

In mathematics, four courses were offered, with tutorials for various levels an every-other-day option. Advanced Numerical Topics served as a first course of high-level arithmetic and pre-algebra topics, for students not yet prepared to undertake algebra. This was followed by Algebra I, Geometry and Algebra II/Trigonometry, with the order determined for individual students by readiness for symbolic logic and spatial relations. Tutorials were used for filling holes or enhancing and accelerating learning.

Science courses began with "Biological Science and the Environment" and "Physical Science and the Earth." These two year-long courses replaced three typical years of study in earth science, biological science and physical science. Next to be offered were a Chemistry/Physics class akin to a ninth-grade offering for Pre-IB students at the nearby high school, with Biology (high school honors level) and Chemistry likely later additions. The acceleration of students in math allows the higher level treatments of subject matter in science; students can handle the necessary formulas and calculations and utilize math as the language of science.

Social studies courses included the following four choices: World Geography, History and Culture; American History; World History; and U.S. Government and History. The courses emphasized both higher order thinking skills and the mastery of basic facts and information in these fields. By the time students left Summit, they would be expected to understand the complexity of these subjects: for example, the effect of different perspectives on history; the use of history as both an explanatory and predictive tool; the influences of geography, resources, and culture on history; the fragmentary nature of historical data; how ideas and individuals can shape history; the interweaving of moral and ethical issues in history; the nature of violence within and between societies; the organizing constructs for society; how to conduct research; and how to argue current issues analytically.

Foreign language courses were offered in Spanish, French, and German with an emphasis on immersion. They consisted of Conversation, Level 1 (typical high school coverage), Level 2 and Level 3. The committee agreed that using the typical middle school Level 1a/1b approach to extend the first year course to two years was too slow. With the Conversation course, a student had the option of beginning with either an immersion approach (without emphasis on correct spelling of vocabulary or a strict grammatical focus) or Level 1, if the student had some experience with a language or were particularly adept at learning languages.

Electives were planned to appeal to the students and support a lively exploration of a variety of fields. Astronomy and Climatology supplemented more typical offerings in arts, drama, and physical education. Music performance classes grouped students by expertise, abandoning the typical orchestra, band, and chorus divisions for string quartets, jazz bands, and other combinations for the particular talent pool each semester.

Placements were based on ability, content mastery, motivation and developmental level (for example, an algebra readiness test was given to ensure readiness for symbolic logic). Students' grade levels were not a factor in placement and parents were allowed to make ultimate placement decisions following an advisory conference.

In the spring of 1996, Summit's principal met with each student and his or her parents to informally assess placement in each subject area for the following year. These initial assessments were augmented by administration of the algebra readiness instrument developed by the principal and by a review of reading comprehension levels on standardized tests to corroborate placement advice in English.

In the spring and summer of 1996, teachers were selected. Those submitting the strongest resumés were asked to teach a class to volunteer students and members of the hiring committee (English teachers were also asked to grade sample papers). Following the class, the students, then the teacher, were interviewed by the committee. The chosen teachers shared a number of characteristics: they had strong content-area expertise, they imposed no ceiling on the level of information they would share with the students, they treated the students as equals and had good rapport, and they stressed critical thinking and a high level of abstraction. Most were high school and college teachers interested in teaching advanced students at this age, who were relatively unaware of "what middle-schoolers cannot do." Some were parents of gifted children who had also struggled to find appropriate educational programs. They were highly intelligent themselves and passionate about their subjects.

Since the opening of the school to 250 students in the fall of 1996, the majority of families has been pleased. Textbooks, chosen to be at approximately the ninth-grade reading level and above (many students had high school-graduate reading comprehension levels), have been appropriate except for a geography book deemed too difficult by some and an ancient history book most feel is too simplistic. The curriculum has proven to be a reasonable match for the student body that is largely in the top quartile of ability. The flexibility to place students at different levels, regardless of age, has met most needs, although an Algebra Plus class has been added to increase the pace and depth needed for some students. Trusting parents to make placement decisions has proven to be reasonable. Some have worried that the approximate two hours per night of homework is stressful and inappropriate for the younger students; others, who have had an older student arrive at high school unprepared for an IB program, feel this preparation is warranted. Students are clearly learning organizational skills necessary to handle their coursework. Minor curriculum modifications are likely to continue as talks progress with local high schools to ensure a smooth transition for Summit students. One course change was brought about by the students themselves, who rallied with placards. Frustrated that their foreign language conversation courses did not include textbooks and more specific help with spelling and grammar, they initiated the elimination of most of the Conversation sections. Their teachers agreed to modify the classes to include the Level 1 curriculum and the students agreed to the extra work in the second semester.

Although evidence of the success of this school is still largely anecdotal, the satisfaction felt by even the most highly gifted students suggests this to be a significantly different environment than public schools usually offer. A science teacher could not contain her joy as she talked to the parents of her Chemistry/Physics students at Back to School Night. "I want you to know what your students did," she said, holding up a small square of foil. After only a few days discussing the physical properties of matter, she had asked her students if they could find a way to determine the thickness of the foil. Each student in the class had been able to figure out independently how to calculate the thickness of the foil. "This is something many college freshmen cannot do and your children did it!" The teacher, who had a Ph.D. in Biochemistry, had come to us from a university and was used to teaching college freshmen. The English IV teacher has taken her class through *The Rhyme of the Ancient Mariner*, *Beowulf*, and *A Doll's House* at a depth most of us experienced in college. While shaping their essay writing, grammar mastery, oral presentations, and knowledge of literary forms and devices, she invoked Joseph Campbell's notions of the universal hero and hero's journey to broaden her students' experience, challenged them with the Anglo-Saxon warrior code and comitatus relationships, and explored issues of individuals who must reject their roles in society. One student commented to his mother that he had never discussed such advanced issues at school, only at home.

A particularly joyous aspect of the new school has been students blossoming socially. Many who were previously isolated for their differences, known to be sensitive and introverted, and girls with a tendency to *go underground* have flourished. One teacher commented, "There are no shrinking violets in my classroom." Summit students both

work and play hard. The school has a volunteer Dean of
Fun, and student council, dances, outings, carnivals, and
sports flourish along with academic competitions. Hundreds
of tickets have been sold for area plays the students attend
together.

The Summit model offers an alternative for the education of
gifted middle level students that is likely to effect more
appropriate programming and social development than can
be provided by modifications in the heterogeneous classroom. The accelerated curriculum is more easily delivered
with instructional approaches geared to these learners,
combining high levels of abstraction and critical thinking
with an energetic involvement of students and hands-on
activities. Teachers can be selected from higher levels of
education who have the necessary expertise in their subjects
to offer instruction without a ceiling when students wish to
move ahead. Students have opportunities to develop socially
with friends who appreciate their similar interests and
nurture their self-esteem. Creating one or more such
schools in a district is no more expensive than maintaining
the same number of students in typical middle schools.
Opening the school to students on a self-selecting basis
allows those most at risk of underachievement or dropping
out a clear alternative. Gifted students may be educated in
what most truly approximates a least restrictive
environment.

Summit Today

Now well-established, this charter school has flourished
from the point of view of its students, parents, and staff. It
has struggled as most do, as well. The school hired its third
principal in its first five years, finding a comfort level

between its parent governing board, principal, and staff not without challenge. Yet, as the school has matured and the interested parties have grown to view their efforts as joint, it has become easier. Likewise, the success of the school increases everyone's confidence and minimizes overreactions as problems arise.

The school has made changes as needed. Curriculum development has been ongoing, with great effort put into meeting specific needs of the student group in various subject areas. Teachers and administrators have noted a change from the first couple of years at Summit when the parents and the students really knew what the mission of the school was, which was to provide a highly academic environment for kids and to make sure that the kids at the top end were not forgotten in the process. Summit has become so popular and the school test scores are so good, parents are now ignoring the mission of the school and choosing to send less advanced students to the school so that they can earn high test scores, too. It has triggered serious changes in the way the school must function.

Below is a description of Summit's curriculum for its seventh year. It has clearly evolved since the school's first year of operation, when parent organizers created an outline of what was felt to be needed. With the help of fine teachers and a standards-based approach, Summit now has a carefully constructed, solid program. However, it is satisfying to note that the assumptions of the parent organizers were very good. The instincts guiding the group to create an accelerated program to fit the level of an advanced student population were on target. Summit has done well offering courses that overlap with high school-level work, allowing students and their families the final say in placement decisions, and, in general, diverging from middle school philosophy to offer many levels of instruction, rather than heterogeneously grouped classes for all.

Current Curriculum

English

In English, the school has retained its four year-long, literature-based courses, with students placed at the level that is appropriate. The school considers the first two levels to cover the content of typical middle school coursework and the third and fourth levels to overlap with high school offerings. The English Level I course will teach students to develop skill in decoding literal meaning in a variety of literature texts while beginning to identify stylistic and structural literary elements including plot, theme, and characterization. In addition, students will use the writing process to develop basic skills: creating and organizing solid expository paragraphs and five-paragraph essays based upon a thesis statement. Formal grammar instruction will include parts of speech and correct use of end punctuation. The coursework will culminate in English Level IV, in which students will respond to literature on numerous levels, considering both universal themes and the particular cultural and artistic traditions that shape a literary work. In addition to the literary elements introduced in earlier levels, students will respond to and analyze stories, poems, plays, and novels with respect to genre, experiences with various rhetorical purposes, including exposition of research, comparison/contrast, analysis of literary style, and narration/storytelling. Grammar units will focus on improvement of writing accuracy and style: spelling rules, internal punctuation, and embedding information using phrases and clauses. To increase flexibility, the faculty has developed two separate reading lists for each course level. The lists are utilized in alternate years the course is offered, allowing a student to remain at the same level, if needed, for two years without repeating the same content. This is especially helpful for the student who struggles in English when

entering the school or the student who begins at a high level
and needs to repeat English IV. This next year, for the first
time, only one section of English IV will be offered, reflecting
the lower proportion of highly advanced students now
comprising the student body. In addition, for the first time,
a remedial reading class must be offered.

Science

In science, Summit will continue to offer two year-long
courses covering three typical years of middle school
instruction: Biological Sciences and the Environment and
Physical Sciences and the Earth. This has continued to work
well, although it is challenging for some students. Those
who have flourished with their instruction will continue on
to Chemistry/Physics, an advanced high school-level
offering. Students who have struggled will take Advanced
Topics in Science, a course designed to revisit selected
content areas.

Social Studies

In social studies, students begin their coursework with
World History, generally taken in sixth grade, which explores
the development of the world's major civilizations on all
continents from pre-history through the Renaissance. This
is followed by American History, which covers the development of our nation from the initial contact between
Europeans and Native Americans to the present. This course
sets the stage for the final course in the sequence: World
Geography/International Relations. The goal of this course
is to help students understand the complex political,
economic, social and environmental problems that face the
world's nations today and to assess the role the United
States should play in shaping solutions.

Math

Courses in mathematics include Pre-Algebra, Algebra, Advanced Algebra and Introduction to Geometry, Pre-Algebra Honors, Accelerated Algebra, Proof Geometry, and Algebra II/Trigonometry to address the need for differing levels of content and instructional pace. Parents and students make the final determination of course choice with school recommendations to assist them. Students are asked to take the most difficult course in which they can succeed. All students will have a solid understanding of algebra by the end of eighth grade (most middle schools allow only some students to take algebra before high school).

Foreign Language

Foreign language instruction is available in French, Spanish, and German. The equivalent of two full high school years of a language comprises the three year-long courses at Summit: Beginning Language, Language I and Language II. Students are prepared to begin high school level III courses after completing Summit's coursework.

Electives

Electives at Summit continue to offer a combination of training in necessary modern day skills, such as computer literacy, support for talent development in the arts, and opportunities for exploration. Advanced students require higher level support for talent development, and their exploratory behavior is more sophisticated. Summit utilizes its talented faculty to provide varying topics of interest (e.g., Introduction to Japan: A Portal to Nihon). Teachers at Summit know well that middle school students in a highly academic program still require their physical education classes (they need to run, jump, bounce balls), and opportunities to express themselves in the arts. Especially in such a program, students need outlets and opportunities to keep stress in check.

Technology is supported with three courses. Applied Technology offers units on structures, machines, energy, materials, flight, rocketry, communications, electronics, and computer technology. Introduction to Programming is a beginning computer programming class, whereas Advanced Programming emphasizes proper program design, including subroutines, data structures, and program control.

Liberal arts electives include Drama, Advanced Reading Techniques, Film as Literature, and Creative Writing. Art electives include Art Forms, Pottery/Crafts, Sculpture, and Splash of Color. Music options continue to include an exceptional range of courses and talent groupings: Orchestra and Select Strings (the latter requiring three years of playing and an audition); Jazz Band I, Jazz Band II, and Jazz Band III (the latter requiring a minimum of three years of playing and an audition); Musical Theatre Workshop; and Choir, Starlight (advanced choir), and Silver Rain (choral ensemble by audition only).

Physical education classes continue to be taught even though the school has only the use of a multi-purpose room for a gym.

Current Politics

With all of Summit's success, it has continued to draw the ire of the school district that fought so hard against it. Continued intense pressure against the school's location, from the middle school forced to share space with it and sympathetic school board members, finally forced Summit to move to another site. It currently resides in a former elementary school building that had been closed. Although the site contains only a multi-purpose room that must serve as cafeteria, gym, and auditorium, and still requires some portable classrooms, the staff is happy to be on their own. There is a sense of relief at having their own space and of not being forced to live with an unfriendly neighbor. The district has stubbornly refused to let the program grow significantly, although it has a lengthy waiting list every year. Interestingly, the school district has not tried to copy it or compete with it, even though this charter school has the highest middle school test scores in the district.

Summit recently appealed to the State Board of Education several decisions made by the local school district. A three-to-three split decision by the board (one member sympathetic to Summit was absent) resulted in Summit's inability to prove its case. Upheld were the district's decisions to restrict Summit's growth to only 50 students within the next five years, restrict Summit from building a gym (one Board member said it was not needed in a highly academic program), make Summit renegotiate its site each year, and force Summit to relinquish all funds raised in internal fund drives to the district (Summit could no longer use these funds, in part, for teachers). The district would decide how much each school would be given. Of significant concern was the fact that Summit was ordered to develop a remediation plan for struggling students, even though the school's stated mission is to support students who require higher challenge and a more advanced program.

Can Charter Schools Meet the Needs of the Gifted?

This chapter began as an effort to familiarize parents with the charter school concept as a viable option for meeting the needs of the gifted. Parents frustrated by their children's inability to learn appropriately in typical school programs need options desperately, and charters have seemed to offer a clear alternative. Charter schools exist to meet myriad student needs. One in Colorado even serves pregnant teens! Certainly, charter schools for the gifted make sense.

However, the problems Summit has experienced emphasize the need for parents to proceed with caution. Certainly charters offer a publicly funded alternative that can, potentially, result in a school with a significantly different educational program. Yet, charter schools are expected to be *open to all* and therein lies the problem. Whereas a school for pregnant teens, obviously not "open to all," is tolerated because it is perceived to meet a need in the community, a school for high ability students may draw criticism because the *need* for it is largely unappreciated.

Summit organizers were initially divided as to whether to create a school for the gifted or a school appealing to a somewhat larger group. Some were clearly uncomfortable with the term *gifted* and felt it would not be popular in Boulder, Colorado. The decision was made to create a self-selecting school "for students who feel they want or need more challenge," hoping that students and their families would choose wisely. Knowing that self-selecting schools for the gifted *can* work, provided the school carefully advertises its program so that parents can make good choices, this approach seemed possible for Summit.

However, the school district recently changed its application process for *schools of choice*, limiting Summit's ability to advertise. Until this year, parents requesting a school of choice were asked to turn in a form at their chosen school. When parents came to the school, they were told of informa- tional meetings and opportunities to visit the program. Now, parents are asked to turn in a request to the district office, listing their first, second, and third choices. If they cannot be granted their first choice, they automatically receive their second. Some new families at Summit have never attended a meeting or learned much about the program. Only a brief description is allowed in the district's brochure on schools of choice. Summit's principal has noted that many of the school's problems could be alleviated if only the parents would visit.

What does a school do when the wrong students attend? Initially, Summit organizers felt such students might need thoughtful "counseling out" because the program would be too stressful for them and other more typical programs would be a better fit. They knew the program was too small for teachers to stretch too much. Teachers also felt that to keep the level of the program high, they could not lower it to the level of the least advanced learner. Yet, pressures such as that by the State Board to develop a remediation plan for next year fly in the face of reason. Each school has a right to stay true to its mission.

Summit's teachers deserve credit for their enormous effort to meet the needs of a student body with ever-widening abilities. For example, science teacher Sharon Sikora, profiled in the teacher chapter, modified her requirement that eighth-graders do Science Fair projects to allow for a less rigorous, group-oriented activity she felt some students would benefit from more. The high-end students overwhelmingly chose Science Fair and individual projects. The lower ability group, which now constitutes 30 percent of the student body, chose a robotics project that was offered as more of a group activity. Critical thinking was emphasized in the group project, as well. All culminated in a "Shine" night, where all students could share their projects who wished to share them with parents. Sharon felt confident that she met the needs of more students in this way than requiring Science Fair for all eighth-graders. A $10,000 grant from Toshiba provided wonderful technology for the robotics project. Students had the opportunity to explain this advanced technology, and the use of it, to their parents, who were often in awe of their children because they were able to do such high-level work. A critical piece in any student's development is the opportunity to shine. Sharon believed that "not every project was awesome, but every kid felt awesome...because every one went up a couple of rungs on the ladder." Some students did not feel confident enough to present their work to parents, but took a strong leadership role in arranging the evening. "You can make it work on so many different levels... now the clientele has shifted from these very gifted kids to a very different group—many emotionally disturbed, many with learning disabilities now," Sharon notes. Summit has always embraced students with disabilities, but advanced students: the twice exceptional and bright students with emotional or physical issues.

The question is: how far can the teachers and the program stretch? In Sharon Sikora's classes, she has found it more difficult to shape critical thinking and been unable to cover as much material as in classes in previous years. She responds, "We're doing well. We're all making adjustments, but I wouldn't want it to go any further. We're still able to challenge those high-end kids." She agrees it would help to make all families come to Summit and hear about the mission and what the school is about. "You are going to have homework; you are going to have to work hard." The school district handling the school choice is a problem. The state board ruled that Summit will have to provide a plan to address the remedial needs of Summit's less successful students. "If you follow the mission statement of the school...," she begins and looks troubled. "Counseling kids out is difficult. Few leave in the middle of the year, but some do leave at the end. And wherever they go, they're happier. It's an interesting challenge."

Colorado does have one charter school specifically for the gifted; another was approved recently, but dissolved due to internal problems. The existing school, which is slightly older than Summit, has continued to use IQ testing as a part of its admissions program—clearly not complying with the *open to all* concept. However, IQ testing is an excellent way of determining *need* for a gifted program. Above all, it measures the degree of asynchrony of the child and is highly suggestive of problems of *fit* in a program designed for average children. This school has come under less attack from its district than Summit, presumably because the district was more amenable to the concept from the outset. It has suffered, however, from problems due to changing staff members. One teacher noted that a charter school, which is usually smaller than regular public schools, is more vulnerable. "They are only as good as the people who work in them," she notes, and may suffer from a lack of checks and balances that regular public schools have. What is their greatest strength, may also be their greatest weakness.

Although the *open to all* concept is more often a point of contention in schools for high ability students, a local charter school attorney points out that a Colorado law allows charter schools to provide any program currently being provided by local school districts. A few school districts have self-contained schools for the gifted, or schools within schools. There are also a number of magnet schools for the arts, computing, International Baccalaureate, etc. Quite interestingly, all have extremely stringent entry criteria and are not *open to all*. The attorney's message is that there is room for some charter schools to meet the needs of specific groups for which enrollment criteria are appropriate.

Parents in all states who may be considering charter school options for the gifted need to be aware of their uphill fight, but the possibilities that remain. Knowing that Summit Middle School continues to support at least a small number of students who would not have other reasonable options, and charter schools for the gifted do exist, seems to justify the effort required to create such schools. However, organizers need to do their homework, choose fellow organizers wisely, be willing to continue their fight, and include lawyers in their groups!

The Colorado League of Charter Schools estimates that there
will be 91 charter schools operating within the state by next
year. Not only in our state, but also across the country, they
are becoming more popular. A law just passed offers help to
charters with building expenses, including requiring districts
to include charter schools in bond issues.

Quinn O'Leary...Summit

*So what can I say about Summit? It's a small school, one of
those unimposing, ambiguously-designed products of an era
bygone in all architectural study save that of schools.
Orangeish brick, a single squat story, ringed with a band of
windows that look like they pivot open from the bottom like
a drawbridge. The surrounding schoolyard is caught
between the philosophies of grammar and middle school
playgrounds, the squatting hulk of the former's requisite
equipment looking small and well-used in the trampled
verdancy of the latter's requisite sports-sized field. It's a
rather dull, cookie-cutter façade considering the ability it
contains.*

*I was frankly tired, a late night and an early morning
ganging up on me, but my exhaustion was tensed and
somewhat dispelled, made ignorable by the stomach-
wrapping tentacles of excitement and the crackle and buzz
of caffeine. My reason for attending, if only for a day and if
only as a ghost, was to watch the expertise of Summit's
teachers.*

*After the usual rounds of smiles and handshakes, I was
shuffled off to my first classroom, moving among the tide of
kids five and six years younger than myself, feeling ancient
and out of place. Walking through the halls of a middle
school is usually like visiting a slaughterhouse long out of
use. It's oppressive and unreal, the lingering flickers of*

simple anguish and elemental fear blending with the forgotten, ethereal and half-imagined smell of animalistic desperation.

Summit, however, was different. The electrical charge in the air was still present, the slightly-needy touch of adolescence, but the fear and angst were absent, replaced by the open, breezy flow of comfortable youth. Abruptly, I found myself wishing I had attended this school.

I claimed a quiet, out of the way seat in my first classroom, English IV, a busily organized place run by a perfectionistic but rather kind and obviously competent teacher. The students were occupied with character dissections, peeling away layers of nuance and exposing desires and fears from the terse text of a short story. It was gratifying to a ridiculous degree to see the intelligence of these children tested and displayed.

In another class, I heard a discussion of Mark Twain that would have put many a high schooler to shame, followed by a discussion of the basis of heroism and a short mention of Metamorphosis, *a book I didn't get around to reading myself until far later in life than this lucky lot, and certainly not for credit.*

As I watched the kids interacting and enjoying their time in what was the least enjoyable of my scholastic eras, I was washed over again with the same soft jealousy and retroactive wishing. I grinned, knowing now that alternatives to the prison camp of most middle schools do exist. It's simply a matter of finding them.

References

Tomlinson, C. (1992). Gifted education and the middle school
    movement: Two voices on teaching the academically talented.
    Journal for the Education of the Gifted, 15(3), 206-238.

For Further Reading

U.S. Charter Schools. Produced with the U.S. Department of
    Education, providing information about currently existing charter
    schools across the United States, state laws, startup and
    assistance, and federal resources.
    http://www.uscharterschools.org/ (18 Feb. 2003).

The Center for Education Reform.
    http://edreform.com/charter_schools/ (18 Feb. 2003).

11

Planning Your Child's Program— Year by Year

Parents call the GDC from around the world, asking what should be done for their children. They call from large cities with more resources, such as the parents who phoned from the Washington D.C. area, whose child once attended a preschool program at the Smithsonian. They call from rural areas, such as the mother from Nebraska, whose son was in a one-room schoolhouse. Virtually none of them have access to a school for the gifted, which would be our first choice to meet academic, social, and emotional needs. Most have only their neighborhood public school, a few additional public schools they might consider, and, possibly, one or more private schools. Not seeing an easy way to meet their child's needs, they seek advice.

They call about how to support the four-year-old, who is an avid reader and is begging to attend school early. They call about the second-grader whose teacher says she is reading at the fifth-grade level. They call about the fourth-grader who seems to have an easy understanding of algebra concepts at home, but is frustrated with arithmetic drill and practice at school. They call frequently because the gifted program at their child's school is minimal or nonexistent, or because being identified for gifted services requires high achievement and their child is losing motivation to achieve.

Parents call because low-level middle school coursework has their son refusing to attend school, or their daughter going underground with her abilities to be more popular. They call because their gifted high school students have attendance problems and are in danger of being expelled from school. The calls regarding older children and teenagers take on more urgency because these kids are considerably more frustrated with their educational options than their younger counterparts.

What role should the parent play? How much advocacy is prudent and what form should it take? Given the fact that this is truly an at-risk population, advocacy is essential. Here is how it can be applied, sensibly and realistically.

The Diagnostic-Prescriptive Curriculum

Gifted children require a *diagnostic-prescriptive curriculum* geared to their advanced learning needs. They master concepts more easily, with little or no drill and practice, so they pace through material more quickly. Even adding depth and breadth (enrichment) to their programs, they still pace faster. Too much of a discrepancy between what they already know and what they are being taught threatens their motivation to learn. So, the parent needs to advocate for accommodations each year that provide the best fit.

Such advocacy takes a different form with gifted children of different ages and levels of giftedness. Children who are moderately gifted will need individual educational plans throughout elementary school to ensure that they are placed at approximately the correct levels in their various academic subjects. Although they stay in one classroom throughout the day, the IEP allows for accommodations within the room and possible opportunities to pursue some work at a higher grade level in another classroom or through a program outside the school.

In middle school, the advocacy focus changes somewhat from ensuring modifications within a single classroom, although this could occur, to obtaining permission from a counselor, teacher, or administrator for the student to take higher-grade-level classes earlier. Appropriate class placement usually involves placing out of some entry-level courses that the student has already mastered and taking classes older students take. This usually results in some high school coursework being taken during middle school. High school advocacy again emphasizes obtaining permission for the student to place out of entry-level courses, take advanced high school classes earlier, and also take college-level courses concurrently.

For children with even higher levels of giftedness, the needed progression is faster. We have seen a wide range of accommodations work for these children, from profoundly gifted children graduating from high school before age 10 and beginning college, to acceleration in the public schools of only a couple of years, provided there are substantial opportunities for high-level work.

With all gifted children, we must constantly assess how their programs are working and make adjustments as needed. We should expect to hear satisfaction from the students about the majority of their courses, even if some will almost inevitably disappoint. Here are guidelines for advocacy at the various levels of schooling, to extend the information presented in chapters 7 (Successful Programs) and 8 (Models of Advocacy).

Elementary School

Early Entrance

For the child who is eager to begin school and has early reading skills, early entrance to kindergarten is an excellent accommodation in school districts that allow it. With such a child, it is a good idea to inquire about the necessary requirements for admission, as this is the easiest acceleration to accomplish. The child begins school with a group of children he or she can remain with for some time. In addition, since reading is not taught seriously until first grade, a child who is advanced is likely to suffer significantly if forced to wait another year before even beginning kindergarten. In some cases, a placement in first grade makes even more sense, but is rarely available.

School districts that allow early admission usually require assessment of some sort. Unfortunately, some utilize a mock classroom situation in which the social maturity of perspective new students is evaluated. When the criterion for maturity is deemed to be willingness to readily join the group, introverted young gifted children may appear *immature*. This is an inappropriate requirement for the gifted, a group that is predominantly introverted and needs time to observe and reflect before joining in. Such children will appear to be no more *mature* in this regard if assessed next year or the year after. They will be slow to join the group initially, but will more eagerly join as they become familiar with classmates. As long as they are comfortable being placed with the older group, and want to begin school early, then early entrance to kindergarten is an appropriate accommodation.

In school districts that refuse to allow early entrance, a child can sometimes accelerate within a few weeks to first grade. The reasoning behind this is that the kindergarten teacher, having observed the child in the classroom, is in a better position to determine the need for acceleration. In such cases, it would be wise to not only have the child tested on an intelligence test, but also on an individual achievement test to document reading and math achievement levels. When the scores indicate advanced achievement, as well as gifted abilities, they can be used to strengthen the case for acceleration to first grade. Many parents worry that their children will not score high on individual achievement tests because they have not been taught higher-grade-level work. However, young gifted children tend to score higher than their classmates because they have learned concepts more thoroughly and can answer more questions correctly. Of course, at some point exposure to new skills is necessary, for example, when learning to multiply or solve algebraic equations. However, these *efficient learners* usually outscore their grade peers, given only the instruction all students have had.

Accommodations in Kindergarten and the Primary Grades

Once children are attending elementary school, regardless of their age, the most common modification needed in the early grades is for advanced reading skills. More young gifted children are advanced in reading than in math, probably because most are read to as young children and have regular access to reading at home. Fewer are taught formal math skills beyond counting. Because the most important early emphasis in school is the acquisition of reading skills, considerable time is spent teaching reading. Although we want to ensure reasonable coverage of phonics and sound blending, the child who is fully reading and sounding out words does not need all of the instruction beginning readers need. Moreover, the advanced child needs to read at a challenging level to progress further.

A plan should be developed with the teacher to substitute more advanced work for material that has already been mastered. If the teacher divides the students into reading groups based on skill level, there may be a group appropriate for the child. If the children are not grouped, or if none of the groups is reading challenging enough material, opportunities to place the child with a higher-grade-level reading group should be sought. In addition, the child may be assigned higher level books to read by the classroom teacher who is individualizing for this child. Or, in some cases, a somewhat lower level book that the class is reading has enough inherent value that it is deemed to be appropriate for the gifted child, as well. When this occurs, assignments related to the book may be modified to increase complexity or level of thought.

Children who read early are also more likely to be aware of the correct spelling of words. Most teachers of kindergarten and first grade encourage inventive spelling to support the early writing efforts of their students. Any reasonable effort to spell a word is met with praise by the teacher. This removes the pressure to be perfect that may hinder some children from writing. However, the gifted child who is already aware of many correct spellings may think new spellings are being learned correctly because of the teacher's praise. Thus, many misspelled words will be committed to memory. Although perfectionistic gifted children also need to be encouraged to write before they know how to spell most words, gently providing the correct spelling, as well, may be appreciated as it helps the child avoid learning a word incorrectly. Some gifted children find this incorrect learning stubborn to rectify.

Children who are advanced in math in the early grades need to be supported to learn at their level, as well. Though reading is most emphasized in kindergarten and first grade, the child who has sufficient interest in math to have learned advanced concepts also needs to continue this wonderful progress. Some children are very eager to learn basic arithmetic operations and question their parents at home to learn more. It is important to support a child's curiosity when information is sought, so we recommend that parents answer their children's questions. However, the child who can add, subtract, and multiply in first grade is going to be underchallenged with a constant diet of beginning addition.

Accommodations must be made so the child can continue to progress.

The IEP

Rather than hope these types of things will be done, perhaps following a conversation with the teacher, it is better to create a written plan. It can be called an *Individual Educational Plan* (IEP), using special education terminology, *Personal Learning Plan* (PLP), or something similar. Some schools carefully avoid the Special Education terminology to underscore the fact that gifted accommodations are usually not mandated by law, whereas Special Education IEPs are. Parents have legal rights relating to Special Education plans and can expect that the school will comply with the accommodations listed. Even though program modifications for the gifted are not usually mandated by law, the written plan is still helpful as it clarifies expectations for the parent, teacher, and student.

The plan need not be complicated; in fact, a simple, straight-forward plan is more likely to be completed and followed. The plan should address the areas of the curriculum in which the child will need modifications. Other areas where the program seems about right for the child need not be mentioned. Forms for the IEP vary. Two examples utilizing a simple form are completed below, but other forms will work well, too, such as those in Karen Rogers' *Re-Forming Gifted Education*, Susan's Winebrenner's *Teaching Gifted Kids in the Regular Classroom*, or Sally Reis' *Curriculum Compacting*. The child's teacher or school may have a form that will serve the purpose. The important thing is to complete a written plan that documents agreed-upon educational goals and lists basic activities planned for the school year. It is not necessary for the plan to contain each and every lesson—the teacher will need freedom to plan as the year unfolds—but general goals should be defined.

For example, let's consider the case of a first-grade girl named Jennifer, who started reading before kindergarten, and currently reads at the third-grade level. She is reading simple chapter books. Her math is at grade level because she has not been exposed to formal, written math calculations at home. She already knows how to spell many words because she is an avid reader. If her advanced reading needs are not accommodated, she may fail to progress in her reading this year. Moreover, she may sense disapproval about her level of reading skill if it is not supported (we have seen gifted children stop reading because they believe the teacher or other students will not like it). Jennifer is moderately gifted with an IQ of 137. Her Wechsler IQ test profile indicated strengths in both verbal abstract reasoning and spatial reasoning. Like most gifted children, she is an introvert who is not likely to complain to her teacher about work that is too easy or to risk calling attention to herself. Her parents and teacher would like to support her strengths in the classroom this year. What might her IEP include?

Individual Educational Plan

Name: *Jennifer*   Age: *6-3*

Grade: *1*

Strong Subject Areas: *Reading and spelling*

Learning Characteristics/Style: *Gifted verbal-abstract reasoner and visual-spatial reasoner*

Subject Areas Chosen to Provide Advanced Study: *Reading and spelling*

Weaknesses to be Accommodated: *None*

Goals: *Jennifer will progress commensurate with her ability this year from her current level in reading and spelling. Her introversion will be supported in the classroom. She will be allowed to pace quickly, if needed, in math* (her gifted visual-spatial strengths suggest she will be good in math).

Activities:

1. *Have Jennifer participate daily in an advanced second-grade reading group.*

2. *Exempt her from pre-reading activities and phonics instruction in the first grade, as her knowledge of phonics is strong.*

3. *In writing assignments, encourage Jennifer to spell inventively, but also offer her the correct spellings for her own information (no penalties for misspelling words).*

4. *Admit Jennifer to the school's gifted program, especially to encourage contact with other gifted girls.*

5. *Have Jennifer participate in the Jr. Great Books program, an extracurricular activity at the school. This program encourages thoughtful analysis of literature, emphasizing abstract reasoning, a strength for Jennifer.*

6. *Assess frequently in math.*

7. *Minimize drill, practice, and worksheets.*

8. *Teach to her visual-spatial strengths: provide a conceptual framework before teaching and use visual aids. Also provide advanced verbal explanations, as needed.*

Evaluation: [Were Jennifer's accommodations successful? Does she enjoy school and feel she is learning mostly new material?]

Plan for Next Year: [Will the third-grade reading group meet her needs next year in second-grade? Or would full-grade acceleration be a better match if her math is becoming advanced, as well? What are the next most logical steps for her?]

Such an IEP for Jennifer should provide reasonable accommodation for her strengths this year; however, it should be reviewed several times during the year to make changes, as needed. Likewise, before the end of the school year, plans will need to be made to continue to support Jennifer's progress next year. She must not simply be placed in a second-grade classroom with the outcome unknown. A plan will be needed to ensure that she will not be asked to repeat material (for example, participate in the advanced second-grade reading group again!). At this point, parents are wise to interview teachers at the next grade level to see which teacher is most anxious to work with such a child and willing to make the needed accommodations. The principal can help, too, by allowing some choice of the teacher or, better yet, suggesting one that would be appropriate. An elementary principal supportive of our sons commented one year, "If you don't like the teacher after a month, I'll put your son into another class." He went on to explain why he thought the particular teacher assignment for that year was a good one and he was right! It is a tremendous help to have such support from an administrator for a special needs child.

Let's take another example. James is a highly gifted third-grade boy with advanced math abilities and interest in science, AD/HD, and poor fine-motor coordination. He can compose stories fairly well if he can dictate them, but hates the physical act of handwriting enough that he will deliber-ately write only brief compositions at school.

He reads at a high level, but rarely reads books for enjoyment. He despises timed math tests because he cannot write quickly enough and his math facts are not fully memorized. He is distractible in the classroom and needs to move around frequently. His teacher wonders if he is appropriate for the gifted program, even with his high IQ score of 146, because he is impatient with classwork and often does not do his best.

James needs significant accommodations to be successful. A very challenging, fast-paced program will minimize his AD/HD symptoms and help him engage in his classwork. Gifted children with AD/HD tend not to show consistent attentional inadequacies, but rather distractibility with low-interest material, usually what they have already mastered that is being reviewed again by the teacher for children who need additional repetition. Gifted children with AD/HD usually have remarkable ability to hyperfocus with high-interest material. If James is taught at a level and pace that is somewhat difficult for him, with material that is largely new and novel, he can engage and focus his attention best. At the same time, he needs modifications for his fine-motor weaknesses.

James is fortunate that he qualifies by federal law for a "504 plan" under the Rehabilitation Act of 1973 because he has AD/HD. He has a legal right to accommodations in school or the workplace to allow him to succeed. Such a plan could also address his fine-motor deficits. The advocacy challenge is that James also needs accommodations for his giftedness and most states do not have strong legal mandates for that. We have actually seen schools refuse to include accommodations for giftedness in 504 plans or Special Education IEPs. However, the appropriate modifications for a child such as James should include both those for giftedness and those necessary to address weaknesses. Particularly with gifted students with AD/HD, there is an interaction between the challenge level of the classroom and the intensity of

AD/HD symptoms. To treat and minimize the symptoms, we must address the giftedness.

Here is a sample IEP for James.

Individual Educational Plan

Name: *James*   Age: *8-5*

Grade: *3*

Strong Subject Areas: *Math, science, and reading*

Learning Characteristics/Style: *Highly gifted, twice exceptional visual-spatial learner with verbal-abstract reasoning strengths; holistic learner*

Subject Areas Chosen to Provide Advanced Study: *Math, science, and reading*

Weaknesses to be Accommodated: *Handwriting, attention*

Goals: *Teach James at the level of his advanced mastery in math and reading. Enrich science study. Accommodate fine-motor weaknesses through reduced writing demands. Address AD/HD symptoms with a challenging, fast-paced program and support for organizational weaknesses.*

Activities:

1. *Place James in the fifth-grade challenge math group for math instruction.*

2. *Allow him to do in-depth projects in science, extending the topics studied by the class. Exempt him from simpler assignments he has already mastered.*

3. *Place James in a fourth-grade reading group.*

4. *Add non-fiction books of his choosing in science.*

5. *Teach to his visual-spatial preference. Provide a conceptual framework before teaching into which James can place new facts learned. Use visual aids and hands-on activities.*

6. *Teach James keyboarding skills.*

7. *Allow him to do writing in class or at home on the computer.*

8. *Also allow James to demonstrate what he knows in other ways, such as through oral reports or class presentations with visual aids.*

9. *Allow him to move around the classroom as needed.*

10. *Teach study and organizational skills, especially the use of a daily planner. Make sure James has his assignments written down adequately or provide assignments in writing.*

11. *Provide a second set of textbooks to be kept at home, if James is unable to remember to bring books back and forth consistently.*

12. *Avoid timed tests.*

13. *Minimize drill and practice. When James masters a concept he should move on.*

14. *Pretest before teaching to avoid teaching what James already knows.*

15. *Arrange a mentor for James in science to support his interests and extend his knowledge of the field.*

Evaluation: [Did the activities planned to challenge James engage him? Did he progress in math and reading from his already advanced levels? How were his science projects? Did organizational skills improve? Is he keeping track of assignments and turning them in? Did composition progress once keyboarding was allowed?]

Plan for Next Year: [It is very important to allow James continuous progress. Avoid repeating coursework when he moves on to the next classroom. Support for AD/HD may need to continue.]

Such a plan for James should be immensely helpful in that it acknowledges his highly gifted learning capacity with accelerated work in math and reading, along with enriched science assignments in the classroom. He will be more likely to engage and do his best work when allowed to stretch. At the same time, the plan supports his handwriting difficulties with an emphasis on keyboarding and demonstrating his learning through alternative assignments. It also acknowledges his AD/HD with opportunities for movement, help with study and organizational skills, and an effort to provide challenging, high-interest, novel material as consistently as possible.

Karen Rogers has done an excellent job describing how particular needs can be addressed in IEP's. Consult her book *Re-Forming Gifted Education: Matching the Program to the Child* for additional examples.

Integrating Outside Coursework into the IEP

What do we do when a child needs a level of instruction that cannot be accommodated within the elementary school (or any level of school)? Although there may seem to be no way around the inherent limitations the school imposes, there are usually a number of options. Consider the students who need algebra as early as elementary school. Such coursework might be available at a nearby middle school or possibly a high school. If the upper-level school agrees to the student attending classes, and transportation can be arranged, younger students can successfully complete such coursework early. Computer-based or correspondence courses provide additional options that might substitute for math at the elementary school. For example, the Education Program for Gifted Youth at Stanford University (EPGY) provides math coursework from the elementary school level to beyond high school. The lectures are available via CD-ROM and can be viewed on a family's home computer or at school, if the school agrees to offer the program. EPGY homework can be done during math instruction in the classroom, allowing the student to substitute EPGY for his or her regular math instruction. EPGY allows students to pace through the coursework as quickly as they wish. The University of Nebraska Independent Study High School also offers correspondence courses that many gifted children have utilized at a young age.

When the advanced needs of a child in a given school year exceed what can be provided through a typical IEP for the gifted, sometimes parents will choose to partially home-school. This may be a solution when the child is quite advanced in several subjects, but resists full-grade acceleration and leaving friends. Parents can offer the advanced coursework needed (in perhaps half of the school day) and still allow the child to attend school for some subjects and social activities. Again, the homeschooling substitutes for certain subjects at school. Students must never be asked to do the regular grade-level work, as well.

Full-Grade Acceleration

As some gifted children progress through elementary school, their advancement becomes more pronounced, requiring more substantial modifications. Acceleration in one or two subjects of a grade level is no longer enough. Consider the child who is advanced in virtually all subject areas. When we see achievement test results that indicate a child is at least two or more grade levels (as indicated by grade equivalents) ahead of age peers in virtually all academic subject areas (we tend to ignore spelling), and the child voices concerns about being bored in school and frustrated by limited options, we suggest full-grade acceleration.

Because the research on grade acceleration is generally positive provided the child concurs with the placement, we recommend that the child make the final decision, once the parents have accepted both the regular and accelerated placement options as reasonable. If the child wishes to accelerate and his or her current teacher concurs, then the school must agree. This usually requires the agreement of a committee of teachers, staff, and administrators within the school. Consider having an expert advocate attend to present the child's case and provide articles about accelera-tion to the committee members because most will not have considered acceleration before. Generally, these committees deal with children who are struggling in some way. There is the risk that each committee member will be swayed by the limited experience he or she has with acceleration—perhaps with a single acquaintance or family member. The committee needs to know that gifted children generally accelerate well and are happy with the results.

Assuming the child to be accelerated next year has a current IEP for this year, that IEP will need to be modified in the spring to include any needed preparation for grade skip-ping. If cursive or long division will be expected, some instruction can be added. Likewise, if the child will miss some material in the next grade level that would be enriching, plans can be made to include it, too, perhaps in the summer. One boy planning to skip third grade would have missed the social studies unit on Colorado history and mining. So, his teachers checked the books out to him over the summer to read.

Enrichment Experiences Outside of School

In addition to the individualized education programs that can be arranged with elementary schools, parents should also consider enrichment experiences outside of school. Many gifted children take summer classes in their areas of interest at local museums and universities. The programs may or may not be specifically for gifted children, but all tend to draw bright children with specific interests in the area the class addresses. They provide one means of finding like-minded peers. Always popular are the science enrichment classes and creative writing groups. Foreign language camps can also be wonderful, such as Concordia Language Villages in Minnesota, which offers summertime immersion learning experiences in many languages.

Talent Searches and Related Programs

Talent Search programs offer advanced educational opportunities for students who can demonstrate high ability on tests. The Rocky Mountain Talent Search website offers this history of such programs:

> *The practice of conducting searches for students who reason extremely well mathematically and/or verbally was begun by Professor Julian Stanley of The Johns Hopkins University in the early 1970's. Giving an SAT or ACT test to students who are much younger than the college-bound seniors for whom the tests were designed, results in scores that measure differences among bright students who all score well on in-grade tests. About 180,000 students participate annually in the four regional talent searches. These talent searches are conducted by The University of Denver, The Johns Hopkins University, Duke University, and Northwestern University.*

Students may want to consider the Talent Search program at the university in their designated area, or may attend the programs of other schools (entrance criteria vary).

To participate in Talent Search, students take the SAT or ACT exams early (usually in the sixth or seventh grade). If they score high enough, they are invited to attend classes at the university in the summer. These are very fast-paced, intensive courses that the students usually love, and that *may* confer credit at the student's home school if requested. Taken as commuter courses or with the students staying in dormitories, they usually offer a wonderful social experience, as well as challenging work. It is important to check with the Talent Searches early for the details. The SAT or ACT must be taken early in the fall prior to the summer in which classes are sought. The Talent Search offices can help with deadlines and information about registering for the tests.

There are also opportunities for younger elementary students, utilizing tests such as the PLUS, EXPLORE and SCAT. A range of classes exists for the children, depending on the program, including distance learning and Saturday enrichment. Contacting the Talent Searches while the child is in the primary grades is a good idea so that options can be anticipated for the future.

In addition to the four major Talent Search programs, smaller regional programs also exist at colleges and universities. These may be accessed by a web search.

The Move to Middle School

Because most middle school philosophy stresses the instruction of students of all ability levels together (*heterogeneous grouping*), parents need to research options carefully. Does a middle school offer honors classes and in what subjects? Is it possible for a student to take a higher-grade-level class if it can be documented that the typical grade-level material has already been mastered? Some middle schools are particularly concerned about their students staying together for the entire school day with a team of teachers. This is felt to provide the support middle-schoolers need. Staff members may be concerned that if a student takes a course with an upper-level teacher and different students, it may undermine the student's confidence. Actually, one middle school in Colorado studied the effects of releasing some of its most advanced students from their within-grade groupings to facilitate their taking higher level classes. A poll taken of the students after their experience documented their overwhelming support for the advanced classes. In no way did they feel their support was undermined!

Providing Accelerated Middle School Coursework

When a student enters middle school, there should already be agreement about placement. If the student is already accelerated, he or she needs to be placed at the next logical level in each subject. Gifted students do not tolerate repeating classes well; this usually produces anger, resentment, and the belief that the school is being unfair. There is virtually never a good argument that taking the typical grade-level class is helpful when the material has already been mastered.

High School Courses for Middle-Schoolers

Because middle schools usually comprise only three grades, there are fewer opportunities for accelerated courses within the building. The advanced student who places out of a course or more in a subject area sequence quickly needs high school-level work. Options must be found to provide it. Most frequently, accelerated middle school students go to the nearest high school to take the necessary course, working it into their schedules more or less successfully. However, transportation must be arranged and parents are usually responsible for it. More than one class period is needed to allow for transportation time, and the middle school student often has little flexibility in his or her schedule.

Computer-Based, Online, and Correspondence Courses

Other options may mesh with a student's schedule better.
Online or correspondence coursework (such as the
University of Nebraska's Independent Study High School or
Stanford's EPGY) might be substituted, eliminating the
transportation problem. This would allow a middle school
program with support for advanced abilities, yet a relatively
normal placement for much of the school day.

College Courses for Middle-Schoolers (and younger students)

Community college and university courses are not out of
reach for many middle school gifted students. Colleges vary
in their admissions policies where younger students are
involved; however, many are open to such possibilities. With
those who are (there are no administrative restrictions
against young students attending), it is wise to speak with
the instructor once the administration has approved the
request. Some teachers are resistant to young students and
might provide a disappointing experience, whereas others
are delighted with the unusual opportunity. It is important
that the child attend a class in which the teacher is
enthusiastic and supportive.

With colleges that restrict younger students from attending
courses, some parents have found approaching an individual
faculty member to be effective. One father reported that his
calls to a university physics department chairman, then
later to the head of undergraduate physics, went unheeded
for months when he wanted his 10-year-old profoundly
gifted son to attend a Physics for Poets class (with little
math). Yet, when he met the well-known professor of the
course at a party, he easily obtained an invitation for his
son to visit a class. The boy's visit went well, and the
professor invited him to take the course. The professor
would simply *tell* his department head, he said. He added

that if the boy wanted credit for the class and the university would not give it, he might be able to persuade them—or he would write a letter describing the young student's achievement that could be presented to an admissions office, if needed.

For the gifted student enrolled in middle school, the goal is usually to provide the next level of coursework in some sequence that is not available within the building, or to provide work of greater depth and interest than is offered. What options exist to meet that need? Which choice would the student enjoy most and be challenged by? The best option should be acceptable to the middle school as a needed accommodation for the student's advancement.

Credit for Accelerated Work

When a younger student takes coursework at the high school level or higher, it is important to ask about credit. Will the course confer credit toward high school graduation? Ideally, it should. However, the school district may have a policy that the coursework counts only for high school placement—the student will not have to take that course again, but will be placed in a higher level course once in high school. It may be impossible to fight such a regulation, but it is better to know ahead of time what will be done.

Grade Acceleration in Middle School

One issue to consider in middle school is full-grade acceleration. There are generally no clear rules about the number of classes that must be taken or credits that need to be earned to complete middle school. However, high school graduation requirements tend to be quite rigid. For example, our school district requires 220 credits for graduation, with a typical semester-long course earning five. This assumes a four-year program in which the student takes 55 credits per year, or 25-30 per semester. To graduate in less than four years requires taking more than the usual five to six courses each semester—not a trivial undertaking. Most districts in our state are reluctant to modify this requirement for any student.

If the gifted student is learning quickly and seven years seems like too many to complete middle and high school, then the *time to skip a grade is in middle school.* In middle schools where few advanced classes are offered, this becomes an even better idea. Interestingly, many gifted students have reached high school grade equivalents in elementary school, leaving little or no gap between their level of achievement and that of typical students entering high school. With some of the most advanced, we have actually suggested skipping middle school, and it has been a good strategy. For others, some reduction of the years in middle school is reasonable.

High School

High Schools Have Different Offerings

When a gifted student needs significant accommodations in high school, it is best to interview personnel at several high schools during the last year of middle school (perhaps in October or November to allow plenty of time). Ask for a course catalog and look for advanced offerings in subjects of interest to the student. Does the school offer a large number of Advanced Placement (AP) courses? A school heavily committed to such offerings will have between 20 and 30 AP courses. Advanced placement courses lead to an exit test taken in May that, depending on the score earned (1-5), can confer college credit to the student. Also helpful for accelerated students, AP exams can be taken *at any age.*

Other high schools may offer the International Baccalaureate (IB) Programme, an eleventh- and twelfth-grade program with similar high-level courses that confer college credit. IB exams must be taken in the junior and senior years, a problem if the student is ready to take the test early. However, there are some excellent, rigorous IB programs that have met the needs of very highly gifted students beautifully. High schools offering IB programs usually have "pre-IB" courses, as well, which ensure advanced coursework for freshmen and sophomores. This can be important. If the student will not be placing out of entry-level courses, are there honors or other advanced or accelerated offerings for underclassmen?

The Importance of Proper Class Placements

High schools usually offer some degree of placement flexibility to entering freshmen. For example, there is often a sizeable group of students that counselors allow to skip the entry-level English class in favor of the sophomore course. Likewise, students routinely take the *next level course* in the typical math and foreign language sequences. If accelerated work was undertaken previously, it is important to make sure the high school course selection will be appropriate when the student enters. Gifted students can usually qualify for such accommodations and should seek them.

For more extensive placement flexibility, the principal will usually need to be contacted, or the school may have a departmental program in place to make placement decisions. When the principal is willing to get involved, he or she can be a wonderful ally for the out-of-sync student, determining placement levels (without the objection of the counselors), offering long-range planning tips, and suggesting appropriate classes or teachers to consider. In our state, the principal has the power to approve the granting of credit for independent studies, mentorships, and internships. He or she can also exempt students from some graduation requirements, so may be an essential participant in the gifted student's planning. Sometimes the principal is pleased to be involved in such a proactive way for a special student; it helps to balance the more negative, problem-oriented aspects of the job.

Bob Martin, former principal of Broomfield High School in Broomfield, Colorado, offered the following help to an accelerated student. He suggested a four-year plan of courses, whereby the student could begin at the correct level in each subject area *based on mastery*. Because the student had completed Geometry 1, Algebra 2, a high school-level Chemistry/Physics class, and was an advanced writer, he would need significant acceleration. The high school already had a suggested "Course of Study With Advanced, Honors, and AP Courses" to help college-bound students plan their schedules. It looked like this:

Figure 11.1

Department	Grade 9	Grade 10	Grade 11	Grade 12
Language Arts	Freshman Core	Sophomore English	Advanced Composition, Shakespeare, ect.	AP English
Social Studies	Freshman Core (English, US Govt. and Geography)	World History	American Studies Honors, or........	AP US History or AP European History
Math	Geometry Honors	Algebra 2 Honors	Pre-Calculus 1 and 2	AP Calculus
Science	Biology	Chemistry	AP Biology, AP Chemistry, or Adv. Physics	Anatomy
Foreign Language	Level 1 or Level 2	Level 2 or Level 3	Level 3 or Level 4	Level 4 or Level 5 (AP)
Electives	PE/Elective	PE/Elective	PE/Elective/ Health	Elective/ Elective or Health
Seventh Class	Optional	Optional	Optional	Optional

However, Bob Martin suggested the following schedule after the English department chair read the student's writing and suggested an appropriate English class:

Figure 11.2

Department	Grade 9	Grade 10	Grade 11	Grade 12
Language Arts	Advanced Composition and Shakespeare	American Studies Honors	AP English	College
Social Studies	US Government and Geography	World History	AP US History	AP European History
Math	Honors Precalculus 1 and 2	AB Calculus and BC Calculus	College	College
Science	Chemistry or Anatomy	AP Biology	AP Chemistry	Advanced Physics
Foreign Language	Spanish Level 4	College or 2nd Foreign Language	College	College
Electives	Stage Band, PE, and Computer Program C++	Stage Band and PE	Stage Band and PE	Stage Band and Health
Seventh Class	Optional	Optional	Optional	Optional

Naturally, the student's final schedule varied from these suggestions, based on course availability and personal preference. The principal served as this student's primary advisor, suggesting courses he thought the student would like. Teacher preference and availability played a role; for example, the student postponed AP Calculus while the favorite teacher took a sabbatical, and took Statistics in the interim. Because he became aware he had missed interesting cultural material in third-level Spanish by beginning with Spanish 4, he took Spanish 310 next (however, it was fairly easy for him). He also decided to take Honors General Chemistry (instead of AP Chemistry) at the university in his first full year on campus after high school. The experienced high school AP Chemistry teacher retired before he could take the course in high school and his university preferred he take their course. Here is what he actually took:

Figure 11.3

Department	Grade 9	Grade ?	Grade 12
Language Arts	Advanced Composition and Public Speaking	AP English [*Masterpieces of American Literature]	Discussion and Debate
Social Studies	World History	AP European History [*History of US to 1865, *History of US Since 1865, and *American Political Systems]	[**World Regional Geography]
Math	Precalculus Honors 1 and 2	Statistics	AB Calculus and BC Calculus (AP)
Science	Chemistry	AP Biology	Advanced Physics
Foreign Language	Spanish Level 4	Spanish 310	AP Spanish 5
Electives	Stage Band and PE	Team Sports	Racquet Sports and Health
Seventh Class	Stage Band		Photography 1 & 2, and Honors Computer C++

*Courses taken at a nearby university in summer school.

** University continuing education course taken in the evening.

The principal had originally suggested a four-year course of study, but the student decided early in his second year to shorten his high school stay, primarily for social reasons. Initially placed with older students, he made friends with them, felt he fit in quite nicely, and was comfortable. He watched many of them graduate at the end of his first year, and soon wanted to go with them. He took four courses at a university in the summer between his second and third years in high school, carefully chosen to meet high school graduation requirements, and another one in the fall of his third year when he had difficulty scheduling it at the high school. His principal approved the courses as meeting various graduation requirements and signed a form for the university stating that the student was mature enough to handle the college work. The school district waived 10 credits toward graduation to enable the student to move on to college (he was 10 credits short). He began college full-time the following fall, with almost enough credits to qualify as a junior (with his college coursework and credit for AP exams) and was well-placed and comfortable. As he was planning on earning a Ph.D. in biochemistry, he figured he would still have plenty of time left in college!

The student who has the support of the school's principal is certainly fortunate. When the school has designated teachers to make placement decisions, results vary. If, for example, a student has a strong enough background to place out of a ninth-grade class, but the department has designated the teacher of that course (who teaches nothing else) to make placement decisions, the odds are that the student's request will be turned down. However, when the department head determines such placements, and teaches classes at several grade levels, there is a better chance of a reasonable placement decision being made. Educators vary in their flexibility and, unfortunately, I have heard some say, "I believe all students will find my class valuable!"

The combination of classes and placements offered, and judgment of teacher quality can make the decision about a high school easy. High schools should be able to grant a request for the student to visit classes, at least in subjects of greatest interest. This way, the student has firsthand knowledge of the teachers, and a feel for the typical size of classes and instructional approaches used. Even a school with an excellent reputation may not have the student's favorite teachers in specific subjects. Meeting them and being students in their classrooms for a period offers a wealth of information. The size of classes not only figures into the comfort of the student, but may also determine admission policies to advanced classes. For example, in very large schools, entry into AP classes can be quite competitive. The underachieving gifted student, without the highest grades, is more likely to be welcomed into the AP class in a smaller high school, that has barely enough students for the school to offer the class.

In our area, high schools vary tremendously. One school is trying to create an AP Scholar program, offering all of the AP classes for which there are tests and flexible placement options. The mother of one very advanced middle schooler was told her son could take some AP classes there as a freshman. Such offerings and flexibility allow the unusually advanced student to take highly challenging courses throughout high school. In contrast, at some other schools, few students take AP classes before their senior year and are forced to take typical grade-level offerings. A gifted student needs to find the right combination. He or she may chose a high school with only moderate AP offerings, if flexible placement is allowed and there are good teachers for favorite subjects.

Maintaining Challenge

Once the student has chosen a high school and the initial placements have been made, the challenge is to ensure engaging coursework that continues to motivate. Gifted high school students flourish in classes that require them to think abstractly, deal with complexity, and occasionally struggle. They will usually gravitate to honors and other advanced courses, unless the teacher requires too much drill and practice (usually in the form of homework). This does not suit the gifted student well. There will be the occasional class that seems ridiculous to these students. There is no way to avoid a few low-level classes that are required for graduation and that seem designed for students who master concepts considerably less well than the gifted. Often these classes have regular homework that seems purposeless. Ask for advice about the most engaging teachers and least frustrating prospects. Gifted high school students perform better for teachers they respect and may put forth less effort for those they do not. The teacher who expects high-level thought and is passionate about his or her subject is the best choice for the gifted student.

Concurrent College Enrollment

When the high school offerings need a boost or a student wants to complete high school quickly (as in the case above), consider concurrent enrollment in college courses. Such classes aim a little higher than most (but not all) of their high school counterparts, asking students to reason at a higher level. They often have more knowledgeable instructors, closer to research and cutting-edge issues in their fields. The students love the discussions, realize how much more there is to be learned, and gain an enhanced view of higher education.

Gifted students are mature and responsible enough to handle college classes and appreciate the fact that very few college instructors value daily homework, but plan their courses around reading, written assignments, and a few exams. These students also enjoy their independence. At the college, they are not usually given unexcused absences for being five minutes late or dogged about dress codes. They like being treated as adults who want to learn and are willing to work hard.

Beyond these benefits, concurrent college enrollment also offers dual credit. If the college course meets a high school graduation requirement or is perceived to be worthy of credit toward the student's high school diploma, it can count for credit towards both high school graduation and a Bachelor's degree. When students realize this, college classes become even more of a pleasure to take. A school administrator will usually have to approve the college course for high school credit. Some school districts will even pay for the college course on the basis that the student needs what the high school is unable to offer. Check requirements carefully for such programs to take advantage of this assistance. Colleges have requirements for the admission of high school students that vary from school to school, but are less daunting than most parents would assume.

College courses can become a large part of a gifted student's program, if the student wishes to graduate early. They are useful when the student is unable to schedule a high school course required for graduation. This is not uncommon with accelerated students who are taking courses out-of-sync and the course is scheduled for only one section. High schools try to schedule classes so that the students who need them can schedule them along with other classes they are likely to take. However, an accelerated student is often taking many classes at an atypical time, so the school's planning does not benefit them. Such students can be flexible about their high school course requests to some degree, but, at some point, must have certain courses. It can be a relief to find an appropriate college class offered, perhaps one night a week for half a semester, that fills such a requirement. Colleges usually offer coursework for high school students through their continuing education departments. Classes are scheduled at times when working people and full-time high school students can take them. Finally, if an accelerated student is graduating early, the experience with college courses is invaluable. The student heading off to college may be young, but is already practiced in getting around a college campus and handling college work. He or she enters with far more experience with college than most older freshmen.

Taking college courses, along with AP and IB classes, can produce an unexpectedly large number of college credits by high school graduation. These credit hours will shorten the time required for a Bachelor's degree, but may also lessen scholarship opportunities open to freshmen. However, most students appreciate having to take fewer entry-level courses when they enter college full time. Moreover, the student who begins college classified as a sophomore or junior enjoys some preference for classes, as seniors are scheduled first, then juniors, etc.

The student may be eligible for a single dorm room sooner (important to gifted introverts) and be offered research opportunities or teaching assistantships quite early as undergraduates.

Other Course Options and Opportunities

Options such as Stanford's EPGY (Education Program for Gifted Youth) continue to offer credit possibilities at the high school level. Likewise, students can consider correspondence courses, although typical high school correspondence programs are usually not challenging enough for the gifted high school student (they work well for younger gifted students). College-level work is more appropriate. Independent study options should also be examined. Peterson's Independent Study Catalogue can be of assistance or contact Duke University's Talent Identification Program about independent study classes.

Internships should also be considered, when an advanced student is anxious to learn more about a particular field or an underachieving gifted student's motivation is waning. A meeting with the principal and/or counselor is advisable to ask that such work be given credit. Student placements for a few hours a week are often possible. The student is usually not paid, but gains a valuable recommendation and, if possible, a few credits for the experience.

A Continued Need for Advocacy

Parents of high school-aged gifted students are needed as advocates as much as ever. Even though the students are older and more capable of advocating for themselves, it is still very difficult for them to gain permission for atypical placements, shortened programs, and exemptions from the usual requirements. Such requests may strike terror in the hearts of administrators who are very concerned about making a wrong choice for the student or diverging from established school or district policy. Parents are needed here to argue for the wisdom of the particular request.

Parents also help their students keep track of graduation requirements, tests that need to be taken, etc., as some gifted students have rather poor organizational skills. Especially when the student will be graduating early, requirements can seem to *sneak up*. Most students who graduate in three years, for example, do not plan to take that course from the outset. It is only after some time in high school that they decide they would rather move on more quickly. It is probably better to assume a likely student will graduate early and to make the decision as soon as possible, so that courses are taken from the outset with graduation requirements in mind. Likewise, the PSAT, SAT or ACT tests must be anticipated and *taken early* to avoid a rush at the end to complete them all. The PSAT (usually taken in the junior year) and SAT (usually taken at the end of the junior or beginning of the senior year) may end up being taken virtually together at the beginning of the third and last year in high school if the student did not know to take the PSAT a year early. This can have one interesting ramification in that the PSAT determines the National Merit Scholarship recipients. Students usually take the test at the beginning of their junior or third year in high school, unless they plan to graduate in three years. In that case, they are allowed to take it in their second year. However, if the student fails to take it in the second year because he or she has not yet decided to graduate in three years, it causes a one-year delay of scholarship opportunities. If the student is granted a scholarship, it is not available until the beginning of the student's second year in college.

Finding ways to shorten the gifted student's stay in high school, elevate the work (through college courses), or offer more responsibility (spending time on a college campus, away from the tight control of the high school) is usually welcomed by the student and is quite empowering. While the intricacies of such options are challenging, they are worth-while for the advocate to pursue.

Twice Exceptional Students

Support Both the Giftedness and the Deficit(s)

Students who exhibit both giftedness and learning disabilities or other deficits require a special type of planning throughout their school careers. As in the case of James, for whom a sample IEP was provided in the section on elementary school accommodations, the child with both gifted reasoning abilities and accompanying weaknesses requires modifications for both. A two-pronged approach, emphasizing and supporting the giftedness, but also accommodating the weaknesses, must be taken. This can be tricky because giftedness is not always well understood by school personnel and some may believe a child with weaknesses cannot be gifted. These are often the same people who believe gifted students are necessarily high achievers. When the achievement is less impressive, especially when deficits are apparent, the child's giftedness may be questioned. In such cases, it is critical to provide high quality testing information that documents the dual exceptionality and provides recommendations for the classroom. Brief or group intelligence tests, the type usually given at school to identify giftedness, often fail to recognize the giftedness in these children—they simply yield scores below the gifted range—so, it is important to utilize a good individual test (e.g., Wechsler tests), administered by a tester experienced with the twice exceptional. It may also be helpful to provide the school with additional articles or other materials about the twice exceptional to clarify the child's needs.

The self-esteem of the gifted child with deficits depends upon his or her strengths being emphasized and supported. Having both gifted intellectual abilities *and* weaknesses can be destabilizing. The child is *smart* and has been told that, but knows that certain classroom activities that other children do easily are difficult. The child wonders if, indeed, he or she really is intelligent. It is critical that the teacher recognize the giftedness and support the child's strengths. Once the advanced math or beautiful creative writing is supported by advanced coursework, accompanying modifications for any weaknesses are more easily tolerated and appreciated, without lowering self-esteem.

Twice exceptional children usually work very hard to compensate for deficits that they may be able to hide fairly well. However, such effort is often exhausting and achievement usually suffers to some degree. These children are typically late bloomers, who master compensatory skills as they mature that allow their giftedness to become more apparent.

Consider IDEA (Special Education Services) and "504" Plans

Some twice exceptional children have access to services for their deficits, but not necessarily their giftedness, at school. If their weaknesses are considered learning disabilities (e.g., reading or writing disabilities) and they show a significant enough discrepancy between higher IQ scores and lower achievement scores, they may qualify for special education services for the learning disabled. Special education can provide not only accommodations in the classroom (e.g., extra time for writing assignments), but also special teaching and therapeutic interventions in a resource room setting until the student graduates from high school. If their deficits fall under the listed disabilities for a "504 plan" under the Rehabilitation Act of 1973 (related to the Americans With Disabilities legislation), then they have access to accommodations in the classroom or workplace as long as they need them. Sometimes weaknesses are significant, but do not qualify for either type of assistance. In such cases, we work to thoroughly diagnose them through initial testing and further evaluation with a specialist, with the goal of parents providing interventions and working with teachers for voluntary accommodations.

Advocating for Children With Higher Levels of Giftedness

How does yearly advocacy differ for parents of children with higher levels of giftedness—the highly, exceptionally, or profoundly gifted? First, gifted children at these levels learn at an increasingly fast pace, easily outstripping their curriculum and surprising their teachers. The mismatch becomes so great at the higher IQ levels between their abilities and their educational programs that increasing angst is to be expected. Some will even find that continued enrollment within typical school programs is impossible. Personality characteristics typical of the gifted increase in intensity and may appear so abnormal to some as to seem pathological. Socially, the highly gifted find it even more difficult to find true peers, or to relate to age peers in meaningful ways. Parents often report that these children prefer adults and considerably older children. Most highly gifted students show strengths in both visual spatial and verbal abstract reasoning abilities, so both learning styles are usually operating fairly well. However, most are holistic, rather than sequential learners. Because teachers have had little or no experience with such children, parent advocates must play a more significant role.

The Need for an Even Higher Level and Faster Pace of Instruction

The level of instruction and pacing necessary for highly, exceptionally, and profoundly gifted children would surprise most. At the highly gifted level (IQ 145 or higher on most tests), students will generally learn upon presentation, if they are paying attention. They do not need drill and practice, so if the teacher is cycling though the material eight or nine times for the average student to master it, highly gifted students are struggling to maintain their attention. At even higher levels of giftedness, the problem is worse. They learn at an even faster pace, devouring teaching materials.

One boy we tested, with a Stanford-Binet L-M IQ score of 192, was assessed on three achievement tests: in the summer prior to first grade, in the spring of second grade, and in the spring of third grade—covering a period of less than three years. While the tests have limited comparability, his grade equivalents can be compared over that period of time to gain an idea of his progress.

Academic Progress

(Measured by Grade Equivalents)

	PIAT-R, Age 6-1	K-TEA, Age 7-9 (Brief Form)	K-TEA, Age 8-10
Math	2.6	10.9	Math Application 11.3 Math Computation 10.7
Reading	3.2	8.5	Reading Comprehension >12.9 Reading Decoding 10.8
Spelling	2.8	5.2	Spelling 10.9

At age 6-1, he earned grade equivalents of 2.6 in pre-algebra math (at the level of the average student in the sixth month of second grade), 3.2 in reading, and 2.8 in spelling. These scores reflect his basic skills before beginning first grade. By the spring of second grade, he earned grade equivalents of 10.9 in pre-algebra math, 8.5 in reading, and 5.2 in spelling. One year later at age 8-10 (third grade), his grade equivalents ranged from 10.7 in math computation to the high school graduate level (>12.9) in reading comprehension. Especially dramatic are the sudden increases as basic skills are learned in reading and math in the primary grades. Few teachers would suspect their students to be progressing this rapidly. Only if the teacher assessed frequently on above-level tests would such progress be discovered. It would not be fully apparent on grade-level achievement tests; such a child would simply earn a score at the 99th percentile for first, second or third-graders and no one would know how high the achievement level actually was.

Provide Achievement Testing

Parents can help by having individual achievement tests administered, perhaps every one and a half to two and a half years, throughout elementary school and somewhat beyond. Be careful to have a test administered with a ceiling score as high as the child's IQ score or ceiling limitations may apply. The Woodcock-Johnson III has a very high ceiling (beyond 200 at some ages, on some subtests) and provides excellent information. The subtests needed include the following: Letter-Word Identification, Passage Comprehension, Calculation, Applied Problems, Spelling, and Writing Samples (or substitute a writing evaluation from another test).

The subtests that measure the speed of reading, calculating, and writing—Reading Fluency, Math Fluency, and Writing Fluency—are less helpful for the gifted. They test very simple skills, not representative of the range of abilities of the gifted: reading simple sentences and answering yes/no, calculating simple math problems, and writing short sentences, all under timed conditions. For the most part, *adequate* speed on such tasks is fine for the classroom and many gifted children are too reflective to be especially speedy. Administering these may lower Broad Reading, Broad Math, and Broad Written Language scores, causing teachers to question the need for higher level work in the classroom. This is an unwarranted concern, unless the child has a serious processing speed deficit and needs accommodations (for example, the child who needs very advanced material, but has a fine-motor weakness that needs to be documented to allow more time for handwritten assignments and tests). Giving the fluency measures in such a case can show that the child has mastered difficult concepts, but cannot show the work quickly on a timed test.

Other major tests, such as the Wechsler Individual Achievement Test (WIAT) and Kaufman Test of Educational Achievement (K-TEA) have lower ceilings (160), but can be used to vary the tests year by year if the child's IQ score is not beyond 160. Individual achievement tests provide additional information for the teacher and student's family to consider in planning each year's program.

Accelerate With Care

The child mentioned above skipped third grade after earning grade equivalents from the fifth through tenth-grade levels in the spring of second grade. His acceleration was easy and comfortable, and permanently moved him to somewhat higher level material than he would have had if he had remained with age peers. When is acceleration appropriate and how much should be skipped? If the child is advanced at least a couple of years in all areas, is concerned about being bored, and makes the final decision to accelerate, then it is usually a very good idea. We generally recommend accelerating a year at a time, but some children have fared well skipping two or three grades at once. Schools tend to be very reluctant to accelerate a child even one grade level, however, so multi-grade skips are unlikely options.

Because subject acceleration and full-grade acceleration are needed more frequently with highly, exceptionally, and profoundly gifted children, parents need to know what to do. After gaining the teacher's agreement with the possibility of acceleration (if the teacher does not suggest it), efforts should be made to provide the child with all of the information needed for him or her to make the final decision. Consider visits to the higher level classroom and an escape clause, whereby the child has a month to decide if the placement is working satisfactorily. A child who is wary should not be pushed, but attending a higher-grade-level class for one subject for a year may ease concerns. Once the child is familiar with the older children, they are considered friends, as well, and a full-grade skip seems less daunting. Parents may be required to attend a meeting with a team of teachers to discuss the potential acceleration. Because most teams do not deal with problems of advancement, they are usually ill-prepared for such a discussion. Providing articles on acceleration and an expert advocate may help. It is important that the parents not be perceived by the teachers as pushing a child, who is otherwise content to remain in a typical grade placement. This evokes great concern about the hurried child and undue pressure to succeed. Only the child's obvious achievement and sincere desire to accelerate can allay such fears by educators. Parents might allow the school counselor to interview the child or bring a letter from the child.

Consider Outside Coursework

Meeting the rapidly advancing needs of the very highly gifted will require other solutions, as well. Consider online and correspondence courses to substitute for one or more courses at school, usually those in which the child is most advanced. Tutoring and partial, or full-time, homeschooling may need to be considered at times. Talent Search summer classes may substitute for some work at school. College courses may be possible, even for elementary-aged students progressing at a very advanced rate. If possible, consider allowing a child to audit a course first, then take the course for credit (which may be allotted when the child is older). We have seen profoundly gifted students successfully taking college courses at six or seven; we know high school graduates of nine, ten, and eleven, and a ten-year-old college graduate. These were all children whose parents capitulated to serving their needs, giving into their requests for more challenging coursework. Such parents rarely push, but struggle to meet the compelling needs of these children.

Most children at the highest levels of giftedness have no access to any program that could come close to meeting their needs. A patchwork of acceptable options must be created to meet their needs each year, with the greatest attention going to supporting their passions. The program needs to be adequate, but not necessarily perfect. Students, teachers, and parents must be flexible enough to combine options and hope they produce a positive result. If something is not working, it needs to be modified, but all need to realize this is a best effort, where there are no firm rules about what should be done.

Of course, parents hope that teachers will compact curriculum and add enrichment, instead of subjecting a very highly gifted student to unneeded and damaging drill and practice. They hope homework will be meaningful, and grading will be flexible and sensible for such a child. Parents can also hope there will be opportunities for in-depth work at school, independent studies, and support for passions. A teacher who is flexible about such things within the classroom and willing to include or substitute outside classes or opportunities is invaluable.

Help Teacher Advocates

Parents can help the teacher by realizing such flexibility may not find favor with other teacher colleagues. The teacher who successfully supports such a student may encounter enormous resistance from other teachers who feel acceleration is inappropriate. Teachers can even have difficulties with administrators and may need support for their efforts.

Parents can also help by understanding that most teachers are not capable of teaching all levels. The child who needs algebra in elementary school will probably have to find instruction outside of the school. Likewise, teachers will not be able to answer all questions posed by such children. The wise teacher will teach the child approaches to finding out the information independently, via the Internet or interviewing experts. The teacher then becomes the guide and facilitator of the child's learning, rather than the authority who knows all the answers.

Support Personality Characteristics

The intensity of highly gifted children, their increased sensitivity and concern for injustice in the world, renders them especially vulnerable to ill-fitting programs. One third-grade girl with a 211 IQ score began to have *meltdowns* in the rest room, with uncontrollable crying. She had simply reached a point where the program required her to be someone else to succeed. She was unable to be a typical third-grader, satisfied with third-grade work; her teacher had decided she was not gifted and had emotional issues. The child was so sensitive and attuned to the need for kindness and fairness that she could not cope. She had to be removed from school and homeschooled.

When teachers become defensive and punishing, these children are undone. They fare poorly in classrooms where there is subtle disapproval for their differences. More blatant criticism can require years of therapy to mitigate. There may be depression and the possibility of suicide where such intense personalities experience extreme difficulty fitting in. Parents need to ensure a healthy psychological environment for such a child. Is the child nurtured and appreciated for his or her special qualities? These children should never be criticized for their differences, nor should their strengths be ignored to avoid hurting the feelings of other children. All children's gifts should be acknowledged, or the message of disapproval is conveyed.

It is helpful to educate teachers about the personality characteristics of the highly gifted. In addition, they need to know that such a child is still able to be a child. The quality of childhood simply changes. Interspersed with a normal love of play, fantasy, and silliness may be a very sophisticated interest in a subject. This is normal childhood for very highly gifted children. The advanced interests go with the territory and are not imposed by pushy parents.

Nurture Social Development

Assuming that the gifted usually gravitate toward mental age peers, it is more difficult for children at the higher ranges of giftedness to find true peers and less likely that those peers will be of a similar chronological age. We have seen remarkable situations in which such children were integrated easily into classrooms of much older children. Indeed, they need mental age peers, who are more likely to have similar interests, in order to form friendships. Such friendships also provide the context in which they learn social skills and confidence to function at their appropriate level. However, when is the age mismatch too great? Probably when the child feels it is. In our experience, the ability of these most highly gifted children to assess what is best for themselves has been impressive. Allowing final acceleration decisions to be made by the children helps to ensure appropriate, realistic plans.

How Familiar are Teachers With Higher Levels of Giftedness?

Because few teachers have had formal training in gifted education, there is little appreciation for the concept of levels of giftedness and even less experience with highly gifted children. One mother of a daughter with a 155 IQ lamented that the seemingly helpful principal of her daughter's school really had no understanding of the young girl's needs when she insisted the girl "would be fine" without special provisions. Very few children were even identified for the gifted program in that school and the principal had had no experience with a child such as her daughter. This is absolutely a concern for parent advocates. If we consider that children with IQ scores in the 150s usually have a need for more radical acceleration, perhaps skipping grades at several points in their educational careers, we know that few schools are willing to consider such a pace. They simply have not seen children progress successfully in this way and prefer to rely on time-tested grade placement strategies perceived to be safe. Most dangerously, schools assume that a decision not to accelerate the highly gifted child is *safer*. It is important to understand that the decision NOT to accelerate is just as serious as the decision TO accelerate, and each option should be weighted equally in consideration.

Becoming the Gifted Advocate and Educational Program Manager

Most parents of the gifted would certainly rather find a perfect school placement for their child than to take on the role of essential advocate and educational program planner. It is a role most accept only reluctantly, once it appears clear a child's needs won't be met within available schools. Happily, letting go of the notion that the "school will do it" can be empowering and actually help us to see options we might otherwise not have considered. Viewing a child's education as a series of potentially interesting years, care-fully crafted with options that come and go as needed, opens up a realm of possibilities. Taking an active role, in partnership with educators, directly meets needs and limits damage.

This is where the parent advocate must be at his or her best, gently educating and cajoling school personnel to try needed accommodations, while releasing them from responsibility if plans do not produce perfect results. All have to make their best guess as to what will work and summon the courage to try.

References

Duke University TIP (Talent Identification Program), Box 90747, Durham, NC 27708, Phone (919) 684-3847; Fax (919) 681-7921. http://www.tip.duke.edu/ (18 Feb. 2003).

EPGY (Education Program for Gifted Youth), Ventura Hall, Stanford University, Stanford, CA 94305-4115. (800) 372-EPGY (3749). http://www-epgy.stanford.edu (18 Feb. 2003).

Peterson's Education Portal (colleges, graduate schools, financial aid, free online). http://www.petersons.com/ (18 Feb. 2003).

Rocky Mountain Talent Search, University of Denver, 1981 S. University Blvd., Denver, CO 80208. (303) 871-2983. http://www.du.edu/education/ces/rmts.html (18 Feb. 2003).

For Further Reading

National Research Center on the Gifted and Talented, 2131 Hillside Road, Unit 3007, Storrs, CT 06269-3007. (860) 486-4676. http://www.ucc.uconn.edu/~wwwgt/nrcgt.html (18 Feb. 2003).

Rogers, K. B. (2002). *Re-forming gifted education: Matching the program to the child.* Scottsdale, AZ: Great Potential Press.

Robinson, N. (1991). Early entrance to kindergarten and grade 1. In W. T. Southern & E. D. Jones (Eds.), *The academic acceleration of gifted children.* New York: Teacher's College Press.

SAT Test Preparation (click on SAT Prep Center and Question of the Day). http://www.collegeboard.com/ (18 Feb. 2003).

Wright, A. L., & Olszewski-Kubilius, P. (1993). *Helping gifted children and their families prepare for college: A handbook designed to assist economically disadvantaged and first-generation college attendees* (RM93201). Storrs, CT: University of Connecticut, The National Research Center on the Gifted and Talented. http://www.sp.uconn.edu/~nrcgt/nrcgt/m93201/wok93201.html (18 Feb. 2003).

Afterword

The Call To Arms

Parents and teachers advocating for gifted children find themselves in the most curious situation. They must advocate strongly for significant educational accommodations to meet the needs of their gifted charges. However, they operate largely in an environment of ignorance about what those needs are. They must learn through their own efforts what a gifted child's education must accomplish. The fact that few states require significant study in gifted education for teacher certification ensures that there will be confusion about what to do with gifted students in the classroom and a dearth of concern about what will happen if the right things are not done.

Advocates battle charges of elitism within a society that is not sure whether it wants to nurture its most capable members or submit them to an egalitarian leveling process. Is it the responsibility of educators to ensure that all children reach the same *moderate* level of education? Or, is it their responsibility to educate each child to reach his or her full potential? The gifted form one last minority group that, in some circles, is still okay to hate.

The message that we must do *something* for the gifted has permeated the American educational system to the extent that there is a plethora of *gifted programs* in schools that superimpose some type of enrichment upon the regular program. Where the gifted student needs accommodations in regular classwork to provide higher level material, faster instructional pace, and a greater emphasis on abstraction, he or she gains no relief. The addition of an hour or more per week of leadership training, thinking skills, art appreciation, or other unrelated enrichment does little to reduce the risk to the student of a vastly inappropriate education, experienced at least six hours a day, five days a week, four weeks a month, nine months a year. Even when add-on gifted programs offer more substantial opportunities to do a project of interest, attend a weekly science enrichment class, participate in a writing workshop, or spend quality time with intellectual peers, they rarely lead to significant and needed changes in regular classwork.

Gifted students usually follow the typical age-grade sequence, utilizing limited gifted programs to the extent possible, but finding access to such programs occasionally quite difficult. The inherent discomfort some feel with the existence of children who are more capable, more advanced, and more efficient learners can lead to restrictive admission policies and demanding, compassionless gatekeepers. It is difficult to forget the boy in Texas who was turned down for the gifted program when he scored low on his school district's creativity test, one of a battery of tests on which he needed to score high, yet he earned a Stanford-Binet L-M IQ score of 180 at the Gifted Development Center. An IQ score from a major individual intelligence test is an excellent indicator of *asynchrony* and need for educational accommodations. Discomfort also appears to drive some school personnel to make gifted children "earn their giftedness" by a show of high achievement, task commitment, or general good citizenship. One parent reported that her son's teacher refused to nominate him for the gifted program, despite a phenomenal test score, because he had a messy desk. It is interesting to note that we impose no such behavioral requirements on children needing to be identified as learning or developmentally disabled. We simply accept their asynchrony—their capacities and limitations—and work to plan appropriate educational programs for them.

Some districts cope with the discomfort of identifying gifted students by trying to include as many children as possible. However, lowering score requirements to identify 10, 20, or even 30% of the school population, can dilute programming options to a degree that they cannot possibly meet the needs of actual gifted children. Perhaps even worse, such a degree of inclusion calls into question whether all of these children actually need differentiation in their programs or whether some are having their needs met already in the regular program. If some do not need the accommodations the special program affords, then there is reason for deep resentment to develop among the parents of children not included. The seeds are sown for the eventual abandonment of all gifted services, poor as many are, due to parent pressure.

The perceived need to include as many gifted students as possible can also result in schools extending their gifted assessment to recognize many *types* of giftedness or *intelligences*. If the candidate must meet a single criterion among *several* to enter the gifted program, perhaps exhibit gifted verbal *or* visual-spatial reasoning abilities, then this is good policy. However, if the candidate must meet a single criterion of giftedness where there are considered to be *many* types of giftedness, the numbers of children and types of advancement to be supported may overwhelm the school and lead to trivial accommodations. The school must be prepared to support children it considers *gifted* in all of the different ways its identification procedures address, yet most schools are unprepared to meet needs in other than typical academic pursuits, the traditional focus of schools. Moreover, the schools who have further extended this concept to believe that "every child is gifted" are effectively ignoring individual needs altogether. A child's needs cannot be met if they are not recognized, and it is no more true to say that "every child is gifted" than it is to say that "every child is retarded."

It is into this daunting world that advocates of the gifted—both teachers and parents—must go, prepared to the extent they can muster to fight for a child's right to a reasonable education. For the gifted, it is the education we seek for a child at any level of ability. It consists of a curriculum in which the child is taught at the appropriate level (based on current mastery) in each subject area, and at approximately the right pace. Such a curriculum is carefully designed for the majority of children in school, but is simply not a good fit for children at the extremes of ability. Advocates for the gifted must attempt to create a patchwork of options each year that comes as close as possible to meeting more asynchronous needs. If they can accomplish this, usually without the benefit of desperately needed legal protection, they may be able to save a child.

Teachers who value these unusual students must do extra work to individualize for them, increasing their own planning time, while they also deal with more typical learners and asynchronous learners at other levels of ability. They must assess frequently to avoid teaching what gifted students already know, and find ways to ensure the continuous progress of the gifted, so that their love of learning is supported. They need to keep ceilings off, concerning the level of discussion or question that is welcomed, encourage abstract reasoning, maintain high expectations, and provide opportunities for gifted students to stretch.

For their efforts, these teachers will face disagreements with their colleagues and encounter inevitable turf battles when a child needs accelerated work and the higher-grade-level teacher disagrees. They must respect each child and his or her gifts, just as they respect all children they teach; but, with the gifted, they must also sensitively deal with a range of personality characteristics from heightened emotions to concern for injustice. They must be intuitive, as well, about the issues these mostly introverted children may experience, but are reluctant to share. These special teachers need to give themselves credit for doing a critical—at times lifesaving—job for their gifted students that other educators will never appreciate or attempt.

Parent advocates for the gifted face even greater challenges because their advocacy continues for the many years of a child's education, with no guarantee—short of pulling a child out of school and homeschooling—of success each and every year. The parent advocate must summon his or her warmest smile and most sincere willingness to work with each teacher, counselor, or administrator to find the best options for the child. Unswayed by superficial enrichment programs offered to gifted children in addition to their regular classwork, the parent must go to the school knowing that significant classroom accommodations are essential. The daily curriculum and instruction in typical schools is simply not designed for such learners. Gifted students are as different from average learners as students who are developmentally delayed, so the regular program must be modified for both. There is no need to apologize for such requests.

Parent advocates must be ready with their testing reports, their portfolios, or records of advanced classes taken to document special needs and qualify their children for modifications. They need to learn to say matter-of-factly, "Here is what we are dealing with. What options do you have that might meet these needs?"

Because they may know more about the educational needs of the gifted than many teachers and other school personnel, parents must be ready to educate with a few well-placed comments about an important topic, or by offering a helpful article or book. They will need to dispel common myths about gifted students. First, the notion that the gifted will be "just fine without special accommodations" is at odds with our experience of gifted students being at the highest risk when their learning is restricted and their needs are ignored. Second, "gifted children need to be with age peers for social development," is countered by seeing gifted children cherish their multi-age friends and learn social skills with all ages. Finally, "grade acceleration is to be avoided at all costs," is nonsense when we can witness a child reengage in his or her studies because the level is finally right. Any child works best at the level of mastery, when mostly new material is being presented.

Both teacher and parent advocates need to remember that a child's program does not have to be perfect to be adequate. Maintaining motivation to learn is the bottom line. We must prevent the gifted student from becoming jaded about education—damaged enough that he or she flees the system and is too afraid to return. It is much easier to prevent such a negative outcome than to repair it, once it is full-blown. Advocates need to know, however, that if they work to ensure a reasonably good program for a child each year, the results can be very good. Even profoundly gifted children, those most at risk of suffering from the poor fit of their educations, complete public school with their love of learning intact. The result is worth every effort.

To accomplish this, the parent advocate must chart a course for a gifted student through school, manipulating the rules of the system, locating supportive teachers, and finding appropriate options. Parents must manage their children's educations or the status quo will prevail. The gifted child will be expected to progress through school in a typical manner. It is highly unlikely that more than a few special teachers will pose the question: "Does this child need any modifications to his or her education?" The number of gifted high school dropouts and depressed or suicidal gifted students is testament to the danger inherent in ignoring these needs.

A friend whose profoundly gifted son, Jeremiah, dropped out of high school sent me this email about him.

> ...for the longest time, he remained adamant about not wanting anything to do with structured schooling. He was hoping to be a success with his band, but the other members weren't as committed to it as he was, and he could see his friends who had opted not to go on to college were settling into lives that were less than what he would want. He finally called me in Tennessee (he was living with a group of friends in Boston) and asked me if he could come to Nashville with the goal of taking the GED, the ACT, and applying to Goddard [College in Vermont]. Goddard was the only school he would even consider applying to. It was the only one that he saw as allowing him the freedom to study what he wanted to study and devise his own program. When he arrived in Nashville, he spent three weeks studying for both tests, took the GED on a Friday and the ACT the next day, aced them both, applied to Goddard and got in. The poor kid didn't have any ready recommendations because he had been out of school for so long. I got one letter from the Pastor of a local church, a second one in handwritten scrawl from Jeremiah's Boston guitar teacher, and a third from a doctoral student/teacher at Vanderbilt University who was a dear friend and offered to interview Jeremiah and write a letter on his behalf. I was SO grateful when he was accepted. And I'll never forget the way he hugged me when they called him. It was as if his life had been saved.

The happy ending is that Jeremiah has been a model student at Goddard—constantly getting high praise from his teachers, who say that now, in his third term at the college, he is working at the Master's level.

As wonderful as this note was to receive, I was struck by the inherent danger in stories like Jeremiah's. Although he seems well on his way now to a life rich with promise, how many others like him never find their way? Our most able students deserve better.

Just prior to this book going to press, students at Goddard College were notified that the school was closing its under-graduate residential degree program that had existed since 1938. Both Jeremiah and Quinn O'Leary were students.

Acknowledgements

So much of this book derives from the loving tutelage of Linda Silverman, Director of the Gifted Development Center in Denver. A one-woman tour de force in our field, she combines a generous spirit with the best diagnostic ability in the business. Over the years, I have seen clients begin a post-test conference in tears because they are at last with the person whose writings touched them most—explained their child. I once watched a long-time gifted school administrator, introducing Linda to a group of parents for a presentation, take 10 minutes describing how she met the qualifications for sainthood! This was unexpected, Linda quipped, as she is Jewish! Hearing her speak just once, I decided to bring my own children to her, and soon returned to testing in her employ. Other employees at the GDC have been drawn to her in the same way, and she has remained our mentor and staunchest supporter. For me, she is the dearest of friends, and she has taught me so much that could be included in this book.

Linda's insistence that we look at children "through the lens of giftedness," that we support strengths first and then accommodate any weaknesses, and that we see the internal characteristics of giftedness, not just external achievement, are integral to the philosophy of this book. No one picks apart the strengths and weaknesses of a gifted/learning disabled child better, or knows with more certainty that such a child *can* become a late bloomer when early indications are to the contrary. She also has a wealth of experience with the very highly gifted, with the personality characteristics and needs that so compellingly argue for educational modifications. Linda views each gifted child from the standpoint of her early training in special education, tutoring learning disabled children. The gifted, like special education children, are simply children with unusual needs who require accommodations. She has never seen accommodations for their needs as elitist. They are simply children, different enough from average children to require modifications at school. What could be more fair than to insist that all children have educational programs that permit them to reach their full potential?

Linda's experience in this field, over 40 years, has allowed her to pursue many areas of interest. Her books and articles have been on the cutting edge of understanding the gifted in such areas as learning styles, especially the visual-spatial learner; the emotional and social aspects of giftedness; counseling the gifted; issues of gifted girls going under-ground with their abilities; underachievement; testing the highly gifted; and on auditory processing, sensory integration, and visual processing problems. I came to adopt these as my own causes, as well, but they were Linda's first, and it was her thoughts on these subjects that were convincing to all of us. I am further grateful to Linda for allowing me to take time away from my duties at the GDC to work on this book, and, over the years, to advocate for my own children on G/T committees, starting a charter school, etc., which all took considerable time. "I'll take you as much as I can get you," she said years ago, and she has kept her word. Thank you, Linda.

Quinn Finnian O'Leary, the wild Irishman, added immeasurably to this book. His powerful writing described vividly the frustration many gifted students encounter in school. While still young enough to remember multitudinous slights, and some truly traumatic events, Quinn writes with captivating maturity.

Originally tapped for an interview in the Underachievement chapter, Quinn graciously gave his permission for consider-able personal information to be disclosed. He also began to share his writing, which led to collaboration on this book. Quinn deserves special credit for providing a sounding board for my work and encouraging me to finish the manuscript. His interest grew as he read and edited succeeding chapters (this was information he needed to have), and that interest helped me to complete the next chapter and the next. When he finally said, "I think this book would have helped my mother," I felt we might have something to offer. The experience forced Quinn to redefine himself, to understand the real cause of his rebellion. There were reasons why he didn't fit in at school, beyond laziness, craziness, or undefined teenage angst. Thank you, Quinn, for providing this book with the richness and brilliance of your thoughts.

Kathi Kearney was especially helpful to me, reviewing the original manuscript and offering suggestions for further reading. Inviting me to her cottage on the Maine coast, after a flurry of book finishing activity, would have been enough. I was exhausted and happy to personally support the local lobster industry. However, she also provided wonderful insights on the book. Kathi is probably the best resource on homeschooling gifted and highly gifted children in the country. She is a longtime teacher of the gifted and there is no better tester. So, thank you, Kathi for your much appreciated help.

I am thrilled to be able to include ideas from the wonderful teachers profiled in chapter 9: Lin Greene, Sharon Sikora, Rich Borinsky, and Betty Maxwell. All generously contributed their time and sincere interest for this book. While there is no cookie cutter "best teacher of the gifted," these teachers demonstrate the essential passion for their teaching and genuine appreciation for gifted children. They expect wonderful things from them. I am also grateful to the principals I have known who modeled a willingness and flexibility to meet the individual needs of gifted students: Bob Martin, Don Groves, and Bob Rea.

Betty Maxwell, one of the teachers profiled, is retired now and serves as the Associate Director of the Gifted Development Center. Her extensive teaching experience (augmented by her later counseling and testing work) lends special weight to her concerns about educational practices that do not support the gifted (e.g., homework that doesn't teach and attendance rules that discourage attendance). Thank you, Betty, for supporting the Quinn O'Learys and Nick Gilmans, whose inherent personal worth begs to be acknowledged and whose educational needs must be accommodated. Thank you also for supporting the parents of such kids to view their rebellion as reasonable and honorable. You have both empowered gifted young people and worked hard to teach other educators best practices for teaching them. Your friendship is precious to me, while your philosophy has become integral to my thinking.

Karen Rogers has my sincere appreciation for reviewing this manuscript and contributing to the book's content. Karen's research on instructional grouping practices should form a basis for restructuring gifted education, in general. It looks unflinchingly at what actually works to accommodate advanced learners. She has also done a wonderful job suggesting individual learning plans to meet the needs of various children in her new book, *Re-Forming Gifted Education: Matching the Program to the Child.* Thank you, Karen, for your help with my book and your years of service in support of gifted students. Your curriculum development efforts, research, and endeavors to teach future teachers of the gifted have been essential to our field.

Heartfelt thanks are due to the many young people featured in this book: Emma, who so beautifully described the challenges of dyslexia, Jeremiah, who generously allowed his college admission to be discussed, and others whose names have been changed, but whose experiences have been described faithfully. Your stories will, I hope, not only move us, but move us to action.

Gracing the cover of this book are three wonderful young people: Alex, Rebecca, and James. I've worked with all of you in the past and thank you for letting me picture real gifted kids—no child models!

Two parents were kind enough to review the manuscript: Carolyn Kottmeyer and Kenneth Arenson. Carolyn is a highly active parent advocate and computer programmer, who created and busily maintains the popular Hoagies' websites, which offer invaluable information to advocates of gifted children. Ken is a trial attorney/parent advocate who is an articulate contributor to the gifted advocacy community, always willing to share his experiences and thoughtful insights with other parents. As busy as both are, I am so grateful to them for considering whether this book could be of help to parents just beginning the advocacy journey. They both provided wonderful suggestions that improved the final product.

Warmest thanks are owed to the staff of the Gifted Development Center, especially Lee Ann Powell, Caroline Klein, and Kattie Birkle for trying to assist me in ways to preserve my sanity, while book, testing, and consultation duties collided. You've always maintained your smiles, while patiently reminding me (as many times as necessary) of what I was doing!

To my husband, Bob, who has never failed to support my endeavors or keep his sense of humor when I needed it, I offer thanks and a big hug. You bought me a laptop and solved each and every computer problem I had! Thanks also to my sons, Nick and Ben, for graciously accepting fast food on many occasions when I was writing, and to my stepson, John, for his wonderful accomplishments and for giving me confidence his brothers will eventually succeed, also. To their many gifted friends, whose daily challenges enrich my understanding of the gifted.

Finally, my thanks to Pam McKinnie for her lovely cover work and to Lisa Probasco for the excellent understanding of the book's topics she brought to indexing it. My sincerest appreciation goes to the staff of DeLeon Publishing, especially Nancy Golon, for her marketing expertise and editing assistance, and to Damion DeLeon, for his diligent work, perfectionism, and fierce defense of my vision of this book.

Bobbie Gilman

References

Essential Resources

 The following resources are popular with parents and teachers advocating for the gifted. The Hoagies' Gifted Education Website (http://www.hoagiesgifted.com/) and search engine Google (http://www.google.com/) are great places to start.

Instructional Materials and Curricula

Creative Learning Press
P.O. Box 320
Mansfield Center, CT 06250
(888) 518-8004
http://www.creativelearningpress.com/

Creative Publications/Wright Group
(800) 523-2371
http://www.creativepublications.com/
http://www.growingwithmath.com/
http://www.wrightgroup.com/

Critical Thinking Books and Software
P.O. Box 448
Pacific Grove, CA 93950
(800) 458-4849
http://www.criticalthinking.com/

Math-U-See
(888) 854-MATH (6284)
In Canada: (800) 255-6654
http://www.mathusee.com/

Science, Math & Gifted Products
N7513 537th Street
Menomonie, WI 54751
(715) 235-1840
http://www.smgproducts.com/

The Teaching Company
(audiotapes of best professors)
(800) 832-2412
http://www.teachco.com/

Instructional Programs for Gifted Children (or that work well for them)

Center for Talent Development
Northwestern University
617 Dartmouth Place, Evanston, IL 60208
(847) 491-3782
http://www.ctd.northwestern.edu/

Concordia Language Villages (immersion foreign language camps)
901 8th St. S
Moorhead, MN 56562
(800) 222-4750
http://www.cord.edu/dept/clv/

EPGY (Education Program for Gifted Youth)
Ventura Hall
Stanford University
Stanford, CA 94305-4115
(800) 372-EPGY (3749)
http://www-epgy.stanford.edu/

Independent Study High School (used for younger gifted children)
University of Nebraska
P.O. Box 839400
Lincoln, NE 68583-9400
(402) 472-4422
http://dcs.unl.edu/ishs/

Internet Academy [K-12]
32020 1st Avenue South, #109
Federal Way, WA 98003-5743
(253) 945-2230
http://www.iacademy.org/

Kentucky Migrant Technology Project ("migrant.org") Very low-cost, standards-based, online distance learning courses
http://www.migrant.org/

Learning Links Program, Northwestern
University
617 Dartmouth Place,
Evanston, IL 60208
(847) 491-3782
http://www.ctd.northwestern.edu/...
programs/ll/program.html

Summer Enrichment Program for the
Gifted and Talented (SEP)
University of Northern Colorado
Campus Box 141
Greeley, CO 80639
(970) 351-2683
http://www.unco.edu/sep/

Virtual School for the Gifted
Street Address:
    70 Watts Lane
    Cottles Bridge, Victoria, 3099 Australia
Postal Address:
    PO Box 549
    Hurstbridge, Victoria 3099 Australia
Phone:
    Within Australia: 03 9710 1558
    International: +61 3 9710 1558
http://www.vsg.edu.au/default.htm

Journals (giftedness in children)

Gifted Child Quarterly (a publication of
NAGC)
(202) 785-4268.
http://www.nagc.org/Publications/...
GiftedChild/index.html

Gifted Child Today
Prufrock Press
P.O. Box 8813
Waco, Texas 76714-8813
(800) 998-2208, Fax: (800) 240-0333
http://www.prufrock.com/...
prufrock_jm_giftchild.cfm

Journal for the Education of the Gifted
Prufrock Press
P.O. Box 8813
Waco, Texas 76714-8813
(800) 998-2208, Fax: (800) 240-0333
http://www.prufrock.com/...
prufrock_jm_jeg.cfm

Journal of Secondary Gifted Education
Prufrock Press
P.O. Box 8813
Waco, Texas 76714-8813
(800) 998-2208, (800) 240-0333
http://www.prufrock.com/...
prufrock_jm_jsge.cfm

Parenting for High Potential
(Quarterly magazine for NAGC members)
http://www.nagc.org/Publications/...
Parenting/index.html

Roeper Review
P.O. Box 329, Bloomfield Hills, MI 48303
http://www.roeperreview.org/

Understanding Our Gifted
Open Space Communications
P.O. Box 18268, Boulder, Colorado 80308
(303) 444-7020, Fax (303) 545-6505
http://www.openspacecomm.com/...
order.htm

Journal (giftedness in adults)

—when you need support for your own
giftedness!

Advanced Development Journal
Gifted Development Center
1452 Marion Street
Denver, CO 80218
(303) 837-8378, fax: (303) 831-7465
http://www.gifteddevelopment.com/
(click on Journal)

Organizations

American Association for Gifted Children
at Duke University
Box 90270
Durham, North Carolina 27708-0270
(919) 783-6152.
http://www.aagc.org/main.html

Belin-Blank Center
210 Lindquist Center
The University of Iowa
Iowa City, IA 52242-1529
(800) 336-6463 or (319) 335-6148
Fax: (319) 335-5151
Email: belinblank@uiowa.edu
http://www.uiowa.edu/~belinctr/

Council on Exceptional Children/Eric
Clearinghouse on Disabilities and Gifted
Education
1110 North Glebe Road
Arlington, VA 22201-5704
(800) 328-0272
http://www.ericec.org/

Center for Talent Development
617 Dartmouth Place
Evanston, IL 60208
(847) 491-3782
http://www.ctd.northwestern.edu/

Davidson Institute for Talent
Development, Northwestern University
9665 Gateway Drive, Suite B
Reno, Nevada 89521
(775) 852-DITD, FAX: (775) 852-2184
http://www.ditd.org/

European Council for High Ability (ECHA)
http://www.echa.ws/modules/news/

Gifted Canada-Douance Canada
http://www3.bc.simpatico.ca/...
giftedcanada/index.html

Gifted Development Center (a service of
the Institute for Advanced Development)
Directed by Linda Silverman, Ph.D.
1452 Marion Street
Denver, CO 80218
(303) 837-8378, Fax: (303) 831-7465
http://www.gifteddevelopment.com/

Gifted Education Resource Institute
Purdue University
http://www.geri.soe.purdue.edu/

Gifted Resource Center of New England
Directed by Deirdre Lovecky, Ph.D.
P.O. Box 40326
Providence, RI 02940-0326
(401) 421-3426
Email: GRCNE02940@aol.com

The Hollingworth Center for Highly Gifted
Children
http://www.hollingworth.org/

Institute for Educational Advancement
625 Fair Oaks Ave. Suite 285
S. Pasadena, CA 91030
(626) 403-8900, Fax: (626) 403-8905
http://www.educationaladvancement.org/

The Mega Foundation
http://www.megafoundation.org/

National Association for Gifted Children
(NAGC)
1707 L Street NW
Suite 550
Washington D.C. 20036
(202) 785-4268
http://www.nagc.org/

National Association for Gifted Children
(NAGC) UK
http://www.nagcbritain.org.uk/

National Center for Learning Disabilities
381 Park Avenue South, Suite 1401
New York, NY 10016
(212) 545-7510, Fax: (212) 545-9665
http://www.ld.org/

National Gifted Children's Fund
HCR 80 Box 42
Venango, NE 69168
http://www.ngcfcharity.org/

National Network of Families With Gifted
Children
http://www.nnfgc.org/

National Research Center on the Gifted
and Talented
University of Connecticut
2131 Hillside Road, Unit 3007
Storrs, CT 06269-3007
(860) 486-4676, Fax: (860) 486-2900
http://www.ucc.uconn.edu/~wwwgt/...
nrcgt.html

Supporting the Emotional Needs of the
Gifted (SENG)
P.O. Box 6550
Scottsdale, AZ 85261
(773) 528-2113
http://www.sengifted.org/

World Council for Gifted and Talented
Children, Inc.
18401 Hiawatha Street
Northridge, CA 91326, USA
(818) 368-7501, Fax : (818) 368-2163
http://www.worldgifted.org/

Publishers of Books and
Periodicals About the Gifted

DeLeon Publishing
P.O. 461027
Glendale, CO 80246
(303) 331-8725, Fax: (303) 331-1116
http://www.deleonpub.com/

Free Spirit Press
217 Fifth Avenue North, Suite 200
Minneapolis, MN 55401-1299
(800) 735-7323
http://www.freespirit.com/

Gifted Education Press
10201 Yuma Court
P.O. Box 1586
Manassas, VA 20108
(703) 369-5017
http://www.giftededpress.com/

Great Potential Press (formerly Gifted
Psychology Press)
P.O. Box 5057
Scottsdale, AZ 85261
(602) 954-4200
http://www.giftedpsychologypress.com/

New Moon Publishing
(800) 381-4743
http://www.newmoon.org/

Open Space Communications, Inc.
P.O. Box 18268
Boulder, CO 80308
(800) 494-6178
http://www.openspacecomm.com/

Prufrock Press
P.O. Box 8813
Waco, TX 76714-8813
(800) 998-2208
http://www.prufrock.com/

State Associations for the Gifted

Search Hoagies' Gifted Education Page
(http://www.hoagiesgifted.com/) or
Google (http://www.google.com/) for
information about your state association
and (possible) city affiliate. Most have
annual conferences and may provide
access to other resources throughout the
year (publications, speakers, support
groups, etc.).

Talent Searches

Johns Hopkins
Center for Talented Youth (CTY)
3400 North Charles Street
Baltimore, MD 21218
(410) 516-0337
http://www.jhu.edu/gifted/

Duke University TIP (Talent Identification
Program)
Box 90747, Durham, NC 27708
(919) 684-3847, Fax (919) 681-7921
http://www.tip.duke.edu/

Northwestern University
Center for Talent Development
617 Dartmouth Place
Evanston, IL 60208
(847) 491-3782
http://www.ctd.northwestern.edu/

University of Denver
Rocky Mountain Talent Search
(303) 871-2983
http://www.du.edu/education/ces/...
rmts.html

Websites About the Gifted

Eric Clearinghouse on Disabilities and Gifted Education (articles on the education of gifted and gifted/LD children). Available at www.hoagiesgifted.org.

Gifted Development Center (comprehensive resource site, including articles about testing issues) http://www.gifteddevelopment.com/

GT-Special List (for families of twice-exceptional children) http://www.gtworld.org/gtspeclist.html

Hoagies' Gifted Education Page (unbelievably comprehensive resource site for parents, educators, kids, and teens, compiled by Carolyn K.) http://www.hoagiesgifted.com/

PG-CyberSource at Davidson Institute for Talent Development (online library of articles on the highly gifted) http://www.davidsoninstitute.org/... pgcybersource.php or http://www.ditd.org/ (click on pg-cybersource)

TAGFAM Home Page (Families of the Talented and Gifted) http://www.tagfam.org/

Uniquely Gifted (twice exceptional resource site) http://www.uniquelygifted.org/

Websites About Homeschooling

Hoagies' Gifted Education Page (gifted homeschooling links) http://www.hoagiesgifted.org/... home_school.htm

Kearney, K. Gifted Children and Homeschooling: An Annotated Bibliography. http://www.hollingworth.org/homebib.html

Home School Legal Defense Association: http://www.hslda.org/

Home Education Magazine: http://www.home-ed-magazine.com/wlcm_HEM.html

Links to summaries of state home-schooling laws: http://www.home-ed-magazine.com/HSRSC/... hsrsc_lws.rgs.html

... Denotes address continues without a space.

Index

A

abilities, crystallized and fluid, 34, 81

ability grouping, 12, 138–139, 141–146, 290

abstract
conceptual learners, 110–111
reasoning abilities, 33, 81, 110–111

academic achievement and learning disabilities, 176

acceleration
and achievement tests, 93–96
credit for accelerated work, 359, 367, 369
decision for, 100, 376–377, 381
in elementary school, 342–343, 353–354
grade and subject, 133, 143, 215–216, 264–266
and grouping research, 141, 143, 145
in high school, 360, 361–369
and higher levels of giftedness, 373–378
holes, 109
and independent learning, 132–133, 256, 269–270, 292–295
and introverts, 215
in middle school, 357, 359–360
preferred over enrichment, 234
research on, 14, 19
scope, 223–224
vs. enrichment, 134–135

achieve, failing to. *See* under-achievement

achievement, high
confusion with giftedness, 35–36
and developmental advancement, 44–45

achievement test score patterns
for older gifted children, 119–129
for younger gifted children, 113–117

achievement tests
and acceleration, 93–96
ceilings in, 375–376
choosing, 118–119
and deficits, 375–376
in elementary school, 375–376
explained, 93–96
individual, 79
and learning levels, 129–130
state standardized, 277–282

AD/HD, 49, 178–179, 196–206, 349–352

adults, gifted, 52–54, 83, 84, 166

Advanced Placement (AP)
courses, 14, 143, 218–219, 233, 360

advocacy. *See also* parents as advocates
in elementary school, 340, 341–356
in high school, 341, 360–371
in middle school, 341, 356–360
need for, 24–25
teacher, 145–147, 272–274, 281, 378–379

age
emotional, tied to chronological, 43–44
mental compared to chronological, 13–14, 42–43

alienation, 155–162

anti-intellectualism, 11

anti-tracking, 138–139

anxiety, sensory integration, 186

assessment aids planning, 229–230

asynchronous development, 29, 35, 41–44, 104

attendance policies, high school, 162–163, 306

Attention-Deficit/Hyperactivity Disorder. *See* AD/HD

attentional deficits, 82, 181–182, 196–206
specialists, 203, 204

W

Z